Committed to Conservation:

50 Years of Work to Help Protect America's Soil and Water

Committed to Conservation:

50 Years of Work to Help Protect America's Soil and Water

R. Neil Sampson and Robert W. Sampson

© 2015 by R. Neil Sampson and Robert W. Sampson
  All rights reserved.

ISBN 9781508604884

Front and back cover photos taken by Natural Resources Conservation
Service

Editing and design by Sara Leeland

Printed in the United States of America

.

Committed to Conservation:
50 Years of Work to Help Protect America's Soil and Water

Part I
by R. Neil Sampson

Part I I

by Robert W. Sampson

Part III

by Neil & Robert Sampson

Preface

"You guys ought to write a book." The speaker was Jim Lyons, talking to Neil and Rob Sampson over dinner in a New Haven, Connecticut café in early 2001. Jim is a former Assistant Secretary of Agriculture who was beginning a new career at Yale. Neil was at the school on a semester's fellowship to teach policy in the School of Forestry and Environmental Services on the campus, and Rob was visiting his dad from his home in Boise, Idaho, and delivering a guest lecture on stream restoration.

The book idea popped up during a conversation about the Sampson's long and almost-continuous service in the Department of Agriculture's Soil Conservation Service. Neil had started with the agency in 1960 and Rob had started his career (which still continues) in 1981. Although their careers had taken different professional pathways, both conservationists had held a variety of positions at all levels of the organization. Both had held positions in Idaho, and Rob had worked in several other states, so there were both shared and contrasting experiences that might make an interesting story, Lyons thought.

But the idea didn't really catch hold at the time. Neil was busy working with partner Larry Walton to launch a new forest management business – Vision Forestry – in Maryland and Rob was up to his eyes in his job as the State Design Engineer with the Natural Resources Conservation Service in Boise. So the book idea lay dormant for a decade.

The idea came back in 2012 as it became obvious that this was a project that couldn't be put off forever if there was going to be time and energy to get it done. Although both were still busy in their professional pursuits, it seemed like the time to start.

We decided to write the book in third-person prose, mainly to keep attention directed to the story and the work that was going on rather than the personalities involved. The idea is to illustrate what it has been like to work in the federal agency whose role is to assist private landowners and communities with land and water management problems. Outside of a few thousand people who have worked in or close to the agency, its ways and the scientific skills and social concepts that lie behind the work are little known by the public. But the agency's impact affects virtually every American citizen as it builds partnerships between federal, state and local government to help assure that our Nation's non-federal lands are managed for the good of the present and the future as well.

We each wrote independently, from our own memories and references collected over the years. Thus, there is a distinct difference between the first and second parts of the book. We were different people, working in different careers, at different times. Hopefully, this helps illustrate the many changes that have occurred in the half-century the book covers. Science and technology have dramatically changed field work, with computers going from non-existent to become the daily work tool that now facilitates virtually everything. New communications tools like cell phones help field workers in rural areas stay as connected to the world as they would be in an office. Global market dynamics buffet farmers and ranchers, and a major event in Europe or Asia can have as much effect as a situation in the U.S. Midwest, and there's not much that any landowner (or policy-maker) can do to change or respond to these massive shifts. And the agency and its programs have seen major changes, including a name change and a significant re-shuffling of program responsibilities and budgets with other USDA agencies as the result of Congressional actions.

Some things haven't changed, however. The wind still blows and water still runs downhill, and if the soil is not protected, it can be permanently damaged as the fertile topsoil is blown or washed off of the land. Where those soils are damaged and degraded, they will be less productive, meaning it will take more expense and effort to get them to produce the food, feed and fiber that is the backbone of any society. The nutrients and pest controls used on US farm fields can assure productivity, but can also be washed into the surrounding surface water or groundwater. A region with poor soils is a poor region – not just economically, but environmentally and socially as well. Similarly, water that is full of sediment, nutrients or other chemicals washed from agricultural land can kill fish, amphibians and insects in the receiving stream. A nation with the resource riches of the United States should feel obligated to develop the best possible ways to keep their lands productive and water clean for the welfare of its citizens and for future generations.

The Natural Resources Conservation Service (NRCS) is the federal agency charged with leading this policy effort. Initially created in the 1930s as the Soil Conservation Service (SCS) before the name was changed to NRCS in the 1990s, it continues to be dedicated to the future of America's land and water, and to the welfare of the people and communities that live on and manage that land and water. We hope this story adequately reflects the dedication and service that have marked the people and the history of the Conservation Service. All opinions and conclusions in this book are those of the authors and do not represent the official positions of the Agency.

-- R.Neil Sampson and Robert W. Sampson

Part I

by R. Neil Sampson

1

New Man on the Job

"The SCS men were not there to dictate federal ideas to farmers; they were there to help solve problems."

It was mid-June 1960 when the new employee showed up at the Soil Conservation Service (SCS) office in Burley, Idaho. Fresh out of the University of Idaho with a degree in Agriculture, he was ready to launch a career as a soil conservationist, helping farmers and ranchers solve their soil and water management problems.

Neil Sampson was typical of the new hires in SCS. He had the required farm background and technical college degree. Newly married, he was ready to settle down and become one of the local "conservation men." Having been too young to go to Korea as a military draftee, he was grateful, both to have a job and to be able to serve the public interest. Although it would be months before the young President John Kennedy would articulate it, he was ready to "see what he could do for his country."

The Burley SCS office was also typical for the times. Burley was a county seat farm town of around 7,500 (1960 population) in south-central Idaho and the SCS office had been recently established to serve two brand new soil conservation districts in Cassia County. Idaho had been slowly expanding the establishment of soil conservation districts and the East and West Cassia districts were among the new ones. There had been opposition to district establishment, based largely on the idea that this new federal soil conservation program was imposing on the turf of the State University and its Extension Service.[1]

---

1. For a background on the history of soil conservation district establishment in the U.S., see Sampson, R. Neil, 1985: *For Love of the Land,* National Association of Conservation Districts.

In addition, opponents raised local anxieties about the "federals" coming in to impose their ideas on the local people. The SCS man in charge was Gordon J. "Whitey" Price, a range conservationist who had seen his SCS career interrupted by service in the WWII Navy and who was an experienced person at working with farmers and local leaders. His job, shared by the staff, was to prove the critics wrong.

The field technicians on the staff were largely local men that had agriculture and technical training. Burke Scholer was an engineering aide who was well versed in all of the engineering needed to solve the local irrigation problems. J.J. McLaws was a native of Oakley who was called "Colonel" for his auctioneering skills, and was known and respected throughout the region. Because of their steady hands and local reputations, an outsider like Neil could come into the office and rapidly learn the ropes.

The timing for problem solving in the valley was excellent. Many of the farmers on the irrigated Snake River Plains and the valleys of the region's smaller streams were still using irrigation systems and techniques that had changed little from the irrigation developments of the early 1900s. Water delivered to the farm by Bureau of Reclamation canals was led across uneven fields in little ditches dug to follow existing contours. Farmers with portable canvas dams and shovels worked endless hours trying to coax irrigation water across the fields. Uneven water application, with dry and soggy spots readily apparent on the field, was the inevitable result, and the hugely laborious work was rewarded with less than top crop yields.

SCS surveyed the fields and designed land leveling projects that were carried out by local contractors with earth-moving equipment. Federal cost-sharing through the Agricultural Conservation Program was available to help defray the large initial costs. New ditches, elevated above the field surface, were designed on non-erosive grades and controlled with irrigation structures or, where needed, lined with concrete. New technology and the SCS men arrived at about the same time, and set about helping modernize the area's irrigation systems.

Water could be siphoned out onto the crop, where it would run virtually unattended for the desired time, while the smoothly graded field let the water gently flow to uniformly irrigate the crop.

Soil erosion was largely eliminated, more efficient water use was realized, yields improved significantly, and costs and labor needs went down. Needless to say, the new SCS men and their surveying gear quickly became very popular with the local farmers.

A concrete ditch and siphon tubes deliver irrigation water to a leveled field.
West Cassia SCD, 1961

In mid-June, however, the first order of business in the Burley SCS office was not field work. The federal fiscal year was ending on June 30, and all the year-end reports needed to be done. In addition, the SCS was about to enter the computer era with a brand-new pro-gress-reporting system. There were a pile of new policy memos and handbooks from the National and State offices and the orders were plain: As of July 1, everyone would switch to the new system. The SCS old-timers in the office were ready to follow orders and learn the new rules, but they weren't looking forward to it.

The solution, Price realized, was straight-forward. Hand it to the new guy. So, with the delivery of the pile of memos and handbooks to Neil's desk, the assignment was made: "Read and learn this new system so that you can help the rest of us learn what we need to do."

Although novel, the new system was fairly straight-forward. A form #253 would be filled out by each employee and sent to headquarters every two weeks when the time sheets were submitted. The handbooks had clear rules, with numerical codes to identify each conservation practice and standard units with which each would be counted. There were codes to identify the state, county, conservation district, and field office so that the computer could provide sorted summaries of accomplishments by a variety of areas.

But before the switch to the new system, there were still the year-end reports to get done, and they would be done the old way. All field work was cancelled, and the entire office staff was put to work in the office for two days. Around a large table, with the new guy in charge of keeping the data on a wall chart, the staff went from drawer to drawer in the filing cabinets, pulling out each district co-operator's file to see what they had done in the past year.

In the process, the files might need updating, and there was a lot of information traded. "I saw John Jones at the gas station a while back and he said he'd be ready to develop that conservation plan as soon as his grain is in." The result was a note on the "work board" reminding the conservation planner to drop by John's place next time he was in the area and see when they could start. Aerial photos would be ordered and soils maps prepared so that the planner could begin talking with John about the details when they met. By the end of the two days, everyone on the staff knew what the office had achieved in the last year, and had a good idea what the workload for the coming months was likely to be.

In July, as ordered, the new reporting system was in place. There were a few fits and starts, as details were worked out so that practices weren't double-reported by two staff members, or overlooked completely. But, aside from normal start-up hitches, things went fine. The problems only began to show up when the computer-produced quarterly summaries started to arrive back at the office six to eight months later. They came in a 2-inch thick stack of fan-fold computer printout paper, about 18 inches wide. In that stack was every possible combination of data one could imagine. Once you figured out where to look, you could see how many feet of irrigation ditch had been installed by the field office, and how much was in each con-servation district.

The problem was, you couldn't tell whether the number was ac-curate or not. There was no way to track where it had come from. The codes showed the office and district location, but not the farm or ranch where the practice existed. Side records were discouraged as a needless additional workload, so you couldn't look to see if all of the practices on a farm were recorded properly in the system. Thus, the summary was impossible to cross-check.

By year's end, the #253 forms on file in the office added up to well over 100, with each employee responsible for at least 26. There might be irrigation ditch codes entered on a dozen or more, so if you had to find that dozen, look up the farm files to see that they were accurate, and then add them up manually to see if there was a com-puter error, it was a huge job. Worse yet, when you got done, you often couldn't tell where the error was made. It could have been someone miscoding something, or just a scanning error when the data were transferred from the #253 form to the computer. Basi-cally, the errors weren't worth finding or chasing. As a result, the numbers on the printouts didn't mean much to field staff, and no-body in our field office paid much attention to the progress summar-ies.

Consequently, the field office staff lost its sense of how much progress was being made, where things were going best, and where additional effort needed to be applied. The bosses at the Area and State Offices used the summaries and followed the trends to satisfy their management needs, but the field office staff seemed to lose touch with its own program—an unintended result of this bureau-cratic improvement.

Neil brought a new skill to the Burley Office, and it was soon put into use. He could type, and he owned his own portable electric type-writer. This was unusual, and it dated back to his high school days in the small town of Worley, Idaho. There, in a 4-year school with 32 students, teachers were taking advantage of small classes to break down stereotypes. Instead of girls being limited to home economics and typing classes, and boys doing vocational agriculture and wood shop, anyone could do anything. So Neil ended up taking both wood shop and typing, and was soon active in writing for the school paper, typing stencils for duplication, and similar work.

In the summer of 1958, while working as a construction lineman in Richland, Washington, a store display for a new Olivetti portable electric typewriter caught Neil's eye. With lots of science classes and labs facing him in the coming year, he decided to buy it. So he went back to the University of Idaho with his new tool, and spent two more years of school gaining proficiency by typing lab reports, research papers, and other assignments. When he carried the little typewriter into the Burley SCS office, he introduced a capability that was uncommon at the time.

Another surprise was also waiting for the new man. Soon after the work had started, Whitey brought out a case about the size of a small saxophone case, and said "we just got this from the Area Office. Do you know what it is?" Neil opened the case and discovered a complete set of camera equipment – a Graflex 4x5 speed graphic camera with all of the attachments needed to make up a professional camera set. While it was a baffling array of parts to the SCS staff, it was familiar to Neil, because of a complete fluke that also had occurred at the University of Idaho.

It just so happened that as a rising senior, Neil's advisor had discovered that he couldn't graduate with his current class group. To Neil, that was a disaster, as he was out of money, engaged to be married, and desperate to get on with his life. The advisor pointed out that more credits in humanities were required, and that while all the necessary technical and science credits were in place, the humanities credits were not. Something had to be done. Out of all the humanities credits available, Neil chose a photography class.

The photography class was taught by Dr. Bell, a photographer of the old school. In his thinking, there were two kinds of cameras – professional (as exemplified by the Graflex 4x5 speed graphic used by virtually every press photographer at the time) and baby brownies (as exemplified by the 35mm cameras that were then winning wide acceptance). So the class was a total immersion in the professional 4x5 speed graphic, including laboratory work that taught how to develop the film and work through the enlargement and printing processes that produced professional photographs.

With that background, the camera case in the Burley SCS office was no mystery, and from that day forward, Neil was the official photographer for the work unit, as well as the designated writer.

Photography in SCS was no light-hearted exercise. The agency was providing professional cameras to each field office and they expected professional results. Photographic workshops and training were part of the training regime. The 4" x 5" film was provided by the agency and, once exposed, sent for development to the regional office's cartography lab in Portland, Oregon. Contact prints were made and returned to the field office. The photographs selected for filing were accompanied by a detailed legend, then sent back to the regional laboratory, where final prints were made and distributed.

In addition to the field offices, the regional office kept a copy and sent copies elsewhere to be filed. Each photo had a unique number, and the legend was copied on the back. The result, no doubt, were huge files of run-of-the mill pictures, but there were also many outstanding landscape and conservation photographs that continue to be seen in publications to this day.

2

Training to be a Professional

"So began a full-scale immersion in the field office work."

Back in 1960, being a farm boy with a college degree didn't mean that you knew anything much about a conservation job. In the Burley, Idaho office, there were two ways to get a new employee going—the SCS way and Whitey's way. Neil got both. Whitey's way was faster and more direct—you threw the new guy into the work and let him learn on the job. With the progress report out the door and two days of work piled up, the field office was back in full action; there was no room for someone who couldn't be part of the team.

"Don Jones needs a ditch surveyed for drop structures. It's an easy job, and he's very knowledgeable about what he needs, so that's a good place for you to start." Neil had no experience in either irrigation or surveying and had never seen a drop structure. No problem. Whitey went to the wall board, drew a ditch profile, and showed how you put a stake in at every one-foot drop so that the contractor knew where to install each structure. Then he opened up the survey level box, took out the instrument, and fastened it to the tripod he had set up on the office floor. A quick lesson in how to assemble the instrument and adjust the leveling screws until it was perfectly level, and the lesson was over. It was time to hit the field.

Don was waiting at the appointed time and, unknown to Neil, had been warned about needing to watch the novice and help with any problems. At least outwardly, the problems were minimal. The work almost certainly went more slowly than necessary, but at its conclusion, there was a staked field ditch line with drop structures, a set of survey notes, and a rough design for the contractor to follow. The landowner had what he needed, and there was a sense of "job done" on the ride back to the office.

So began a full-scale immersion in the field office work. Often in the company of an experienced engineering aide, the irrigation work progressed in complexity. But there were also other activities. Land leveling surveys had Neil in the role of note-taker while the engineer read off the elevations and the farmer carried the survey rod. That experience progressed into doing solo surveys, then into learning how to convert the field notes into final land leveling designs.

Soil surveys with soil scientist Glen Logan leading the way on soil mapping expeditions or digging pits to develop soil profile descriptions led to maps that could be explained to the landowner as part of a conservation plan. Range surveys with area range conservationist Boyd Price showing Neil how to map vegetation types and conditions, then develop a new grazing plan for a ranch. The work was varied, and the technical training intense.

In the meantime, the SCS training was gearing up. This was a more structured and formal training experience, based on workshops, field trips, and experienced instructors. A training plan made sure that all the necessary SCS topics were covered and events were scheduled. One of the first big events would occur in October of 1960 – a month in residence at the SCS Western Training Center in San Luis Obispo, California.

Using facilities on the campus of California Polytechnic, SCS maintained a year-around training program under the direction of Boyd Murray, an experienced SCS field man and educator. Some 12 young SCS field men from the western states, along with a visiting woman forester from Yugoslavia, were in that 1960 class. The work was about half academic and half practical. Classroom work led by experienced trainers included soil science, range science, forestry and conservation planning. Field trips drove home the classroom lessons with practical exercises designed to teach the day-to-day field skills that students needed to develop.

Evenings held either more formal programs or social time that was also a learning experience. The participants all had from three months to several years' experience in the field, and so the topics were nearly always about the experiences encountered in doing SCS work. Ranging from practical to humorous, the stories expanded everyone's understanding of what they were trying to achieve in the agency. Friendships were made that would be renewed over many years in other jobs and locations ranging from Portland, Oregon to Washington, DC.

Although the Training Center program was the keystone of a new employee's formal training, it was just the beginning. Formal and semi-formal training workshops and field days were regular occurrences, often held at a nearby University of Idaho Experiment Station or the SCS Plant Materials Center at Aberdeen. Their objective: keep everyone up to date on the latest research or new plant variety that could be used for conservation work.

The result was a field staff that could best be described as technical generalists. Although each person had been educated in one field, such as engineering or soil science, by the time they had worked a while in an SCS field office, most had been trained in virtually every scientific field affecting land management in agriculture and forestry. They weren't experts in the academic sense, but they could encounter about any problem with a good mix of practical science and solution development.

In the process, the young professionals were also learning their limits, and that would be critical as they encountered situations in the field. If an engineering challenge was over their head, they could call the Area Engineer for assistance. The same held true for the Soil Scientists, Range Conservationists, Foresters and other technical specialists. Knowing how to solve problems meant not only being confident about what you could do, but also knowing when you needed help and what other skills were required. The landowners being assisted often didn't know or care who came up with the final solution, just as long as it worked.

One of the early learning experiences for any SCS employee is the unique relationship between the federal agency and the local soil conservation district (SCD). These districts are a special-purpose unit of local government formed under State law, so although they vary somewhat state-by-state, generally they are similar.[2] They are guided by a locally-elected board of supervisors (or directors, in some states) and their purpose is to bring local leadership to the soil and water conservation program.

More important than the legal aspects, however, are the personal relationships. In the Cassia districts, all of the supervisors were working farmers and ranchers. They varied from very large operators to small, struggling ones. To a person, they were dedicated to helping the local soil and water conservation program, and they devoted many hours of volunteer time to contribute to its success.

Like all new SCS employees, Neil learned that working with these local people was the key to building support for the agency within the local community. Without them, the SCS would have been seen primarily as a "federal" agency, and the criticism that it was pressing federal ideas on local people would have been an obstacle. With the district supervisor's leadership, it was clear that this was a cooperative program, and that local views were important.

There were, of course, ways to confuse *who* was doing or saying what. For example, on one occasion the West Cassia district board decided to send a letter to their Congressman in Washington, urging him to vote for an SCS budget bill then coming up in the House. Since neither the SCS nor the district supervisors had a clerk, Neil, who could type, was given the task of writing and sending the letter on behalf of the district board. He did—on official SCS stationary!

It didn't take long for that to bounce from the Congressman's staff to the Washington Office of SCS, then the State Office, then down to Whitey Price in the local Burley SCS office. Neil was in the soup! A stern lesson on the prohibition on SCS directly lobbying Congress for funds was administered. The issue faded away. Apparently the SCS was able to convince the Congressman that a novice who didn't know better was learning the ropes!

---

[2] See R. Neil Sampson, 1985, *For Love of the Land*, League City, TX: NACD, for a background on conservation districts and their national association.

11

3

Surveying Snow

"That [snow survey] information, as disastrous as it was, proved to be a saving grace for the farmers who took the SCS predictions to heart."

As winter closed in and farm field activities in Burley began to slow down, another work season – Snow Survey – opened up and with it, a whole new set of training and experiences.

The snow survey program was born out of the critical role of summer stream flow in shaping the irrigated agriculture of the West. Following the pioneering work of Dr. James E. Church of the University of Nevada in the early 1900s, SCS hydrologists and engineers had been working since the 1930's to develop snow survey courses throughout the mountain watersheds of the region.

A rather simple and straight-forward measuring device was designed in Dr. Church's work. It was a hollow aluminum tube marked off in inches, with a sharp cutter bit on the end. Thin slots in the tube allow a view of the snow inside. The tube is driven down through the snowpack until it meets the ground. The snow depth is recorded, and then the tube is carefully extracted with the internal snow core intact. The depth of the core is noted to make certain a full core is there. Then, the tube is weighed on a set of handheld scales. Subtracting the weight of the empty tube gives the net weight of the core itself. The tube is calibrated so that, for every ounce of weight in the snow core, an inch of water is contained. Each sample collected records both snow depth and water content A series of samples – usually 5 to 10 – were made at each snow survey site at the same time each month on a schedule from December to May.

The results from the sample readings were averaged, and used in the monthly forecast formula. Data from the monthly measurements were compared to summer stream flows, and correlations were developed so that the monthly measurements in February could be used to give a rough estimate of the amount of stream flow that would be experienced in the coming summer. The correlations tended to get better each month, so that by April 1, the stream flow forecast would be in the 95% accurate range.

In that first year, Neil learned exactly how important these forecasts were to the region's farmers. South central Idaho had been experiencing drought conditions in 1959, and the winter snowpack had been light as a result. One of the West Cassia farm areas was the Oakley fan, where desert soils were irrigated by water from Goose Creek, a stream that flowed out of the South Mountains toward the Snake River. The stream had been dammed in 1911 by a private company, operating under provisions of the Carey Act. Water from spring and summer stream flow was held in the Oakley Reservoir, then released through canals for summer irrigation. When the dam was full, everyone had plenty of water. But when it wasn't, which had been most of the time since the dam was built, the available water didn't fill everyone's needs, and the deficit had to be shared.

This was one of those extra bad years, and SCS's Whitey Price had been forced to tell a meeting of Oakley farmers that they could only expect a 10% water delivery during the 1960 irrigation season. The reservoir had been drawn completely down at the end of the 1959 irrigation season, and the snow pack in the hills was below normal again in 1960.

That information, as disastrous as it was, proved to be a saving grace for the farmers who took the SCS predictions to heart. Many fields were left idle, and low water-using crops like grain replaced those like sugar beets and potatoes with a higher water demand. Farmers faced reduced profits and difficult times. A few refused to believe the SCS water supply forecast, however, and prepared their land as usual. In some cases, it was reported, those farmers had used their entire year's water allocation by the time their crops germinated and, as a result, lost everything — including the costs of land preparation, seed and fertilizer — as their crops withered in the summer desert sun.

The result was that by the winter of 1960-61, there was great interest in the SCS snow survey program. Everyone was now convinced of its value in predicting summer irrigation supplies. The regional drought was not over, so interest was keen.

From the SCS perspective, the challenge in operating the snow survey program was to get the monthly readings on a regular schedule, and to do it safely. The snow courses lay high in remote mountains with no winter access, so had to be reached either by foot travel or with special over-snow machines. In order to make accurate forecasts, the readings had to be made on about the same day each month, so the snow surveyors went out regardless of weather conditions. Most of the snow courses involved a long day's travel for two people, and those people had to be both physically fit and trained for winter travel and survival.

The Snow Survey Supervisor in the Boise SCS state office was Morlan W. "Morley" Nelson, a career SCS employee whose World War II service was in the Army's famed 10th Mountain Division. Morley brought his experience in surviving combat in the Italian Alps to the SCS, so the training was intense and the safety rules clear.

Morley's "common sense" rules included: no "solo" traveling, no traveling without minimum survival gear and clothing, and no untrained people on the survey team. "With proper training, a set of basic equipment, and a cool head, anyone can survive the worst winter conditions," Nelson told the writer for the November, 1969, issue of Snowmobiling magazine. He was justifiably proud that SCS snow surveyors had traveled over one and a half million miles on the snow in the remote western back country without a single fatality from exposure or freezing.

Neil's first experience in SCS snow travel started at a local ski area south of Twin Falls, Idaho, in a regional snow survey training session. War surplus Army ski boots (way too large) and old Army skis were provided, and the lessons began. Rough mastery of cross-country and modest downhill skiing technique was accompanied by classroom sessions on winter survival (staying dry, layering clothing, keeping hydrated, etc.), and a field session on how to build a snow shelter for overnight or blizzard survival.

Armed with their training, the work began. On the first week of each month from January to May, a two-man crew would leave the SCS office to make the snow survey runs.

Often led by Burke Scholer, the team would travel in an Army surplus truck that was carrying a "Sno-Ball" snow machine. At the end of the maintained road, the Sno-Ball was unloaded for over-snow travel to the snow course.

The Sno-Ball was a custom-converted Chevrolet pickup, with the original axles and drive train replaced by a tractor differential and wide rubber-belted tracks. The wide tracks gave it adequate flotation to handle the deep powder snow often encountered in the moun-tains. With plenty of power, it could handle steep hills and snowed-over roads through rough terrain. But it was not a fool-proof ride. Lots could go wrong on the back country trips, and the Sno-Ball pickup was always loaded with the gear needed to safely ski or snow-shoe out in the event of trouble. It also carried a load of tools so that minor repairs could be made in order to get back home.

Neil joined the regular snow survey team, and became familiar with the general forecasting methodology, a set of skills that would come into play regularly as he continued his career in Idaho. The job involved, at times, serious surprises.

In the fall of 1961, deer hunting season in the South Hills of Cassia County was scheduled to open on a Saturday morning. Friday was a balmy fall day, with pleasant temperatures and weather; then Satur-day brought an unseasonable (and unpredicted) snow storm that dumped up to 18 inches of snow in the hills south of Oakley. Hunt-ers that had traveled into the mountains with passenger cars and 2-wheel drive pickups found themselves snowed in and unable to get out. Some had made the error of wearing light clothing, and were woefully under-equipped for the situations they faced.

On Monday, when it became apparent that there were dozens, if not hundreds, of people stranded and in trouble, the Cassia County Sheriff asked SCS for assistance in helping to find and extricate strand-ed hunters. The SCS staff took turns for two days with the Sno-Ball, driving snowy roads searching for and helping people in the back country. Tragically, not everyone was found; two people died as a result. Many others, however, were grateful to see a strange red machine heading up the snowbound road toward where they were stranded.

Burke Scholer and Jim Chapman prepare to leave the Sno-Ball to measure snow at Howell Canyon Snow Course. (1961)

Morlan W. "Morley" Nelson, SCS Snow Survey Supervisor, weighs a snow sample on scales held by Keith Higginson, Idaho State Reclamation Engineer, near Boise, Idaho, 1970.

4

Multiplying the Effort

"By 1961, SCS engineers were running a winter surveying school."

As winter's grip held field work to a minimum, the SCS staff in Burley continued to chart a new way of doing the irrigation system work that was threatening to overwhelm the staff. In the first days of the new district program, two SCS men would go out to a farm and drive wooden stakes into the field to establish a 100' x 100' grid, then survey the elevation at each stake, take the survey back the office, draw the existing field contour map, create new contours to the desired field slope, then calculate the cuts and fills needed at each stake. These would then be flagged and marked on each stake in the field so that the equipment operator could move the topsoil correctly. It was a laborious task, taking many hours in the field and office to get a job done. By the 1960s, this method was too much work for too few SCS technicians.

The first to go were the two-man crews. One SCS man would go to the field, and the farmer (or his wife) would provide the second person on the crew. Next to go was the staking operation. A job sheet instructed people how to properly lay out the grid on the field and install the stakes. The farmer (or contractor) would get the field ready for surveying and call the SCS to schedule the job. After the job was designed, the layout drawings were given to the farmer and he or his contractor marked the stakes for the amount of cut or fill at each location. SCS surveyors came out when the job was completed and did a final survey to assure that each job met the specifications that had been established.

As contractors got more experience, and became interested in doing a more professional job, many of them bought their own survey instruments. By 1961, SCS engineers were running a winter surveying school, teaching contractors all they needed to know about surveying in the field. Those contractors started to bring professional-quality field notes and contour maps to the SCS office, where the professional conservationists could do the design work. On simple jobs, the contractor would bring in a proposed design for the SCS to review and approve. Before long, the bulk of the field survey work done by the SCS technicians was the final survey to assure job quality.

By restricting their field work to the more difficult design jobs and the final surveys, the SCS crew was able to expand its impact tenfold, and in the 1961 field season, something like 100,000 acres of new irrigation layouts were installed in the Cassia conservation districts, using the technical expertise of SCS and the cost-sharing available through USDA's conservation programs. An irrigation "revolution" was achieved in spite of the small size of the SCS crew.

5

Getting Conservation on the Land

"The conservationist...saw himself as trying to treat
the whole land use malady, while the client mainly wanted
to be rid of a troublesome symptom."

Although it is hazardous to describe an "average" person in any situation, it was possible, in the 1960's, to make some generalizations about SCS field people. Most of them carried the job title of "Soil Conservationist," a Civil Service classification used widely by SCS. Qualifications for this job historically included: (1) a farm or ranch background; and (2) a college degree in soil science, agronomy, range management, or some closely related subject.[3] Recruitment and placement was done primarily at the state level. Because of low budgets and slow staff turnover rates, recruitment was very deliberate and selective.

The average SCS field professional had been carefully recruited from a Land Grant or agricultural college, had a rural background, and was placed in his home state to begin (and often end) his career.[4] It is probably safe to estimate that a clear majority of field office personnel were still located within 200 to 300 miles of their family's home. For this and other reasons, a clearly local bias was predictable. National or State policy which trampled local values could meet highly effective internal filters on its way to fruition.

---

[3] This section is taken from a paper analyzing Soil Conservation Service management policy written in 1974 as part of a management course at Harvard University taught by James Q. Wilson. Many of the conclusions and interpretations might not be germane today, but do reflect an assessment at that time.

[4] At that time, SCS field people were overwhelmingly male.

On the other hand, policy which was accepted seemed to be carried out very effectively. SCS employees carried the rural work ethic, rural self-reliance, and a great deal of personal commitment to the cause of conservation into their work. Morale, in general, appeared to run high. One indicator of this was a history of exceptionally low personnel turnover. Dr. William R. Van Dersal, formerly Deputy Administrator for Management, told the author that SCS consistently enjoyed the lowest turnover rate within the federal agencies and the second lowest rate in a national survey of large organizations, both public and private.

When the SCS man arrived at a client's land, he was there on the invitation of the land user, who had joined the local conservation district and requested help with his land use problem. Although more and more assistance was being rendered to urban and suburban landowners and organizations, the predominant client was still rural – a farmer or rancher.

Typically, the client had a troublesome erosion or resource problem. It might be a gully or an eroding hillside, or the need to develop adequate water for livestock. His interest was usually limited to the solution of that particular problem.

To the trained conservationist, however, such problems are rarely isolated, and more likely are symptomatic of a land use system that was failing to meet the complex demands of the natural environment. The land was being used beyond its physical capability or the user was neglecting the conservation practices and management techniques the land required, or both.

The conservationist, then, would often propose a more comprehensive "cure" than the client requested. He saw himself as trying to treat the whole land use malady, while the client mainly wanted to be rid of a troublesome symptom.

There were other differences, as well. The conservationist viewed the land and water as having public resource value which justified his job and efforts to preserve these resources. The farmer viewed land mainly as a private economic resource, the basic capital stock in his business. As well, the conservationist tended to be future-oriented, attempting to save the land for the sustained use of future generations. The farmer tended to be more present-oriented. He was concerned for the land and its conservation, too, but he had this year's cost and return picture to worry about. He might recognize that continued erosion was robbing the capital stock from his business, but prices and costs were beyond his control, and he might feel he needs to maintain his current methods to have a chance of remaining solvent.

By the 1960s, one earlier difference between the SCS conservationist and their clients—the level of education—had been rapidly disappearing. That farmer was not the hayseed stereotype of the comic strip. He typically operated a large, complex business involving large cash flows, huge investments in sophisticated and specialized machinery, highly technical agricultural chemicals, and very complex management techniques. He might hold one or more college degrees, play the commodity futures market to hedge risks in his business, and be active in community and political affairs. He did not stand in awe at the professional expertise of the SCS and often considered himself more of an expert in land management – particularly on his own land with which he was intimately familiar.

The SCS conservationist, then, faced the task of selling the client on the idea of a comprehensive land use and management system which met the needs of the land, solved the immediate problem, was compatible with the management ability and personal goals of the land user, *and* was economically sound. Not only must the idea be "sold" to the client, it must be fully internalized. Once the SCS man drove away to serve another of the clients he needed to see, the only real benefit to the quality of the environment came from the *client's* continued, day-to-day land use management. Technical discussions that involved a lot of good ideas being thrown around, without any being applied to the land by the client, were a waste of everyone's time and did nothing to further the public benefit goals of the SCS.

SCS policy and philosophy developed a generally-accepted way to get this task accomplished. The client is encouraged to develop their own personal conservation plan with the technical assistance of the SCS technician. It is written up, with details recorded on maps. Following completion of the plan, the SCS technician would be available to provide help as needed for implementation. That system worked, and in the early days of the agency, there were even those who forecast that if every farm could have a conservation plan, the erosion problem would be "solved." Experience tempered that expectation, but there was little doubt that the system had proven effective.

Some problems, however, were readily apparent. Each plan had to be tailored to the soil and water situation, economics, personality, and management ability of the individual client. The plan must be developed rather slowly and tediously in order to be fully internalized by the client. This makes attempts to mass-produce good conservation plans very difficult, and often casts a shadow of doubt on the SCS conservationists that are noted for producing high numbers of plans each year. Those plans may be excellent, or they may be the result of selecting easy units where few problems exist—while avoiding the tough challenges that really need help, but which slow production.

Since so much of the soil conservation task is educational in nature, considerable time may be required to develop the client's understanding and commitment to the conservation program laid out in the plan. Much of this time is difficult to justify in terms of output, and it might take many hours to get one person to understand what another had quickly grasped. Thus, one conservation plan, even though it might cover the same amount of land as another, might take much longer to finalize. That difference in time was hard to explain to management.

In addition, the time just may not be available. Staff limitations in field offices often meant that each staff person needed to assist several hundred clients a year. Geographic dispersion in rural areas – particularly in the West – means considerable travel time. This leads to some difficult trade-offs in the management of an SCS field office. Do you see several hundred clients, doing each little or no good? Or do you restrict service to a smaller client list, attempting to improve effectiveness with each? How many fewer? Carried too far, this begins to smack of discrimination, unacceptable in a public function.

The primary external influence on the SCS field office is the Soil Conservation District, a local unit of special-purpose government formed under state law. Governed by an elected board of 5-7 people, the district is charged with the development and promotion of a conservation program tailored to the locality. Through a memorandum of understanding, the SCS agrees to furnish technical assistance to help carry out the district's program.

District officials (who serve without pay) develop strong commitments to the conservation ethic and the program that provides local assistance. The main demand they make on the SCS field office is that it be effective in meeting locally-perceived needs. This effectiveness is normally judged by the informal contacts between neighbors and friends. If the SCS person begins getting a local reputation for being unhelpful, lazy, rigid, unimaginative or impractical, District officials will soon know it. Even worse is a reputation for ineptness. Woe to the careless employee that lays out an irrigation ditch that won't carry water or a pond that doesn't hold water. It won't take much of that and the District will be contacting the State or Area Conservationist to see that people are trained, disciplined, moved, or terminated.

Another outside influence growing in importance since the 1970's is the environmental movement. Growing public awareness of the dangers in crude tampering with the natural environment led to criticism of some SCS historic work, such as wetland drainage and stream channelization. It came as a profound shock to many devoted SCS professionals to hear their work criticized by the public for being environmentally destructive. This movement made SCS field people more sensitive to the full range of the environmental implications of their work, and more attentive to the voices of new, vocal, non-agricultural, and often critical outside groups.

6

In Charge of the Local Office

"...we had evidence that the Chinese were doing nuclear testing. Radioactive particles...are being washed down in this storm."

In 1962, Neil got the news that he had been promoted and transferred to the Orofino, Idaho field office, where he would be the Work Unit Conservationist (WUC) and also be assigned part-time to lead an accelerated conservation planning effort in the surrounding conservation districts that made up the Palouse region. So with his wife, Jeanne, and baby Rob in the car and Neil and the bird dog in the pickup, the 400+ mile move was done on icy and snowbound February roads.

An old house on a hillside farm near Orofino was rented, and Neil was ready (at age 23) to take on the task of organizing and running a local SCS office. The office had been vacant for several months, so there was little opportunity to find out what was where, as the prior WUC was long gone. Don Phillips, a native of Tekoa, Washington and an experienced Palouse farm hand, was assigned to the Orofino staff, so with two natives of the region (Neil had been raised in the northern Idaho panhandle), the staff was ready to take on the work in the Clearwater district as well as the extra Palouse planning.

Orofino was a small (2,500 people in 1960) river town at the confluence of Orofino Creek and the Clearwater River. The primary economic activity was logging and a little bit of agriculture. It was the county seat of Clearwater County, which was a large (some 1.5 million acre) county made up primarily of forests and mountains, much of it in the Clearwater National Forest that extended to the Montana line on the East. Agriculture was limited to the lower-elevation ridges and plateaus above the river canyons and consisted largely of dryland grain and livestock operations, intermingled with private forest lands.

In early 1962, the area was anticipating a significant expansion of economic activity. After years of planning, including several years when it looked like nothing would happen, Senator Henry Dworshak of Idaho had succeeded in getting Congressional approval to build the Bruce's Eddy dam on the north fork of the Clearwater, about 5 miles west of Orofino. Construction on the Dworshak Dam (renamed in his honor) was to begin immediately. The Corps of Engineers had begun establishing offices and preliminary work was beginning. The town was braced for a population/construction boom. Housing was tight, and expensive.

The small, one-room SCS office was a challenge. Finding where things were, what the backlog of work might be, and getting acquainted took a while. One of the nice things about it was the neighborhood. It was upstairs in the Orofino Post Office, surrounded by the staff of the Clearwater National Forest, and next door to Norm Fitzsimmons, the Clearwater County Agent for the University of Idaho Extension Service. None of them could help figure out where things were in the SCS office, but they made the place a welcoming work environment. Norm knew all the farmers in the county, so teaming up with him made meeting the people and learning the area a lot easier.

Neil hadn't been in the office long before the past arrived, in a hurry. An intense gentleman strode up to his desk one day, flopped down a string of credentials, announced that he was a fraud investigator from the Department of Agriculture, and that Neil would work for him from that moment forward. A shocked Neil was directed to open the cooperator files for a certain farmer and find any records of a cost-shared grassed waterway. The records were promptly turned over, and the investigation moved to the Agricultural Stabilization and Conservation Service (ASCS) office a couple of blocks away.

Neither Neil nor Don, his staffer, knew anything about the job under question, so they went to the farm and found that the waterway was, indeed, in place as the documents indicated, and looking pretty good. The farmer in question was a member of the local ASCS

Committee that had approved the payment, so the key question was whether the payment was legal or was an "inside job." After several days of nervous time during the intensive audit, the problem appeared to be that one of the documents ASCS had needed to certify the payment had been mislaid in their state office. When the proper documents were finally found, the investigator lost interest and wrapped up his work.

Neil was left with a lasting impression about the importance of getting the paperwork right, along with being technically right in the first place.

The other lesson, learned first in Burley, was really driven home during this field office experience: the importance of saying "no" when things weren't right. SCS had to provide two certifications on a cost-shared conservation practice. The first was that the practice was needed on the land, was the right practice for the problem, and was designed correctly. The second certified that, after installation, the practice had been installed according to the design and specifications. The worst mistake an SCS man could make, in either circumstance, was to try to be a "nice guy" and let something go that was on the margin, or that shouldn't be approved.

Farmers are, in the main, honest, straight-forward people that are a pleasure to deal with. But money was involved and they could be counting on that cost-sharing check (many farmers were in pretty dire financial situations). If they couldn't see the need for all the detailed specifications that SCS was insisting were important, they might conclude that if a detail or two slipped by, so what? That situation could get difficult.

The SCS answer had to be firm and straight-forward. If it wasn't right, it wasn't approved. No exceptions. That was especially true for a 20-something kid trying to get a foothold in the local farm community. You couldn't be arrogant or pushy about it, but you had to establish a reputation as a straight-shooter who did things right. The only way to do that was to be consistent in pushing to get jobs right, and being willing to say "no" when they weren't. Both Neil and Don were in full agreement on that one, and worked together to make sure that each job was handled right.

The snow survey program in Orofino consisted of one low-elevation snow course that often had little snow in mid-winter and was reachable off a maintained road, another course in the trees behind the Pierce Ranger Station, and a mountain course on Hemlock Butte, the small mountain behind Pierce. SCS maintained a Snow Cat (this one a jeep on tracks) at the Pierce Ranger Station for the monthly trip to measure Hemlock Butte. In 1962, the snow survey wasn't much of a job at Orofino, but that was soon to change.

With the impending construction of Dworshak dam, the Corps of Engineers needed river flow forecasts on the Clearwater River, and those forecasts didn't exist. SCS was funded to install a new snow survey network that could become part of the river forecasting system. The Clearwater is part of the headwaters of the Columbia River, so the entire river system and its dams were affected by the Clearwater flows. Here, over-snow travel, as difficult as it was in the rest of Idaho, was out of the question. In the steep, remote Clearwater Mountains, the distance from a useable road to a snow course could be 50 miles or more. The only possible access was with the use of helicopters.

Jack Wilson, Morley Nelson's assistant in the SCS snow survey office in Boise, had studied the watershed on USGS maps and picked out some candidate spots for snow courses. Maps in hand, he came to Orofino, where he and Neil hired a local helicopter service out of Lewiston for the task. Flying in winter conditions, over a vast mountain region, with little more than a topographic map for guidance, they spent a week locating appropriate places for the new snow courses.

Often, upon finding the right topographic and elevation conditions, the challenge was finding a nearby landing spot. The pilot, Ned Gilliand, was an exceptionally skilled mountain flyer, and at times he would put the chopper down in a spot that was too tight for safe take-off, so in addition to marking out and measuring the new snow course, the task involved cutting enough trees and brush to open up the site for a safe departure. That caused a little friction with the Forest Service people, who were glad to get additional hydrologic data on the National Forest, but not too happy about having their trees cut down!

Neil won those arguments, on the basis that it was his neck on the line, but the Forest Service guys weren't always pleased. It was interesting to come back to those landing sites the following summer to put in the permanent snow survey course markers. The winter landings were made on top of 6-8' or more of snow, but the summer site was a jungle of cut-off brush and tree stems that was impossible to navigate! So the crew had to hike in from wherever a safe landing could be made, then use chain saws to cut down the "stubble" in the landing zone before the helicopter could ferry in the pipes, concrete, etc. required to install the permanent markers.

Snow courses were marked with permanent pipes on each end, then (usually) five sample points were located at intervals between the end markers. On one end, the marker was a pipe with cross-bars welded on it at measured intervals. At two foot intervals, the cross-bar was 6" high and 24" wide. At the one-foot markers in between, small 2" x 8" bars were located. The result was a tall, ladder-looking affair that, when painted fluorescent orange, was easily visible from the air. This allowed the snow surveyors to read the snow depth from a fixed-wing airplane when desired. Those aerial depth readings didn't register the amount of water in the snow as a ground measurement could do, but if rapid assessment was needed, the average water content could be estimated quickly at a reasonable cost.

The other end of the snow course was marked with a plain pipe, also painted orange. The sample points between were cleared of small trees and brush if it existed so that the snow tube wouldn't get hung up on a buried stick. With all the new snow courses marked, the SCS program was ready for the winter season.

SCS also worked with the Corps of Engineers in the summer of 1962 to re-build the experimental isotopic snow-measuring station at Hemlock Butte. This device was designed to register radioactive measurements and relay them automatically to the Corps office in Walla Walla, Washington.

The idea was fairly straight-forward. A radioactive source was buried in a leaden container at ground level, with an opening pointing straight up. A metal trestle about 15 feet off the ground supported a Geiger counter, and a box off to the end of the trestle contained a battery-driven radio transmitter to send the readings. An early-generation solar array provided power to charge the batteries. A high fence and warning signs kept wandering wildlife and humans from getting too close to the radiation source.

Pilot Charles "Frenny" Frensdorf carries the snow tube on a snow course in the Clearwater Mountains. Note the aerial marker in the foreground.

As water molecules in the snow accumulated between the source and the counter, the rays from the radioactive source were deflected, so the readings in the counter went down as more water accumulated in the snow pack. The readings could be correlated directly with the amount of snow water between the source and the counter.

For a couple of months, the system worked fine. The SCS crew manually measured the snow at the nearby permanent snow course each month as a way of correlating the radiological data, and Walla

Walla was getting the radioed data readings in fine shape. Then the readings from the remote site stopped. Totally. The Corps technicians went to the site with SCS and recovered the transmitter box, where it was discovered that a temperature recorder showed something like 150° F difference between the high and low temperatures that had been registered within the box! Those extreme temperatures led to expansion and contraction, damaging the wiring connections and transistors in the device. The transmitter was ruined.

The re-build of the snow course the following summer reversed the structure. The leaden case with the radioactive material was mounted on the overhead trestle and the counter and transmission equipment were put at ground level, where a covering of winter snow would keep the temperatures uniform and, would hopefully allow the system to run through the next winter. It ran just fine, but not without some surprising results. That's a story for later.

Meanwhile, Neil and Don were settling into the work routine in the Orofino office. After the Burley experience, with its heavy work load of irrigation system improvements, there really wasn't much local conservation activity. The dryland grain and cattle operations built a few farm ponds, developed some springs for livestock water, and installed some grassed waterways. Most of the work involved developing conservation plans to help landowners improve their crop rotation, tillage practices to reduce soil erosion on cropland, and adoption of better grazing practices to improve pasture performance and soil protection.

Most of the farms had patches of woodland, and this was often the most frustrating part of the conservation planning effort. The forest types were largely slow-growing mixed fir-pine stands that required something like 40-80 years to produce merchantable timber. Many of the landowners had purchased their farms after the prior owner had removed all the saleable timber, so the woodlands were a mess.

Those harvesting techniques had usually been highly destructive, and the remaining stand was struggling to recover anything of value. Selective thinning to remove poor trees and unwanted species was needed, but it was expensive and there was no hope of any economic return for decades. Struggling farm families that usually needed at least one job in town to help support the farm had very few resources to devote to those investments. Often, their forest management plan was to "wait 10 or 20 years and see what happens." Not a very satisfying conservation approach!

But it was important for we SCSers to learn basic forestry techniques and do our best to help improve woodland management wherever possible. Mel Carlson was the SCS State Forester who came to teach Neil and Don basic forestry techniques. Mel was an old-school forester who had worked in logging camps on the Clearwater before starting his SCS career in the old CCC camp at Worley, Idaho (Neil's home town) in the 1930's. He taught the basics—how to map and sample stands, measure trees for diameter and height, drill cores to get ages and estimate growth rates, and estimate stocking density with the use of a "foresters stick."

With this information and a set of growth and yield tables for the forest types in the region, the conservationist could estimate growth rates for a landowner and show them what kind of economic return to expect from managing their forest. This was highly useful to the owner with a manageable stand; less so for those with the torn-up remains of a destructive timber harvest. For Neil, this work was training that would come strongly into play decades later.

One thing the SCS asked of its field people was to conduct good information programs to tell the public about soil and water conservation. This was a task that Neil really enjoyed. As with most SCS field offices, Orofino had a 4x5 speed graphic camera, and it got a lot of use, documenting both conservation scenes and, at times, local flooding events.

One of Neil's early stories was about a local farmer who had decided to convert his operation from grain to hay and livestock. Henry and Mary Hasse ran a medium-sized farm in the Cavendish community, and were building up a significant hog operation that relied on purchased grain rather than home-grown feed. On the rolling forest soils of the farm, this was an excellent conservation system. In the March 19, 1961 issue of *Idaho Farmer*, Neil's front page story ended with "Henry is proving in his operation that it is possible to run prof-

31

itably a small diversified operation on the cutover lands of North Idaho. He is also proving that the land doesn't need to be 'farmed to death' to get economical returns if livestock and soil management principles are properly applied."

With that story, plus work to get snow survey results printed in the local paper and many speeches to local service, school and agricultural groups, Neil started to hone his information skills—later to become a key part of his professional life.

Conservation education was an important part of the job. Under the leadership of County Agent Norm Fitzsimmons, a group of local professionals was formed in 1962 to conduct a 6th grade Forestry Tour for Clearwater County school kids. For three days, school buses full of 6th graders toured the Clearwater back country, looking at the Potlatch Forests' logging town of Headquarters, seeing forestry operations in action, staying in logging camps, and getting field lectures and demonstrations from foresters and other professionals. Fifty years later, the program continues, having shared the forest conservation story with thousands of kids stretching over three generations.

In May of 1966, Neil was pleased to be informed by Jim Golden of *The Lewiston Morning Tribune* that the Palouse Empire Chapter of Sigma Delta Chi, the professional journalistic society, had named him as one of five regional news sources that were rated 'outstanding' in their 1966 Freedom of Information report.

Another aspect of the SCS work that might sound a bit strange to today's conservationists was Civil Defense. In the early 1960s, the United States was steeped in Cold War fears. That led to a huge government effort to try to foresee and respond to a nuclear attack. There were county Civil Defense programs that included fallout shelters, air raid drills, and all kinds of ideas for what needed to be done in preparation for the unthinkable horror of a nuclear attack. The University of Idaho worked with the Office of Civil Defense to conduct workshops and conferences on the topic.

For the SCS, as the technical agency serving agriculture, the assigned Civil Defense role was radiation monitoring. The Orofino office, like all field offices, was equipped with a set of radiation monitoring instruments and its staffers were trained in their use. Regular training drills, with the instructors hiding minute pieces of radioactive material, were conducted so that the SCS monitors knew how to locate and identify dangerous situations.

Theoretically, the job for SCS was to go out in the countryside after a nuclear incident and see if vegetation and soils were safe. Could cow's milk be used safely? What about vegetables and fruits that might be contaminated? Could farmers safely cultivate soils without stirring up damaging radioactive dust? Those were some of the questions to be answered for Civil Defense officials.

What wasn't clear was what happened to the SCS person who ventured out of their bomb shelter and discovered that the surrounding countryside was lethal. There was no protective clothing—only the little instruments whose clicking sounds and dial faces could tell you if you were toast or not. That possibility was not widely discussed in the training conferences or manuals, but it was on everyone's mind. A major problem was that, if you were directly hit, there probably wasn't very much you could do about it.

But the SCS was ready, just in case. New batteries were purchased every month, and the instruments were tested—just in case. Then came October, 1962, and the Cuban missile crisis. High-flying U.S. planes photographed the Soviets installing nuclear-armed intercontinental ballistic missiles in Cuba, and the U.S. threw a naval blockade around the island nation. It became a most serious confrontation between the world's super-powers, and the threat level went over the top.

For the SCS, even in Clearwater County, Idaho, it was a new level of readiness. Instead of leaving the monitoring instruments in the office closet, Neil had to carry them with him full time—24 hours a day, 7 days a week. A steel army surplus ammunition case provided the container, and was always within easy reach. Happily, the Soviets and the U.S. reached an agreement that each would pull back some of its nuclear installations, and the threat gradually receded. But it didn't go away, so the Civil Defense preparation continued. The monitoring meters were kept in working order and always within easy reach.

Which brings us back to the snow survey program. One morning, in the midst of a mid-winter blizzard, Neil was awakened by a phone call from the Corps of Engineers at Walla Walla. "What's going on up there?" the voice inquired. "We just recorded a 10-inch loss of water at the monitoring station at Hemlock Butte!"

"I don't have any idea what's going on," Neil said, "but you didn't lose any snow water on Hemlock Butte. It's been snowing like crazy all night."

"Well, get up there right away and see what's happening. Something's not right."

So an unscheduled trip to Pierce was in order, and Neil set out in the SCS pickup through snow-covered roads to carry out the task. At Pierce, he got the Snow Cat out of the Forest Service garage, loaded his ammo box of radiological gear in it, and headed for the Hemlock Butte snow course.

At the course, he found what he was expecting—about 2 feet of new powder snow from the recent storm. Curious, however, about why the radiological readings were so strange, he got out his counter to see if the station's source had somehow been damaged.

What he found was surprising. The counter went off immediately, registering high levels of radiation even at the snow machine. A second meter was turned on to make sure there was no mistake, and it began registering radiation as well. Taking the two meters, he began to snowshoe around the snow course site to see where the radiation was coming from. The levels weren't dangerous, but they were the same everywhere, no matter how far from the radiological station he walked.

Puzzled, he loaded up the gear and drove down the mountain. Back in the office, he called Walla Walla to report on what he'd found. The response was quick and direct. "We were afraid that was what happened," the Corpsman said. "We've been monitoring the Chinese and we had evidence that they were doing atmospheric nuclear testing, in defiance of the worldwide treaty banning that action. Radioactive particles have blown this far and are being washed down in this storm. This is top secret information, and you are to tell no one at this time."

Neil measures snow at Hemlock Butte 1964

So, as the mountains of northern Idaho (and who knows where else) lay under a beautiful blanket of radioactive snow, thanks to the the Chinese, Neil and the SCS staff went on about their daily tasks, including the snow surveys every month. The radiological snow measuring station was, however, history. New measuring devices called snow pillows were just coming on line, and promised to do a reliable job of remote snow water measurement without all the radiation problems.

The conservation work in the Orofino office was, as noted earlier, fairly limited. There was plenty of work to do, but much of it was not recognized by the SCS progress-reporting system. Thus, while other offices were reporting lots of officially recognized progress, Orofino was tied up with a lot of questions created by the rapid growth of the community.

Neil was advising on runoff and erosion control on new subdivisions and roads, along with helping with the layout, soil mapping, drainage and erosion control on a new community golf course. He was also working with a group of forest owners to set up the

Clearwater Valley Christmas Tree Growers Association so that land-owners could see a few dollars coming out of the little trees in the cutover timber stands in their woodlands.

The work was addressing local natural resource concerns, but there were no "progress" codes for this type of work, so there was nothing to put on the bi-weekly 253 reports or the SCS progress reports. "Urban development" work wasn't the standard conservation work on farm and ranch land that the agency had concentrated on in the past, and was still doing in more agriculturally-intense areas.

The Clearwater area suffered severe low-elevation flooding in December of 1964 and January of 1965, and Neil was right in the middle of it. The snow surveys had shown very high levels of soil moisture and snow at the lower elevations and, although it was beyond SCS's mission to try to forecast flooding, Neil made sure that local officials went with him to inspect snow and soil conditions so that they could come to their own conclusions as to the situation.

The result was that the community was as well prepared as possible when rainfall events created significant flooding in the side streams running into the Clearwater.

Preparation could only do so much, however. When Orofino Creek erupted under the double flow of rainfall and low-elevation snowmelt runoff, much of the downtown area was affected. The Clearwater River was running high, and while the dikes keeping it from flooding the town did hold the river water out, the high water blocked the outlet for Orofino Creek, which backed up and flooded the downtown.

Neil was busy taking photographs and measuring flows to establish a data record in the event of a future watershed stabilization or restoration program, but there wasn't much else to be done. Similar work was done at Peck, a small community on Big Canyon Creek, where the flooding was also severe. As the waters receded, the communities worked together to clean up and repair what had been damaged. The role of SCS, while minor, was appreciated by many.

The aerial snow survey work in Orofino differed somewhat from the traditional ground-travel methods that Neil had learned in Burley. For one thing, the weather really mattered. You might brave a snow cat trip in a storm, but you didn't fly a helicopter. So, as the last week in the month approached, it was important to keep an eye on the weather as well as the calendar. The weather forecasts were only of marginal help. There were no weather stations in the back country mountains, and satellite weather imagery was not yet developed, so it was often more important to look out the window than to listen to the forecast.

As a result, a lot of time was spent waiting for weather to clear before attempting a survey flight. The flights started in December with aerial surveys. These were always an adventure, depending on which flying company won the annually-awarded federal contract to provide the planes and helicopters. If the pilot was a skilled mountain flyer who was familiar with the landmarks in the Clearwater, it could be fairly straight-forward. If the pilot was new and lost, it could get interesting. This put Neil in the role of navigator, with little more than USGS maps as a guide. Having not seen the mountains for six months, it required close attention to the terrain and the map to keep from getting confused.

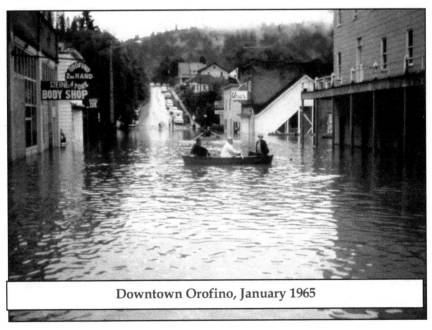

Downtown Orofino, January 1965

Upon arriving at the snow course, the pilot was shown (if needed) how to approach the fly-over so that the aerial marker could be clearly seen. Neil would concentrate on counting the rungs on the marker that were above the snow, and marking a line across a drawing of the marker to indicate the snow depth. If he got a good reading on the first pass, it was thumbs-up. If not, it was go around and try another approach. If that didn't work, you did it again.

That was no problem if the air was smooth, but when the winter winds were howling over that mountainous terrain, creating major up-and downdrafts, the pilot had his hands full with the airplane, and getting a good look at the marker was a challenge, as well.

Neil's stomach had to hold on as he concentrated on getting a good reading, but at times it was a near thing. If weather permitted, all the courses on the route could be read in 2-3 flying hours, and the team could be comfortably back in the Orofino airport by mid-afternoon. If the weather turned bad, some of the readings might have to be delayed a day or two until flying conditions were better.

One day the back country weather looked favorable, but the Orofino airport was covered with 6" of new wet snow. The airport was a fairly short strip, on a river bar across from town, with the mountains rising on one side and U.S. Highway 12 running between the runway and the Clearwater River on the other side. This day, the airplane was a Cessna 172, with tricycle landing gear. It was a fairly small single-engine plane, and it took several attempts down the snow-covered runway to get wheel tracks packed down in the wet snow so that the plane could get up enough speed to take off.

Upon take-off, the snow course readings were done without incident. Upon return, the pilot was uneasy about landing on the snow-covered runway. He slowed down as much as possible, and with the stall warning blaring, gently set the plane down. As the main wheels touched the ground, however, they seemed to lock up, slamming the nose wheel down and putting the plane into a sickening horizontal spin. In a matter of seconds the plane came to a stop, with its propeller right at the very edge of the busy highway.

Everyone was safe, but not breathing easily. As was later discovered, one of the main wheel brakes had packed full of wet snow during the takeoff attempts, and with that snow frozen solid during the long flight, the wheel had locked up on the landing.

From February through May, the snow courses were sampled on the ground. Travel by helicopter is significantly slower than with a light plane, so these trips often involved a full day or more. After landing near the snow course, the pilot and Neil would don snow-shoes, gather up the snow tube and scales, and head for the course.

The snow tube was made up of 30" sections that screwed to-gether to make up the necessary length to reach through the snow pack to the ground, and it was common to use 150" of tube to collect the samples. (The total kit was 180", but that length was only seldom needed.)

Getting a clean core sample without having the snow freeze in-side the long tube took some technique. The tube was cooled (or warmed, depending on the air temperature) to snow temperature by laying and spinning it on the top of the snow. The survey team then tried to push it down through the snow pack in one smooth, rapid movement, without stopping. When the snowpack was 10-12 feet deep, or had ice layers inside, this was not always easy. The weight and strength of two men were sometimes fully needed.

While it was critical to get high quality samples to maintain the accuracy of the survey and the resulting water forecast, it was often important to get the sampling done as quickly as possible. When it was bitter cold, the helicopter engine would cool down rapidly as it sat on the landing spot, and there was the threat that, if it got too cold, it might not start. That possibility drove the team to move as fast as possible, since the prospect of spending overnight (or longer) in a dead copter on a remote winter mountain was not appealing. That problem never arose, although a few times when the engine seemed to turn over very reluctantly before starting, there were some nervous moments.

Other nervous moments arose when the contract was awarded to a flying company that used pilots unfamiliar with mountain flying. All of the pilots were flight-qualified and experienced, as the con-tract required, but some of them had gained their helicopter experi-ence as contract pilots flying over the jungles of Laos or Cambodia in military situations. The mountains were something else. An experienced mountain pilot could read the wind and the terrain below and either avoid or compensate for the violent wind shifts that regularly occurred. Jungle training wasn't very helpful in those situations.

Although Neil was not qualified as a pilot of any sort, many hours of mountain flying had taught a few lessons. His advice, however, was seldom welcomed by an experienced pilot. After one adventure trying unsuccessfully to land at Forty-nine Meadows, high on the divide between the Clearwater and St. Joe drainages, Neil called the SCS State Office, who notified the flying service that the one particular pilot was no longer to be utilized. "Watching his knuckles turn white on the controls and seeing the sweat beads pop out on his face didn't build confidence," Neil had reported. Over 5 years and 100+ snow measurements, the Orofino office upheld the SCS safety record in snow surveys, with no injuries or accidents of any kind.

7

Conservation Frustration

*"...conservation planning transitioned from being
a rather "loose" agreement by the landowner to improve
certain management practices into a solid plan...."*

It is never much fun to be a noodge*, but to be a soil conservation noodge in northern Idaho in the 1960's was downright depressing. To understand why, it helps to know a bit about the land and the agriculture of that time and place.

The Palouse region of eastern Washington and northern Idaho is a land of rolling hills that look a lot like sand dunes because they were formed the same way—soil blown in from the south and west had formed them over the eons. The silt loam soils had grown grass or mixed grass and trees for centuries, and the result was dark, rich, fertile soils that pioneers began plowing out for cropland in the late 1800's. The Mediterranean climate was great for growing crops of grass, wheat, barley, peas and lentils. Some 24 to 40 inches of annual precipitation fell, mostly as winter and spring snow and rain. Summers were dry and hot.

Winter wheat was king of the crops because it gave higher yields than spring-planted crops. The soft white kernels were highly prized as pastry flour, so prices were usually decent. It was often planted after summer fallow, a practice where the land was clean-cultivated throughout the growing season to kill weeds and store additional moisture. In September or October, wheat was planted. If soil moisture and weather cooperated, the wheat plants would grow a few inches tall and cover the field for the winter.

---

* A 'noodge' is 'one who nags or nudges another'

But the small plants often did little to stop soil erosion and with the soil finely pulverized from a summer's cultivation, any runoff could melt the topsoil like sugar and move it off the slopes. Erosion rates in the range of 100 tons of topsoil lost per year were routinely observed, and the combination of moldboard plowing (which threw a 6-inch layer of topsoil some 18 to 24 inches downhill with each plowing) and soil erosion were rapidly depleting the fertile topsoil and revealing the lighter, less fertile subsoil on the surface, particularly on the hilltops. To a soil conservationist, the lesson was clear: this type of agriculture had no long-term future and would have to be changed.

Changing wasn't easy, however. The mechanization of agriculture, which began in earnest after World War I, really accelerated after World War II. Tractors got bigger and faster, machinery got larger and more efficient and a farm family no longer needed a stable full of horses and a bunch of hired hands to get field work done. It was, in the eyes of the farm community, unalloyed progress.

Instead of growing hay and pasture in rotation to feed animals and re-build crop-depleted soils, farmers could tear out all the old fence rows, create larger fields that were more efficient to farm with the large machinery, and concentrate on growing cash crops. With that transition made, turning back to a mixed crop and animal agriculture was very unlikely. Constant cropping, supported by clean cultivation and high soil erosion rates, was the new paradigm.

In a social sense, it became a point of pride when farm fields were cultivated as clean as a pin, with the topsoil finely pulverized and as smooth as a dance floor. The locals called these the "good farms," owned by industrious people who were taking full advantage of their control over the land and its production. Farmers who left crop residues on the soil, or rough-tilled their land so that water erosion was reduced, were often derided as "lazy" or "sloppy" farmers.

Coffee-shop pressures are very important in affecting farm country behavior, and selling conservation tillage methods in that social atmosphere was difficult. The improved machinery was also accompanied by improvements in crop varieties, featuring more disease and insect resistance, a higher grain-to-straw ratio, and higher yields.

Commercial nitrogen fertilizer was readily available and economical to apply. Legume cover crops, once used to restore soil fertility and structure, were no longer needed to support high yields, so their use was reduced and their soil-conserving value lost. Dryland winter wheat yields in the Palouse were hitting 60 bushels per acre and more—much higher yields than in the pioneer days—and going up steadily.

So the conservation story was a tough sell. It was plain that the topsoil was being damaged and, in many cases, virtually obliterated. As the subsoils became more prominent, water holding capacity and soil fertility went down. But crop yields kept going up due to the improved varieties and increased use of fertilizer! So the trend lines were going in absolutely opposite directions. One could argue the illogical conclusion that maximum yield would be realized when the topsoil was completely washed away. Nobody really believed that, but the evidence pointed that way.

As difficult and frustrating as it was to try to sell soil conservation methods in this situation, it was even more frustrating to have national agricultural policy driving directly against the conservation efforts. While the SCS soil conservationists were trying to develop more effective soil-conserving methods compatible with the ongoing agricultural technologies and convince farmers to try them in the name of protecting future productivity, other forces in Congress and USDA were creating significant economic incentives that promoted soil-damaging behavior.

Crop surpluses drove national agricultural policy, and wheat was a major surplus crop. The response was to put acreage limits on the amount of wheat a farm could produce. Acreage allotments were calculated on the farm's prior wheat production history. As a result, the farmer who had been concentrating most heavily on wheat got a better allotment than the one that had been conscientiously rotating crops, growing cover crops, or including livestock as a means of protecting the soil. It's not rare for new regulatory programs like this to penalize the good actors, and this was an example. The lesson to farmers was clear: protecting your fragile economic foothold meant ignoring conservation needs and growing as much wheat as possible when the controls were not in place.

When the controls were in place, it was still important to grow as much wheat as was allowed. In addition to limiting the acres of wheat a farm could grow, the new rules made it imperative to always grow the full allowed amount if you wanted to maintain your acreage allotment.

If you voluntarily reduced the acres of wheat planted, you lost that crop history, and with it, the future allowance to grow your previous wheat acreage. So the surplus-reducing "ceiling" actually became a "floor," that forced farmers to protect their wheat allotment. If a better soil-conserving rotation was available with some cropping adjustments, the risk of future limits on wheat planting was too high, and farmers wouldn't risk it. So adjusting the crop rotation was a limited conservation opportunity. Soil conservation took a back seat to the economic reality created by the federal farm program.

The conservation cost-sharing program—then called the Agricultural Conservation Program (ACP)—wasn't helpful in this situation, either. One of the cost-shared practices at the time was clean cultivation for weed control. The program paid farmers to summer fallow their land, provided that it was kept weed-free by regular cultivation. This, of course, was a major contributor to the soil erosion problem, so while the SCS people were out there trying to get farmers to cultivate less, the ACP program was paying them hard cash to cultivate more!

That incongruous and frustrating situation made inter-agency relations prickly. As one looks at the conservation policy changes that began to be realized in the 1980's, it is easy to see how this history—repeated in one form or another in many parts of rural America—was a major factor in the new approaches to soil conservation that have since emerged.

The Palouse conservation planning work was spread out over three other counties—Lewis, Nez Perce, and Latah—and involved a lot of coordination with the other SCS offices and people. It also involved a lot of road travel, so was not terribly efficient. Regardless, it was half or more of the job, so it got underway as soon as the jobs could be organized.

Farmers in the region grew wheat, peas, and barley on the rolling hills of the region. Soil erosion rates were some of the highest in the nation, particularly where annual crops were grown with conventional tillage. The machinery and methods needed for no-till were not yet developed and the economic and policy obstacles to conservation described above were all in place, so most of the conservation planning was around limiting tillage as much as possible, building and maintaining grassed waterways, and avoiding up-and-down hill tillage where possible.

Wheat was the most profitable and dependable crop, and the annual planting acreage each farm was tightly controlled by the USDA commodity control programs, so there wasn't much that could be done to change the farm's cropping patterns to help reduce erosion. Many of the conservation plans proposed very little change in the operations on most farms, and the impact on soil erosion rates was modest, at best. It was difficult, if not impossible, to see much progress as a result of the extra effort.

The Palouse, in addition to being a high-erosion area, was also a marvelous opportunity for training young soil conservationists.

The Moscow work unit had two "sub-units" that were located in the small towns of Genesee and Kendrick. Staff at the three offices included three conservation technicians whose experience all dated back many years. As veterans of the CCC and SCS program since the 1930's, these men were founts of experience and skill. Larry Sorenson at Genesee was widely known as the regional expert on tile drainage; Manning Onstott at Kendrick was without peer at designing and laying out farm ponds; and John Nicholas at Moscow was an all-around conservationist and grassed waterway expert. Turning to men like these for help on special jobs, and working alongside them as they did "their thing" was a conservation education in itself.

In the 1962 Farm Bill, a pilot program called the "Cropland Conversion Program" was designed, and USDA implemented a testing effort in 100 counties in 13 states. Clearwater County was one of those chosen, and by 1964 Neil and Don were immersed in the new program. A local farmer and former county commissioner, Clifford Anderson, was hired as a part-time addition to the staff.

The program was designed to help farmers make the transition from cropland producing surplus crops (wheat, in this case) to other uses such as trees, grass, water storage, recreational facilities or wildlife habitat. The idea was to reduce both surplus crop production and convert marginal soils into a more conservation-oriented pro-duction system. The land was not to be "retired," as in the Soil Bank Program, but remain in an economic use while avoiding the produc-tion of surplus crops.

It was based on a conservation plan developed in cooperation with the SCS and the local conservation district, and backed by a 5-year contract that guaranteed cost-sharing for installing the needed conservation practices and providing a rental payment for the dura-tion of the contract. The long-term contracting feature had been done in the Great Plains Conservation Program, but was a completely new experience for Idaho farmers and USDA agencies.

The program worked well in Clearwater County, and conserva-tion planning transitioned from being a rather "loose" agreement by the landowner to improve certain management practices into a solid plan that could become the basis for a 5-year contract. Every-one got a lot more serious in that process! As a result, Neil, Don and Cliff spent a very active summer in 1964, doing a lot of conservation plans, working with the Agricultural Stabilization and Conservation Service (ASCS) to get the contracts established, and working with the landowners to get the initial practices installed. It was a very positive experience, and (as will be seen later) had a lot of influence on the initial concepts in the Conservation Reserve Program that was cre-ated in 1985 and is still an important part of USDA's conservation program today.

But good things don't always last long, and at the end of the pilot program period, the Cropland Conversion Program was not con-verted to a permanent program, and a good opportunity to improve conservation work in Clearwater County was lost.

The other conservation work done in Orofino was a mix of agri-culture, forestry, and development-related challenges that Neil en-joyed. But to some in the SCS hierarchy, the numbers in the progress reporting system were what mattered. Orofino didn't produce them. So there was steady criticism of the Clearwater district program, and in 1965, Neil began to think that his career with SCS had come to a dead end. He resigned from the SCS and went into private business locally, running a drive-in movie theatre in the summer, selling and brokering Christmas trees in the fall, and working on a logging crew in the winter. Those were dead-end jobs, producing little income and no family security.

In 1966, local talk was that his replacement in the Orofino SCS office was ready to be transferred, so Neil let word get around that he would consider coming back to the agency. Lee Morgan, the SCS State Conservationist in Boise, called and asked if it was true that Neil was ready to return. "Yes," he said, "but with two conditions."

"What are they?"

"I can come back to work now (in early summer) but I need to stay here until the end of the year to finish off the obligations I have with the Christmas tree business. So I'll need to take some leave without pay from Thanksgiving until Christmas. Then, I need to move out as soon as possible, because there's no SCS future for me in this area."

"I'll agree to those conditions," Lee said. With a few quick paper transactions, Neil was back at work in the Orofino SCS office, with 6 months in which to tie down loose ends and get the office in shape for a successor.

Lee Morgan was, in the eyes of some, a demanding and difficult boss. But to Neil he was a highly respected mentor and person who would always keep his word. And he did. By February, 1967, Neil, Jeanne, Rob and Eric were on their way to Idaho Falls, where Neil would be assigned as the Dryland Specialist in the Eastern Idaho Area office with an additional assignment of learning as much as possible about the information and education business because Morgan wanted him to come to Boise in 18 months and assume a new Information and education role on the state office staff.

For Neil, it was back to SCS work with a new energy and commitment to a career with a future.

8

Midwest Technology Comes to Idaho

"Neil was learning to be more proficient
in providing information to the local news media."

Dryland cropping in Eastern Idaho was different than that of the Palouse. These were high-elevation grassland soils with low annual rainfall, most of which occurred as winter snow. The rotation was grain-fallow, growing primarily wheat and barley every other year. The slopes were less steep than those found in the Palouse, but there was significant soil erosion during the spring snowmelt as well as in summer storms on the fallow land.

The new SCS approach to erosion control here was to adapt the terraces that had been developed in the Midwest to the topography and soils of Eastern Idaho. Neil worked with John Ozmun, a soil conservationist with extensive terrace experience in Iowa, to design terraces that would work in the hills east of Idaho Falls. Their first efforts were broad-based level terraces designed to be farmed over. By spacing the terraces the proper distance apart, runoff water could be retained on the hill slopes instead of building up to cause erosion and water pollution, and crops would benefit from the additional water.

The problem was, no one was certain about how to calculate the proper spacing under these new conditions in Idaho. So the first systems were done mainly by trial and error, starting with one terrace near the top of the slope and monitoring it carefully during the runoff season to make sure it was working as planned. Since there were no experienced local contractors to turn to, it was weekend work with John on the survey gear and Neil on the landowner's dozer to put in the initial trial terraces.

Farther north, in the Green Canyon region of Teton County, the soils were much different. They had thin topsoils over a rocky base, and the topsoils were getting thinner each year as soil erosion took its toll. Here, the terraces were built higher, dug down to a rocky base, and put on a grade so that the water was carried into the rocky gullies that bisected the fields. Because these terraces were not meant to be crossed by farm machinery, cultivation operations were forced to work on the contour between the terraces. This may have had as much impact on reducing soil erosion as the terraces themselves. Many of the farmers in the region were skeptical of these new terraces, but were at the point where they knew something had to be done or their soils would soon be beyond cultivation. So again, the experimental structures were put in one at a time, and watched closely.

The goal, if the terraces proved successful, was to install a complete runoff control system, starting at the top of the long slopes and eventually getting to the bottom. Beginning in 1967 and proceeding slowly to allow adaptation to the new conditions, as well as the limits to the farmer's and the USDA's available funds, it was the start of a multi-year effort.

A road grader builds terraces in Teton County, 1967

49

The Idaho Falls Area had a snow survey program, as well, and that area's preferred method of winter travel was the small one-person snow machines that were beginning to become very popular as winter recreational vehicles. When the snow machines weren't busy on the monthly snow course measurements, Neil could use them to observe snow and runoff conditions on the new dryland terraces in the region. This was a first, because the dryland fields were large and fairly remote, and few people ventured out to observe the winter conditions. Watching snow accumulate in the terraces, then melt and either fill them or run off, was educational, and resulted in modifications where needed.

At the same time, Neil was learning to be more proficient in providing information to the local news media. The local television station, KID-TV, had an excellent farm program and their reporters and photographers were quick to pick up on conservation stories when Neil would call them up with a story idea. At the time, the station used 16mm film cameras to shoot news footage, and Neil bought a used 16mm Bolex camera so that he could be part of that action.

After some training by the station's head photographer, a deal was made. KID-TV would provide a new roll of film for Neil to carry with him in his field work. When he saw an interesting story, he would shoot the roll of film (about 2-3 minutes worth), write up the story particulars, and take the package to the station. They would give him a new roll of film, process and edit the exposed roll, and use the story whenever they had available time in their newscast.

It was a great deal for Neil. Free film, good experience in what TV stations needed, and a raft of soil conservation stories on the local news that would not have otherwise happened! It was a good deal for KID-TV, as well. They got free stories that didn't have a deadline, so they could use them as "filler" when the news was slow.

As was common in SCS, not all the requests for assistance came from the farm community. In May of 1968, a local community development group in Eastern Idaho was seeking a loan from USDA to assist with the construction of a new recreational and skiing area near Driggs, Idaho, on a site near the state line in Wyoming. One of the USDA's concerns had to do with snow cover at the site. Would there be enough snow for a long winter ski season to support the financial success of the venture? It wasn't clear why Neil was assigned the task of checking out the site, but he was, so a snowmobile trip was organized.

Armed with a map and description of the proposed lodge site, Neil and John Ozmun headed up the snowbound mountain road from Driggs. Arriving at the site, they measured something on the order of 9 feet of snow. In May! Whatever financial risks the proposed venture faced, the lack of late-season snow did not seem to be one, and this was duly reported back to the USDA agency in charge of the loan application. The sponsoring local development organization proceeded to build the project which opened in 1969. Today, the Grand Targhee Resort proudly brags on its web site about receiving an average of over 500 inches of snow a year, putting it among the top four ski resorts in North America!

9

Information and Education

*"It is always interesting to start a job with no previous history,
and Neil set out to define the work as it unfolded."*

In July 1968, with Lee Morgan holding to his earlier commitment, Neil was transferred into the Boise State Office. He began a new position that was a split between being the SCS information specialist on the state staff and providing staff support to the new programs SCS was beginning to test, efforts that helped local governments with land use planning and management challenges.

Because he was still a GS-11, the position was slotted under Assistant State Conservationist for Watersheds Blaine Morse and supported by the unit's secretary, Sharon Stevenson (now Norris). In addition to being an extremely talented secretary, Sharon was very interested in information work, so she was, in effect, an assistant information specialist. (Later, she finished her degree at Boise State University and served for many years as the Public Affairs Officer on the state staff prior to her retirement.)

It's always interesting to start a job with no previous history, and Neil set out to define the work as it unfolded. Initial efforts included making sure to meet all of the key news media people working in Boise, and it wasn't long before Neil's movie camera case carried a fresh roll of film from each of the two major television stations in town. Story ideas didn't come along as often when much of the work was tied to a desk in the state office, but there were still enough stories to keep media interest alive, and to help tell the conservation story in Idaho.

With his new responsibilities so heavily involving writing, Neil felt justified in leaving his old Olivetti portable at home and asking for an

SCS-provided electric typewriter at his office desk. That was met with resistance, as SCS policy and practice were that only high-grade clerk-typists could be provided with such an expensive and specialized machine. But with Lee Morgan on his side, Neil prevailed over the objections of the administrative staff, and soon was outfitted with a professional writing tool.

Information work is one of the more pleasant tasks on an SCS staff, because for the most part, you deal with the good news in the agency. The idea is to search out where people are doing things right, where land and water resources are being conserved and improved in the process, and where people are finding answers to their everyday problems on the land. The local partners in the soil and water conservation districts were often good sources of these stories, and it was Neil's role to help the field staff recognize good news when it happened and get stories out to the local press.

But, as anyone who has been in public service knows, not all the news is good all the time, and periodically someone would take a shot at SCS in the news media for one reason or another. When that would happen in Idaho, it was hard to keep Lee Morgan in his chair. He wanted to jump up and hit back at someone. Often, Neil would argue that there was little that could be done that wouldn't have the effect of simply inflaming the issue and keeping it in the public's mind, whereas, if it were ignored, it would go away quickly. But those points of view were not always absolute, and one had to become sophisticated in judging which issues might have "legs" and stay around for a while, and which were going to evaporate. You tried to weigh in on the lasting ones and let the instant ones die as quickly as possible. Only experience (and sometimes, good guessing) can teach those lessons.

It wasn't always outside critics that created an agency PR flare-up. Some were also home grown. Neil hadn't been in the job very long when Lee Morgan asked for a slide show presentation to give before a large agricultural audience in Lewiston. This was an important group of stakeholders that weren't always as supportive of SCS as Lee wished they were, and he wanted to make a good impression to win their favor.

Neil worked for a day or two gathering up slides from all over the place since, prior to his coming, there wasn't much of an organized filing system. He put together a slide show and speech script for the occasion. Carrying the Kodak Carousel projector and the written material into Lee's office, he suggested that it would be good for Lee to go through the presentation a few times to become familiar with how it went and fix up any spots that weren't to his liking.

"It will be fine," was the response. "I'm too busy to do that today." So that was that. When time came for him to leave for the airport, Neil again carried the Carousel projector and the slide tray into the office for him to take to Lewiston. "I won't need the projector," Lee said. "Frank Dickson, the Lewiston Work Unit Conservationist, has a good one, and he can run it for me. I'll just take the Carousel tray." Neil argued that it was safer to have the projector that had been tested, had a spare bulb, etc., but as a lowly staff person, that was a losing argument. The decision had been made.

In Lewiston, it was reported later, the large meeting was well underway when Lee's turn to speak came. Frank was running the projector and Lee was at the podium. At the signal, the projector came on, and all the lights went out. Unfortunately, Lee couldn't read the script in the pitch black, and he didn't want to stop and ask for a little light, so he plowed into the unfamiliar text using the reflected light from the screen behind him.

The picture on the screen, however, was on its side! Frank's projector was a different brand with a slide wheel that mounted on the projector vertically, while the Carousel slide wheel mounted horizontally. As a result, simply transferring the slides from one wheel to the other turned everything 90 degrees. Lee was struggling ahead with a near-blind script, while Frank was scrambling to get the next slide turned into the right position. The second one came in upside down, but pretty quick he had the system down, and the presentation went on.

Lee was both embarrassed and furious about the mess-up. The following Monday morning was a State Office staff meeting and his first item of business was to jump on Neil for setting him up wrong. Reminded that he had been asked to do some dry runs, and to take the projector with him to the presentation, he calmed down and acknowledged that it was a lesson learned. When mixing people and mechanical equipment, it is best to always remember Murphy's Law: "If anything can go wrong, it will, and at the worst possible time."

One of the delights in working the information job was to help the Idaho Association of Conservation Districts with their annual convention. The Association's leaders were local SCD supervisors that had been elected to regional and state office, so many of them were the same district people that Neil had worked with in his field assignments. The association operated on a shoestring budget, with volunteers doing what needed to be done, so they were both gracious and grateful for the help Neil and others could provide during the meeting. Lifelong friends and a lot of meeting management experience came out of those conferences.

The political implications of information work were also felt from time to time. In 1969, the community golf course in Orofino was attracting attention. Its development dated back to 1965, when the USDA received authorization to cost-share rural community recreational facilities. A community group formed under the leadership of Orofino mayor A. B. Curtis, and the search for a site began. That was no easy task in the narrow, steep canyons of the Clearwater valley, but there was a local farm for sale on a riverside bench close to town. As the local SCS man at the time, Neil had made a quick survey and determined that it was large enough, and had suitable topography for a 9-hole course.

With a purchase option in hand, the group began site investigations. Neil and others worked weekends to do a topographic survey for planning purposes and a local contractor donated a backhoe to dig soil pits so that SCS soil scientists could make a detailed soil survey of the property. The Orofino Golf Association (of which Neil was President) became a cooperator with the Soil Conservation District so that SCS could assist them in the planning process.

The soil survey illustrated some wet soils that would need tile drainage to be able to be used year around, and this was designed and presented to the architects. Other heavy usage areas such as roads, parking lots, and drain fields were located away from wet soils to more suitable land. Once the course was designed by the architects, spot soil inspections assured that the tees and greens were on the type of soil indicated, rather than some small inclusion of problematic area that might cause problems.

So in 1969, with the golf course in full operation, Neil wrote up the story for *Soil Conservation,* the official magazine of SCS. His write-up focused heavily on the contribution of other USDA agencies—financing from Farmers Home Administration, engineering and accounting expertise from local Forest Service volunteers, and technical help on grass seeding and other factors from the County Agent. The Forest Service fire control officer, Clem Pederson, had assisted with timber removal and slash disposal advice in the early phases of construction. It sounded like a poster story for cooperative USDA assistance to a rural community in need of help.

Then a problem emerged. By the time the story was submitted to SCS in late 1969, the federal policy had changed, and USDA was no longer in the business of funding community recreation facilities. The story had to be re-written to adjust to the new realities and avoid the mention of the interagency success. In his return memo to Neil transmitting a seriously chopped up manuscript, *Soil Conservation* Editor Ben Osborne said "Sorry we didn't find a slot for it before the wind changed."

10

Flying Conservation Ambassadors

"The conservation story is easy to tell with a bird on your arm."

Morley Nelson, in addition to being the SCS Snow Survey Supervisor in Boise, was internationally recognized as a leading expert in falconry. His home in the Boise foothills had a large hillside lot that was full of buildings, pens and shelters for a variety of birds, including golden eagles, prairie falcons, and hawks. He had enough open space that he could fly and train the birds there, so that was his usual after-work activity.

Neil had started to work with Morley through the snow survey in 1960 and in his role while learning information work in Idaho Falls had begun to team up in conservation education efforts involving the birds. Few things get the attention of a crowd of restless students like staring into the unblinking eyes of a fearless raptor. So Morley would take a bird and travel to do educational programs with Neil.

When the move to Boise was done and Neil's primary job included conservation education, that work became more intense, and Neil became one of Morley's local partners and helpers. Summer evenings were spent feeding and flying the birds, and Neil began to learn a bit about their care and handling. This also opened up many avenues for good photography, both movies and stills, so those skills continued to develop.

Morley was also widely known for his ability and willingness to care for injured or stranded birds, some of which could be nursed back to health and either released into the wild or trained as part of the environmental education stable. The problem he faced was an overflow that he could not house, so he was always looking for "out-placement" opportunities. That resulted in Neil's backyard becoming a refuge for homeless or injured hawks and owls. These birds, much calmer and easier to handle than eagles and falcons, became a training ground for learning the ancient art of falconry.

The conservation story is easy to tell with a bird on your arm. It all starts with the soil, and its productivity that supports a diversity of microbial and plant life that produces the food, water, and shelter that all animals, including humans, require. Maintaining the diversity and productivity of the soils and the communities that live on them is essential for the long-term survival of all life on earth.

The birds of prey, while well-adapted to live in the environment, must have a food base that is provided by their habitats, and if they can't succeed, it could be that humans will begin to find survival hard as well. Kids "get" that, and the bird's presence makes the lesson more memorable and real.

One of Neil's favorite birds was Bubo, a female Great Horned Owl that had been brought to Morley when a power line crew accidentally knocked down an owl nest with chicks too young to survive. Bubo came to Neil's back yard, where she soon became the queen of the roost. Owls are quiet and gentle to handle, so she also became a staple of the conservation education team.

She would sit quietly on Neil's gloved hand, but if he would clench his fist slightly, she would give a low call or hoot. That led to some different approaches, where Neil would have the kids ask Bubo a question, and she would answer appropriately. That caused all kinds of enthusiastic participation!

Bubo had a practical presence as well. When roaming neighborhood cats attempted to climb a backyard trellis to get at the baby birds in a nest there, and the raucous screaming of the parent birds woke the family at dawn, there was a solution. Neil just staked Bubo at the foot of the trellis for a few nights, and the cats came back no more.

In July of 1969, the Boy Scouts of America (BSA) brought their National Jamboree to Farragut State Park in northern Idaho and requested assistance from the SCS to provide teachers for the environmental education displays at the Jamboree. Walter Jeske, then SCS's national leader in environmental education, asked Neil as the Idaho leader and Morley with his birds to be a major part of the SCS team. They would be joined by others from SCS who would then work alongside other resource experts from Forest Service, Bureau of Land Management, Fish and Wildlife Service, and state agencies. It was a big show, with some 50,000 Scouts and leaders expected, and a large cadre of resource people to teach outdoor skills.

Preparation for the Jamboree took many months. Neil coordinated the creation and construction of a large model watershed, where water ran in streams and instructors could point out the land management features and practices that were affecting the flow and quality of the water. Tons of soil samples were collected and prepared so that each Scout could use a clear plastic tube to build their own soil profile with layers of subsoil and topsoil illustrating how soils are formed and how they function.

But the star of the show was Morley, with an evening display of falconry using two trained prairie falcons that would fly over the assembled Scouts, climb to a high elevation, then swoop down at speeds approaching 100 miles an hour to hit a lure that Morley would swing over his head on a rope. That, along with the chance to hear the conservation story in the presence of Otis, a giant golden eagle, made for memorable outdoor learning experiences.

The young falcons had been captured and trained specifically for the Jamboree. With an appropriate permit from the Fish and Wildlife Service, Morley and Neil had located and monitored a falcon eyrie on the cliffs bordering the Snake River south of Boise. Here, the Snake River canyon was renowned for supporting one of the densest populations of birds of prey in North America. The canyon walls were perfect for safe spots to build an eyrie, and the surrounding desert lands provided an abundance of ground squirrels, jack rabbits, and other prey species. The result was a proliferation of hawks, owls, falcons and eagles not found elsewhere, and that stretch of canyon would soon become nationally designated as the Snake River Birds of Prey Natural Area in recognition of its unique character.

At first, Morley and Neil were only interested in capturing two young falcons, a task that involved not just cliff climbing, but also good timing, since the young birds should not be taken from their mother too young but cannot be caught once they learn to fly. The appropriate time is only a few days long, so the nest was closely monitored until the time was right. At that point, Morley broke out the climbing ropes and descended the cliff. Neil was "rope minder" up top with his camera at the ready.

Mama falcon was very unhappy with the whole process, and kept diving at Neil's head to try to drive the intruders away. Keeping the rope appropriately tight, trying to take pictures, and ducking an angry falcon made for an interesting dance, but disaster was averted and Morley was able to come back up the cliff face, bearing two of the three chicks that had been in the nest. We had our trainer birds, and the adult falcon soon settled back down to parent the remaining chick.

Training the young birds was the daily after-hours work through the summer, but when the Jamboree rolled around in late July, they were ready and the show was a great success. The Boy Scout administrators were happy, and we felt like SCS had successfully provided a high-quality environmental education show for a huge crowd of young men who would become influential adults that could understand why conservation was an important part of life.

The Jamboree experience led to another unique conservation education opportunity in 1970 when the BSA asked Morley and Neil to become part of the educational team at a Conservation Encampment for American Indian Youth to be held at Camp Asaayi in northern New Mexico. Some 300 Indian youth would be involved, along with many Indian and Scout adult leaders. Nine SCS conservationists were invited, along with experts from the other federal resource agencies to make up a team of 23 conservation educators. The boys were split up into clans of 15, each led by an Indian adult, and spent a week at the encampment.

Preparations once again had Morley and Neil training the falcons and preparing for the trip. Boise Cascade was one of the commercial sponsors and Larry Jackson, a retired major league pitcher who worked for their public relations department, would go to the camp to present a program on forestry. One of Boise Cascade's executive aircraft would fly the team and the birds to Gallup, New Mexico.

When the time came, all but three seats were removed from the cabin and replaced with specially designed perches that were fastened to the floor. Floors were covered to prevent soiling, and the birds were loaded.

In addition to the two performing falcons, Morley brought Otis, the golden eagle. Neil had Bubo, along with an American Roughleg hawk, a young barn owl and a sparrow hawk from the backyard. The owls went into special boxes and the rest were fitted with hoods to keep them calm during the transit.

Jackson, Morley, and Neil took the 3 remaining seats and the three-hour flight was under way. Watching the birds "fly" inside the airplane cabin was amazing. They would lean, bank, and adjust to every movement of the craft. It was clear that their flying instincts worked as well inside the airplane as when they were on the wing.

After some initial nervousness, all the birds settled down nicely for the ride except Otis, who got increasingly bored and agitated in the back of the cabin. Something needed to be done to calm him, and it turned out to be Jackson's morning paper. Proving that a newspaper is a valuable traveling companion for owls as well as people, Otis spent the rest of the flight happily reducing the *Idaho Statesman* to confetti.

At the Gallup airport, the team was met by a car and two Navajo police paddy wagons, which looked like pickup trucks carrying a large piece of metal culvert with bars and a door welded on the back end. Jackson got the car while Morley took Otis and the falcons in one paddy wagon and Neil took the rest of the troop in the other. The 60-mile drive to Camp Asaayi was made over rutted and pot-holed mountain roads. It was impossible to tell what the birds thought about those rattling, clanging, jouncing steel cages, but to the SCS'ers it was apparent that a Saturday night ride over the rough roads common to the Reservation would have to be a sobering experience.

The conservation education program during the week was similar to the one that had been done at Farragut the year before, but with a different twist due to the religious and mythical affinity the Indians have for the eagle, owl, and other birds of prey. Every effort was made to involve the boys in the conservation activities, and the Indian outlook was the route.

Lessons were discussed in terms of how the Indian looks on man and nature and helping them see how important they could be to their people if they would combine their Indian background with the white man's education to become qualified for professional careers. Coming from men such as Bob Tsiosdia, SCS engineer (Navajo), Ben Murdock of BLM's Washington, DC office (Ute), or Bob Tippeconnic, Forest Service Ranger (Navajo), it made a readily apparent impression on the Indian students.

Because of the trained raptors, the class where Morley and Neil discussed the inter-relationships between humans and nature often got side-tracked into other subjects. The almost-universal use of the eagle as a religious symbol by the Indian tribes gave rise to discussions of the Indian religion and mythology. These could lead to discussions about how young Indians felt about the conflict between the ancient beliefs of their people and the dominant culture they must either reject or assimilate into. The youth were, in general, frank in discussing these issues and optimistic about their people's future. Neil, while not Indian by birth, had been raised on the Coeur d' Alene Reservation in northern Idaho, and found these boys and their attitudes consistent with the friends of his youth, making discussions free and easy.

The old ways were still critically important, though. Otis was molting, and in the process, one of his large primary wing feathers was coming visibly loose. One young man noticed it and asked Morley if he could have the feather when it was released. Morley agreed, and the boy spent hours sitting silently and watching Otis move about on his perch. When the feather finally dislodged naturally, Morley retrieved it and gave it to the boy. The next morning, that boy arrived back at the gathering to proudly say that he had walked the 20 miles to his home, delivered the precious feather to his family where it would be used in religious rites, and walked back to the camp.

Otis, the golden eagle is not too sure about being carried on the arm of BSA Executive Walt Wenzel while Morley Nelson looks on. 1969 BSA National Jamboree.

An unidentified Boy Scout holds a sparrow hawk while Morley Nelson holds a Prairie Falcon at the 1969 National Boy Scout Jamboree at Farragut State Park, Idaho.

Neil and Bubo ready for another conservation education outing.

11

Middle Management

"Doing more with less is not easy for a staff that is already stretched, and abandoning old priorities to make room for new ones is never easy."

In 1970, Neil was selected as the Area Conservationist in the Boise Area Office. This was a middle management line officer position, situated between the State Conservationist and the District Conservationists (as they were now called). The job was to help administer SCS programs and policies across 12 SCS offices serving the conservation districts in southwestern Idaho. It is a large area that meant a lot of driving to get back and forth between offices that were many miles apart.

The job was totally different. Instead of dealing with all the good things that were happening in the conservation field, it usually dealt with the administrative minutia and problems that were regularly encountered within agency operations. It also entailed a lot of evening meetings, as the AC needed to maintain good relations with the conservation district board members in the area. Since many of the small rural towns where the district meetings were held had little in the way of overnight accommodations, that often meant driving 100 miles or more to get home after a night meeting.

The government cars operated by GSA and SCS were plain as possible as the agencies tried to keep costs at rock-bottom. In the hot desert heat of southern Idaho, the lack of air conditioning was a topic of much conversation among the overheated employees. "Instead of air conditioning, we got black vinyl upholstery," was a common comment.

Also noteworthy was the lack of any entertainment media, as radios were not included and the installation of a personal device was discouraged. So if you couldn't entertain yourself, those long drives between offices and meetings were not much fun, and staying awake was job one.

One good part of the job was the quality of the field staff. Most of the DCs were older than Neil, and they were a talented lot that knew the ins and outs of running field operations. Supervision was not so much a task of guiding them, but of communicating the changing needs and desires of the agency's leadership in a way that was both understood and accepted. That wasn't always easy when then, as now, the word from on high was often about reduced budgets, new limits on staffing, and new responsibilities that needed attention.

Doing more with less is not easy for a staff that is already stretched, and abandoning old priorities to make room for new ones is never easy. But that was the reality facing the agency, and the field staffers were the front lines in implementing what needed to be done.

As anyone who has had supervisory responsibilities knows, personnel problems are often the most vexing situations to be faced, and the ACs job was no exception. SCS was only rarely able to hire new people, and it was incumbent on the supervisor of each new person to see to it that they were a good fit for a career in the agency. That usually meant a lot more about attitude and ability to get along with people than it did about technical proficiency. SCS recruited carefully, and most of the time, the new hires were quickly assimilated into the staff. But there could be exceptions.

One of the latter came to the Boise Area Office as an engineer in training, working under Neil's supervision. As the end of the 6-month probationary training period drew closer, it became clear that there were real questions as to the young man's future with the agency. Sending him out to work with the field offices usually brought back more complaints than words of praise. Once those flags were raised, it was important to carry out both a formal and informal review to decide how to handle the situation.

The staff really needed the extra help, and the prospect of losing an engineer was not welcome. But if the probationary period was completed successfully, the employee would be much more firmly entrenched, and it would take serious violations of agency policy or procedure to release him. Better to do it early, take the medicine, and try to recruit again.

This was never a pleasant prospect, and at an area-wide meeting, Neil sought counsel in an executive session with the DCs. The consensus was clear—as unpleasant as it was, the employee should be terminated before the end of the probationary period. One of the older and wiser DCs demurred, and urged that more time and training be allowed. With only a month or so left of the probation, Neil had a solution. "I'll assign him to your field office for 2 weeks, and then I want your honest and frank recommendation," he said.

With that agreed to, the assignment was made and two weeks later, the recommendation came back. "As much as I don't like to say it", the DC said, "I don't think he has a future in SCS." So the personnel decision was made, and the young engineer was terminated, hopefully to find a better "fit" in which to pursue his career.

12

SCS Management Policy

*"Goals can be represented by numbers, percentages,
completed actions, target dates, or in other ways."*

In 1971, SCS published a new mission statement as part of *A
Framework Plan: Soil and Water Conservation for a Better America.*
The new focus was clearly aimed at environmental quality as an
agency goal:

> *"The Mission of the Soil Conservation Service is the conservation,
> development, and productive use of the Nation's soil, water and
> related resources so that all Americans may enjoy:*
> - *Quality in the Natural Resource Base for Sustained Use;*
> - *Quality in the Environment to Provide Attractive, Con-
>   venient and Satisfying Places to Live, Work, and Play;
>   and,*
> - *Quality in the Standard of Living Based on Community
>   Improvement and Adequate Income."*

Shortly after the publication of the Framework Plan, SCS constituted a Management Task Force of field people under the chairmanship of Verne M. Bathurst, the Assistant Deputy Administrator
for Management, to update the agency's management policy. [5]

---

[5] Neil was a member of the committee, along with Chester Bellard, Herb Grimes, Bob Hallstead, Jerry
Hytry, Ray Margo, and Don Robertson. He became disconnected from day-to-day SCS management
soon after the committee work was finished, so was not aware of many of the practical ramifications of
the committee's work. This section is taken from "The Soil Conservation Service: Management for Environmental Quality", submitted as a class paper to James Q. Wilson at Harvard University on January 30,
1974.

The other seven members selected represented a broad range of geographic, technical, and organizational backgrounds within SCS. Along with Bathurst, who began his career in a small field office in rural Kansas, they represented a broad knowledge of how things really worked out in the field. As a result of the Task Force's effort, staff work within the Washington Office of SCS, pressures from the Office of Management and Budget, and considerable internal review within SCS, management changes began to emerge.

The primary focus of the committee was on the field office's Annual Plan of Operations (APO), a document prepared by the District Conservationist in consultation with the Conservation District, the local staff, and the Area Conservationist. This APO becomes the device upon which the field offices activities were judged for adequacy during the AC's periodic progress reviews. Achievement of the goals was considered important, and falling short was not good for one's organizational future.

But the most basic question facing the management review committee involved the quandary the SCS found itself in: How does an agency whose mission is based on achieving *quality* encourage its employees to pursue that goal with a management system based on performance measurements that all focused on *quantity*?

Summaries from the progress reporting system provided one way of judging performance, but as Neil had learned in his Orofino experience, they didn't measure everything a field office achieved, and there were few or no quality indicators in any of the numbers. A worthless conservation plan counted as much as one where the landowner had done significant conservation work and made a noticeable difference in environmental quality.

The progress reporting system (launched in 1960 as earlier described) had proven itself valuable at the national and state levels. A Congressman or Legislator could call the national or state office and find out how many people were being served by SCS in his/her district, and what kinds of conservation work was being accomplished as a result.

At the field level, it was far less useful. Because of time delays in punch-coding and computer access, the quarterly summaries arrived in the field office some 6-8 weeks after a quarter ended. In addition to being summary numbers with no trace back to individuals or individual jobs, some of the information was almost 6 months old by the time the field office received it. With small staffs, often heavily loaded with field work, there was little time or patience to try and figure out what, if anything, the summaries indicated.

The Management Task Force met for a full week, spending many hours working on incorporating changes (most of which were minor modifications that had become common practice since the older versions were written) into the agency's management memorandum. The most basic disagreement concerned the reliance on numerical goals from the progress reporting system as the primary yard stick of accomplishment.

Proponents for abandoning these goals argued that past efforts had too often ended up in a "numbers game" with field people selecting work specifically to meet the goals rather than to solve problems. They proposed more reliance on personal management by the Area Conservationist who should be able to realize better performance from his District Conservationists by expecting better performance.

Opposing viewpoints were based on doubt that the District Conservationists could be expected to reach peak production with- out some sort of numerical quantity goal to strive for. They agreed that the "numbers game" could be a problem, but thought that skilled management could overcome it.

The argument was rendered somewhat mute, however, by a concurrent development beyond the control of SCS or the Task Force. The President's Office of Management and Budget (OMB) was attempting to install input-output budgeting and management in the federal agencies, and was insisting that SCS add annual goals to the computerized progress reporting system. If, their argument went, SCS already had a progress-reporting system, why not have the system keep track of progress toward identified goals as a management tool?

Thus, while the Task Force recommended that numerical goals be downplayed in favor of more quality-based measures, such a move would have been unacceptable to OMB, so couldn't be considered a viable option.

The result was stress in the Washington office, as the national staff was pushed to follow the OMB dictates, while Task Force members Jerry Hytry and Bob Halstead held out for a version closer to the Task Force recommendations. When the new policy finally emerged after a year of review and re-writing, the numerical goals had been added to the progress reporting system as per OMB's guidance, but the agency's policy added some flexibility.

"Goals", the new management memorandum said, *"are the amounts of work expected to be accomplished toward meeting the established objectives or local needs and are identifiable or expressed in measurable amounts. They may be items reportable in the Progress Reporting System, or other measurable increments that permit determining progress toward established objectives Goals can be represented by numbers, percentages, completed actions, target dates, or in other ways. "*[6]

So did the agency work to reconcile its mission seeking quality improvements with a federal push to get hard number results to justify federal spending. Whether this proved to be a positive step in the agency's management efforts is not known, but it clearly represented a learning and growth experience for a young professional from Boise, Idaho.

---

[6] Management Memorandum-3 (Rev. 3), March 30, 1973. USDA Soil Conservation Service.

13

Entering the Land Use Fray

*"As we now interpret private ownership rights,
the landowner is free to utilize, use, or misuse his land...."*

In spite of the administrative work that dominated the Area Conservationist job, Neil remained interested and involved in the conservation challenges facing the state and area. Southwestern Idaho was a bustling growth center, and much of the growth continued to sprawl across the fertile and flat irrigated farmlands of the region. The results of the 1967 Conservation Needs Inventory became available and in 1971 Neil was instrumental in bringing some of those results to the attention of the Idaho public.

A seminar on the Snake River Basin sponsored by the Idaho League of Women Voters provided one such forum. Excerpts from Neil's keynote address, published in *The Statesman* on June 11, 1971, give some ideas as to the type of conservation message that was involved, and that would characterize his work in the future.

"The 1967 Conservation Needs Inventory indicates that Idaho's irrigated cropland is not receiving very good treatment. About 21 percent of the land is all that has adequate conservation treatment. Another 35 percent needs a new irrigation system before it can be properly irrigated. The sad part of the land use pattern, however, is that 42 percent of Idaho's irrigated land has an adequate irrigation system, but is not being managed and utilized properly. In other words, 42 percent of Idaho's irrigated land has an adequate system, an adequate water supply, and a suitable land use pattern for good conservation treatment.

"The operators involved, however, have not faced up to their responsibility to manage and control their water in such a way as to prevent erosion, sedimentation and water pollution. Referring back to the Conservation Needs Inventory, this survey shows that about 20 percent of the dry cropland in Idaho has proper conservation treatment.

"Thirty-eight percent of this land needs a better crop rotation and better management of crop and stubble residues to provide soil protection during erosion seasons. Forty-two percent needs terraces, strip cropping or other mechanical controls to adequately protect the soil from excessive loss. Over 100,000 acres of dry cropland which is simply too steep and rough to be farmed should be converted back to grass, trees, and wildlife habitat.

"Another category of agricultural land use which affects water quality is animal feedlots. Feedlots...have been growing in size and intensity for greater efficiency. It is common to find feedlots capable of handling from five to 15 thousand head of cattle throughout the Snake River Basin.

"A feedlot is ecologically impossible. The food necessary to sustain the animals can't be produced on the small amount of land they occupy, so it is all trucked in. The bodies of the animals could not possibly be decomposed or utilized by other creatures living in the area, so they are trucked out. It is obvious, of course, that a feedlot requiring one fleet of trucks to carry feed in, and another fleet of trucks to carry fat cattle out, should have a fleet of trucks to carry out waste products.

"Too often, however, a good local stream has substituted for this purpose. Locating feedlots near drainage systems greatly reduces the manure problem. What doesn't wash into the stream naturally can be bulldozed in whenever necessary.

"The only logical answer is to recycle manure back to the soil where it can be utilized again in the life cycle. To do this requires a great deal of land. About 15 to 30 tons of cow manure per acre is a beneficial addition to soils, providing organic matter, nitrogen, phosphate and other elements needed for soil building and crop production. A beef animal produces about 10 tons of manure a year. As a general rule, then, about 1/3 to ½ acre of cropland is needed for each animal in the feedlot. With some of the very large feedlots handling around 100,000 head a year, the magnitude of the problem becomes great indeed.

"A listing of land use problems such as we have been discussing is of little value unless some constructive suggestions can be made as to how to overcome them. We can talk of the various conservation practices which can, and should, be utilized to control erosion, runoff and the resulting inevitable pollution of our state's waters through sediment, pesticides, herbicides, manures and other natural and foreign contaminants.

"This is not the real cure for the problem, however. The cure for the land use and conservation problems in the Snake River Basin will probably require a basic reorientation of our entire approach toward land use rights on the private lands of the state.

"As we now interpret private ownership rights, the landowner is free to utilize, use, or misuse his land in any way he pleases. If, as a result of his management, damages occur to the state's waterways or to its air, or to other lands downstream, the landowner incurs little or no liability.

"If we are to become serious about maintaining the quality of Idaho's environment, this view of land use rights must be slightly altered.

"It must, however, be altered very, very carefully...with an eye out for practical, workable solutions. One approach ...might be the establishment of land use regulations which require the landowner to be responsible for any damages that he might create off his property. The approach...could say that any type of irrigation system and any type of management is acceptable so long as the rest of society is not subject to the effects of excessive waste water or underground water contamination.

"In a parallel situation, the farmer on dry cropland could be asked to keep any sediment produced on his own land.

Technically, the methods for doing this exist. There are ways to define the portion of erosion which can feasibly be prevented and which portion is inevitable and beyond reasonable control. Methods of monitoring runoff streams for sediment content exist and could be carried out if we wished.

"Feedlot owners who were expected to be responsible for any pollutant allowed to leave the feedlot area would simply have to design adequate waste management systems into the original feedlot design. Many are doing so today. The technology certainly exists.

"There is only one small catch to this whole suggestion—that is, when we decide to impose any type of restriction such as this on agriculture, we have to be fully committed and ready to pay the bill. The costs of erosion control and conservation cannot be borne out of thin air, but must come from the consumer. If federal cost-sharing is used, it will have to pay about 75-80% before the farmer can break even. Farmers cannot be expected to apply all the conservation treatment needed on their lands so long as the man who does a good conservation job is liable to be penalized in the economic market place while he who creates erosion, sedimentation and pollution problems sees a greater net profit as a result.

"If we ever decide that we are going to hold landowners uniformly responsible for the performance of the conservation systems on their land, placing everyone on a uniform economic footing in the matter, the farmers and ranchers in Idaho will gladly apply far better conservation treatment to their agricultural lands. The future quality of the Snake River system may rest on that decision."

In retrospect, those opinions don't seem so far off the mark, as national and state policies have progressed, along with conservation science and technology. Forty years ago, however, when those ideas were not yet common, there is no record of any pushback in the form of complaining letters to the editor or complaints to Neil's bosses at

SCS. But neither was there any great rush to change land use regulations in the State legislature!

That is not to say that there was not a lot of attention to the topic of land use and land use regulation, both at the national level and in Idaho. What was termed a "quiet revolution" in land use regulation had started in the states–Minnesota, Vermont, Maine, Hawaii, and others–in the late 1960's, and by 1970 had resulted in a new state law in Vermont. Most of the new laws seemed to be a spontaneous response to some triggering event, like a huge development proposal or a natural disaster that galvanized state legislatures into responding. The laws differed, depending on the issue involved and the political history of the state, but many were patterned after the Model Land Development Code published by the prestigious American Law Institute.

A federal law—the National Land Use Policy and Planning Assistance Act—was introduced in Congress under the leadership of Senator Henry M. Jackson (D-WA) and Morris K. Udall (D-AZ). The bill, which proposed that states take the lead in developing land use legislation and regulations with federal financial assistance, passed twice in the Senate but was never able to overcome opposition in the House of Representatives. It was, however, a hot political topic for most of the early 1970's and Idaho was strongly considering how to respond to this new challenge.

Glenn Nichols was the new Director of the Idaho Planning and Community Affairs Agency under Cecil Andrus' first administration. In his 1972 State of the State message, Governor Andrus called for the passage of state land use planning legislation, but the understaffed state agency was having trouble getting started on the challenge. Nichols got tired of Neil making speeches about the need for the State to do something about land use, and issued a challenge: "If you want to help, don't just stand out there and criticize. Come on over and help us design something that works." Neil agreed, if a way could be found.

The solution was found in a fairly new federal law called the Intergovernmental Personnel Act that would allow a federal agency to loan an employee to a state agency. As the details were worked out, by mid-September of 1972 Neil was on his way to the Idaho State House as the new Program Manager for Land Use, on loan from the Soil Conservation Service.

14

A Tour in the State House

"We need to hear the message of mayors and housewives, farmers and lawyers, environmentalists and miners, service station attendants and students, foresters and pipefitters."

State Planning and Community Affairs (SP&CA) was small— about 10-12 staffers—and new—having been established in 1970. It was charged with the preparation of a statewide comprehensive land-use plan and the provision of services to local towns, cities and counties in their local planning efforts. City and community planning was not widely done outside the larger cities in the state, and it was woefully underfunded everywhere. Local efforts were mostly involved with administering zoning laws in the cities, where the main effort was to keep objectionable development out of residential areas. In small towns and rural counties, zoning was non-existent and there were few efforts at comprehensive planning of any kind.

The new land use staff was assembled cooperatively. The SCS provided Neil to serve as program manager, the Idaho Soil Conservation Commission hired David Alvord as an assistant manager and SP&CA hired a clerk. In an agency that was brand new, had minimal budget resources, and whose key staffers were young (most of them were around 30 at the time), Neil was the most familiar with Idaho's land and water resources, so he was the "expert" in the group. His IPA assignment was scheduled to end on July 1, 1973, so time was short. David was an Idaho native who was recently back from a volunteer commitment in the Peace Corps, and Debbie, the unit clerk, was a young woman with the asset of a good artistic flair.

The first challenge in this assignment was to clarify what was to be done. This was somewhat complicated by the fact that SP&CA had not yet been formally designated as the lead agency for developing the state's comprehensive plan, and there were other older, larger, and more influential state agencies that were pressuring the Governor to designate them. So SP&CA had to prove it was up to the task, and do it rapidly.

Neil had been thinking and working with others on the land use question for some time, including serving on some advisory committees as SP&CA was established, so he was ready to propose a direction for the project.

"Let's start with Land Use Policy, our immediate concern.[7] Just what do Idahoans prefer to see done with the limited and yet bountiful resources of our state? What are our general intentions? What kinds of value judgments will we make today—in 1972—about the future use and development of our resources? What kind of an Idaho do we want to see emerging in the next decade or two? We know what has gone on in the past, to bring our state to its current condition. We tip our hats to the valiant pioneers and men of courage and vision who developed Idaho and her resources to the point where ¾ of a million people think this is one of the finest places in the world to live.

"We also realize that we can't re-live the past. This is 1972, and it is time to try and define our preferences for the Idaho of 1980, 1990, and 2000. We start this project with an assumption: Idaho already has a Land Use Policy. Pieces of it exist in current legislation, and other pieces are found in expressed or implied 'operating policies' of state and local agencies. Some policies are set by the make-up and past decisions of various commissions and boards, and some policies are simply assumed because no one has seriously questioned them and 'we've always done it that way.'

"So the challenge is not one of inventing a State Land Use Policy, it is one of identifying the set of pre-

---

[7] Excerpts from a speech by Neil Sampson to the Idaho Soil Conservation Commission, Boise, Idaho, September 5, 1972.

ferences, intentions, and value judgments that informed Idahoans express today. To do this, we will have to go to the people—tell them what current policies exist or don't exist, show them some proposed policies, and give them the best possible forecast of the outcome they can expect from each policy.

"Then we'll have to listen. We need to hear the message of mayors and housewives, farmers and lawyers, environmentalists and miners, service station attendants and students, foresters and pipefitters. Then, the challenge: to take this broad, confusing, and often conflicting set of value judgments and focus in on a policy statement that appears to reflect the feelings of the majority of Idahoans.

"Without really asking for the preferences of the majority of the people, we have agencies today planning to build dams in order to irrigate new lands while, at the same time, private interests are developing these same lands by tapping ground water supplies, and other agencies are gearing up to provide recreational opportunities on free-flowing rivers. Each group is certain it is doing its work on the side of the angels, but too often they can be found guilty of only asking their friends what should be done next. Getting a predictable answer, they proceed with vigor, and are shocked and offended if serious questions are raised about their proposals.

"Around our cities, land is caught up in a speculative whirlwind that is completely out of control. Builders and developers, reacting to economic opportunities and pressures, make independent decisions, and permanent communities are designed on the basis of today's development economics.

"Meanwhile, planning and zoning commissions simply find themselves unable to cope with growth and development's speed and intensity. Not knowing for sure what the community expects from them, never

certain whether they are being too lenient or too re-
strictive, snagged most of the time on questions of le-
gality and procedure, and nearly always hampered by
the lack of facts, or staff help, or both, they spend
many frustrating, unpaid, nerve-wracking hours hoping they can help guide their community toward a better, rather than worse, condition. Alone in their effort, they plead for help from the State today.

"What kind of destiny does Idaho want? Can we define our preferences for the shape, size, and quality of
the city of Boise for the year 2000? Do we want it
sprawled in disconnected patches of houses reaching
to Caldwell? If so, all we need to do is sit back and re-
lax, because that's where our current trend is heading. If we don't want that, we have work to do.

We have to try and identify an alternative future
that people want, then give our cities and counties the
backing they need to plan it and the help they need
to carry out their plan. It's not an easy task and having
the policy identified is only the beginning of the job. It is,
however, the beginning we must have if our plans are
to lead to anything productive at all."

The work got under way immediately, with the team developing
a slide program that could be carried out to audiences around the
state. Using the art talents of Debbie, Neil and Dave rounded up
slides from across the state and began outlining a set of policy issues
to illustrate. The slide show actually developed from meeting to
meeting, as new illustrations were found, new photographs taken,
and new issues raised by the attendees. The presentation spoke
about land use change and some of the possible ramifications. It was
accompanied by a questionnaire the people could fill out and turn in
at the end of the meeting.

In spite of efforts to keep the program non-controversial, it didn't
always work. Land use is a prickly topic in a rural western state, and
there were people who came to the meetings determined to chal
lenge or attack any suggestion from the state agency. In the process,

Neil learned a few things. In the most rural areas, state agencies and employees attracted much the same response as federal agents—distrust and, in some cases, anger.

The slide show mixed artwork and Idaho scenes to pose issues.

The most important thing was learning how to listen and respond. Most of the time, if you listened very carefully to an angry comment, maintained a respectful attitude, and tried to turn the comment into something positive—whether through a factual answer, a follow-up question, or an invitation to convert the point into a recommendation that could become part of the input to the project—the anger was often diffused. In most of the meetings, any belligerence at the beginning was not apparent at the end, and in some, it had been converted into support for the project and its goals. That didn't always work, of course. In one meeting, a man got so loud and disruptive that his neighbors threatened to throw him out bodily if he didn't sit down and shut up! Neil was grateful to those neighbors because he wasn't about to go that far as the only representative of the state government in the room!

Between Neil and Dave, the slide show was repeated dozens of times in the following months. Policy ideas on agricultural issues, water issues, suburban sprawl, and wildland management were proposed and tested at the meetings. The approach was always: here's what seems to be happening, here are some of the probable outcomes, here's what else might be done and the possible outcomes there. What seems to be the best approach?

The meetings lasted anywhere from 30 minutes at a luncheon session to over 3 hours where people really wanted to get into the discussion. After tabulating the results from the questionnaire, we would report back to the group as soon as possible.

As the end of the project drew near in 1973, Neil was informed by Guy Nutt, the SCS State Conservationist, that he had been selected to attend graduate school at Harvard University as one of three SCS employees chosen for the one-year scholarship. That was a huge honor that could not be rejected, but it made for an awkward time gap between the end of the State IPA assignment on July 1 and an August move to Boston. Nutt and Glenn Nichols agreed to extend the IPA so that Neil could remain with the Land Use project until school started.

The final months of the assignment were focused on making a movie to replace the slide show. Neil contracted with Norman Nelson, who had just returned from an Army tour where he had been a military film maker. Norm was the son of Morley Nelson, the SCS Snow Survey Supervisor who was also deeply involved in making wildlife movies with his falconry skills, so Norm was well versed in both outdoor and land use issues as well as film making.

With virtually no budget, the film was written and planned by Neil and Dave. It was shot in 16mm color, with the project buying the film and each filming sequence carefully planned and shot so that there was little or no film wasted in the editing process. Norm and, when needed, a sound man, were contracted on an hourly basis. As Neil was getting packed up to move East, the final narrations and sound editing were completed, and *Look to the Land* was ready to be shown around Idaho. Because of the tight timeline and the trip to Boston, Neil never saw a showing in front of a live audience, but he was told the film was quite popular and well-received.

What did the project achieve? Without being in the state in the following years, Neil was never fully sure. State legislators took many ideas from it, some of which showed up in new state legislation over the next few years. Some of the ideas that emerged from the meetings were hard to reconcile. There was strong sentiment, for example, that people should not be allowed to build in flood plains. There was equally strong sentiment that the rights of private landowners should be respected. Thus, if a landowner wanted to build in a flood plain, what to do? These are the kinds of land use binds that local planning officials find themselves in, and there was not much to be learned from the project that could ease those conflicts.

Local planning groups may have benefitted as well, but those gains take a long time and are very incremental in nature, so are hard to quantify. Neil's personal and professional benefits, gained by managing new programs and presenting public programs on a controversial topic, were many.

15

Cultural Retraining:
A Country Boy Goes to Harvard

"Taking an economics course from an environmental economist that had written the text (Robert Dorfman) was a privilege."

As the time for the start of the Harvard school year got near, Neil was able to talk to the SCS Washington, DC Office and learn that there was a home in the nearby town of Needham, Mass, that SCS students with families had been renting for many years. The current occupant was Glen Loomis, and Neil contacted him to learn the details of the property. Upon hearing that it had a good place to park a travel trailer and could probably be rented over the phone by talking to the landlord in Florida, the deal was struck and the temporary living arrangements for the school year were solved.

August found Neil, Jeanne, and the family on the road, heading east. Traveling in a large van, pulling a 22-foot travel-trailer, with 4 kids and a bird dog, their pilgrimage was aimed at Needham, where the furnished home awaited. The house was right across the street from the train line into Boston, so an easy commute seemed in the prospect, and Neil was ready to jump back into the business of being a student. At age 35, and far away from any prior experience, it promised to be a very new and different endeavor.

The curriculum in the Kennedy School was fairly open. The degree was a Masters in Public Administration and, while there were a few required classes, students could also sign up for classes in other schools that allowed them to focus more on specific interests. Because of his recent work in land use, Neil signed up for classes in land use law, planning, and economics.

Surprisingly, the first problem to be faced was the abrupt change of pace in daily life. Coming from the Idaho State House, where activity was always hectic and hurried, and the daily calendar tended to rule activities, student life at Harvard consisted of a lot of sitting around in the library, reading papers and books, and preparing for one or two (and sometimes no) classes a day. Instead of feeling hectic, the work felt totally dead.

Class work, particularly in the early part of the semester, was easy if you paid attention and kept up on the readings and assignments. The daily calendar, instead of ruling your life with its appointments, became almost unnecessary. The telephone never rang, the Governor never called down with an emergency, and nobody cared whether you were in one place or another except during class hours. Instead of being a welcome relief, the sudden inactivity made Neil feel like he'd been banished to an outside-the-action realm.

Compared to his youthful studies at the University of Idaho, Neil's Harvard experience was vastly different. The professors were highly respected experts in their field, and not accustomed or willing to recognize that their students might have some practical experience to bring to the classroom. As a mid-career student with several credit hours of graduate study along the way, Neil often felt that the attitudes he encountered were condescending, even insulting. That was, however, just something else to get used to.

It took a while, but gradually the essential difference in the Harvard experience and his undergraduate studies became apparent. At Harvard, nobody cared what you were taking or how you were doing. Instead of being a student in the sense of going to school and having information poured out on you, at Harvard you needed to become an active consumer. You were spending your time (and the SCS's money) to be there, and you had to reach out and insist on getting what you wanted and needed to further your own goals in life.

With that mind-set, it was much easier to appreciate the remarkable resources available at Harvard. Taking an economics course from an environmental economist that had written the text and was being talked about as a Nobel Prize candidate (Robert Dorfman) was a privilege. Likewise, a land use course from an internationally-recognized expert (Charles Harr) in land use law and one in organizational design and management from one of the nation's most brilliant organizational and management thinkers (James Q. Wilson) were opportunities to be savored.

Neil decided to write a book on land use planning at the state level and what it could entail, both technically and politically. With that in mind, and a beginning outline in hand, he spent the final semester at Harvard actively seeking out classes designed to help further that work. Every class, and every assigned paper, became a part of the book effort.

By the end of the school year, a three-ring binder of chapters was filling up, and because there was a theme and purpose to the class work, the experience became much more rewarding and productive. That book never emerged, but virtually every page of manuscript developed in the project became part of either a professional paper or some subsequent effort.

The major uncertainty in the year at Harvard was the question of where the SCS would assign Neil at the end of the school term. It had been obvious from the start that a return to his beloved Idaho was not in the cards, but nothing else was certain. As a condition of the scholarship, Neil had agreed to continue to work for SCS for three months for each month of school attended, so he would need to go wherever they wanted him for the next three years to pay off that obligation.

During the Christmas holidays, Neil and the other graduate students in that year's class were requested to come to the SCS Washington Office for consultations. The leadership wanted to know how things were going, and get a more personal feel for their capabilities and desires. When Norm Berg, the Deputy Administrator of SCS, asked Neil where he wanted to go, Neil said "Anywhere but DC."

"Well," Norm said, "we need you here to help us with this whole land use situation. Congress is liable to pass the Jackson Bill, and USDA needs to be ready for what comes out. As one of the few people in SCS with actual land use planning experience at the state level, you're going to be our expert."

So the die was cast. Neil and family were headed to Washington, DC, for an assignment in the SCS national office. Another house-hunting trip in the spring resulted in signing a contract for a house in nearby Alexandria, Virginia, and another professional adventure was set to begin.

16

The SCS Washington Office

*"Neil was involved with other staffers in planning
a major "Prime Lands Seminar" to be held in 1975."*

Neil's aversion to Washington, D.C. was real, and the most dreaded part was the commute from Virginia. Raised on a farm, working in small towns most of his career, he was definitely not looking forward to the traffic congestion and frustration of an urban commute. That had been, in fact, a major factor in choosing the house his family purchased. The idea was to get close as possible to the city with an affordable house, and get in a location where there were plenty of access roads to provide options for avoiding traffic.

As it turned out, he had some luck. This new house was within a block of the real estate agent he was using, Bill Moore, who was retiring from SCS and taking up a real estate career. Along with the house, Neil received Bill's vacant seat in the community car pool.

As a result of that gift, Neil was immediately incorporated into a well-organized commuting process. The car pool was made up of SCS people Dick Leisher, Karl Klingelhofer, and Dick Hogue. John Wright of USDA made up the fifth. The car pool had a free reserved parking spot inside a courtyard of USDA's South Building, and the routine was well established. Driving chores were rotated, and travel schedules were accommodated. In addition to good company for the 12-mile, half-hour trip each way, Neil had experienced advisors on everything from local doctors, insurance agents and local landmarks to where to buy house repair materials. A previously-dreaded part of the work turned into an enjoyable part.

Car pools and buses were the most common way that agency people commuted, and that had a major effect on the Washington D.C. work day. Whereas, when working in the field Neil had often kept with a job until well after quitting time to see things get finished up, that didn't happen in the Washington office. At 4:30 sharp, every person that was dependent on a car pool or bus got up and headed for the door. Meetings ended abruptly, whatever the subject matter, because missing the ride home was simply not an option for most people. There were seldom any options other than an expensive cab ride. Since much of the office work revolved around meetings, this provided a discipline that helped keep things on track and on time.

In the Washington headquarters, Neil was slotted within the Conservation Planning Branch as a staff specialist. This was a branch in a division under a Deputy Administrator, so it was about as far down the organizational chart as one could go. The real job, however, was to serve at Deputy Administrator Norm Berg's pleasure.

Norm was the #2 person in the agency, providing leadership in many of the complex inter-agency efforts that the SCS was involved in. High on the list at the moment was the pending land use legislation that was working its way through Congress. Norm was also the USDA representative on the Great Lakes Commission and served on many other federal inter-agency boards and commissions as well. There were 4-5 staffers sprinkled throughout the headquarters who worked as Neil did, essentially as staff support team for Norm.

Norm's career in SCS had been long and distinguished. A native of Minnesota, he started his SCS career at a field office in Downey, Idaho in 1943, then moved to the Pocatello Office as Work Unit Conservationist and then as District Conservationist (a position similar to today's Area Conservationist). After a year in graduate school at Harvard, he became Assistant State Conservationist in South Dakota, then held several staff positions in the Washington headquarters, culminating in the Associate Administrator's position in the early 1970's. (Later, in 1979, Norm became the SCS Chief.)

Working for Norm was, Neil found, a great pleasure. A highly intelligent and insightful person, Norm was nonetheless very unassuming and mild-mannered. He gave you a job, then basically stayed out of your way until you had something ready for him. His office door was open to his staff assistants day and night, and you could always depend on wise counsel when you asked for it. Neil found himself monitoring land use legislative activities on the Hill, preparing brief-ing papers for use with the USDA leadership, and providing staff support to a USDA Land Use Committee that had been constituted so that the various USDA agencies could remain jointly abreast of new developments in the field.

The conversion of prime agricultural lands to non-agricultural uses was a major concern of the Land Use Committee, and Neil was involved with other staffers in planning a major "Prime Lands Seminar" to be held in 1975. The staff invited expert papers and published them in a 257-page background report entitled "Perspectives on Prime Lands" for the eighty experts invited to the seminar.

The seminar produced several recommendations to USDA, urg-ing the department to become a stronger advocate for the protec-tion of prime lands, working with states and localities to attempt to stem the rate of conversion to non-farm uses. Neil worked to get the seminar proceedings published and wrote up a summary story that appeared in the October, 1975 issue of *Soil Conservation*, the monthly magazine produced by SCS.

Since his job once again involved a lot of writing, Neil again re-quested a personal electric typewriter. That request ran counter to the usual practice. The entire Washington staff was accustomed to producing paperwork in the most difficult way possible. A hand-writ-ten or typed draft from a staff person went to a clerk, who typed it up in final form. The typed draft went back to the staffer, where it was proofed for mistakes or typos. If any were found, it went back to the typist for a new version which could, if the typist were not expert, contain new mistakes or typos. The finally clean   copy would start up the chain of command, where every step could find a mis-take or require a change. If that happened, the marked-up version would come back to the originator, and the process would start again. Often, a simple letter to a Congressman or a speech text would take days to get from draft to final, with untold hours of work and stress involved.

But new technology was emerging and Neil was involved in get-ting it purchased for the office. The first to arrive was a Mag Card typewriter. It was essentially an IBM Selectric typewriter hooked to a magnetic card reader. As the writer typed in the document, it came out of the typewriter and was simultaneously recorded on the card. If there were errors to correct, the typist could run the machine to that point in the text and re-type the correction. When it was completed, the machine would rapidly (and very loudly) re-type the entire document in its final format. In addition to speeding up the process, this technology dramatically reduced the introduction of new errors. It was a revolution, and the start of the whole word processing phenomenon.

Then-Assistant Secretary of Agriculture Robert Long had leadership for the land use efforts in USDA, and he looked to Norm Berg for technical expertise. As a result, Neil soon found himself in policy and strategy conferences at the Departmental level, as well as writing papers and speeches for Berg, Long, and Secretary of Agriculture Earl Butz. With the new word processing capability, he could produce volumes of work rapidly.

While this was heady staff work for a young professional, it was not without its hazards. Norm had little patience with the bureaucratic elements of agency operations, and was adept at seeing that things got done in spite of them. As a result, one of Neil's briefing papers or speech drafts could end up in the hands of USDA leaders without ever having been reviewed by the four layers of SCS overhead that showed on the organizational chart as being his superiors.

That did not always go over very well, and Neil was periodically chastened for "going around" his bosses. They all understood the way Norm worked and they couldn't change it, but they didn't like it. That situation began creating Neil's reputation for being a maverick, something neither Norm or Neil intended, but which came nonetheless.

As one of the exercises carried out when Jimmy Carter was elected President and Bob Bergland replaced Earl Butz as Secretary of Agriculture, SCS Administrator R. M. Davis asked every staff person in the DC office to justify his/her position and job description.

Neil wrote a brief page suggesting that his job could be eliminated, on the basis that it mostly consisted of generating paper that fed the internal bureaucratic machinery, but seldom did much to get conservation on the land or improve resource quality as stated in the agency's mission statement. Apparently somebody read that paper in the SCS leadership staff conference and they were not amused. It did not help diminish Neil's "maverick" reputation.

Excerpts from "Will the real land use planning please stand up?"
Journal of Soil and Water Conservation, Vol. 30, No. 5, Sept-Oct 1975.
R. Neil Sampson

"The three different types of planning commonly called land use planning are similar in that they deal with land and related resources, have many common techniques, use similar data and are all 'planning.' They are vastly different in the amount of control available to the decision-makers, the way in which goals can be established and used in the process, the types of decision-making processes involved, and the degree of certainty that can be ascribed to achievement of any plan.

"If land use planners are never going to get the type of control or data reliability enjoyed by project or land management planners they must search for planning techniques that accomplish something worthwhile despite these shortcomings. If, as I have suggested, land use planning is much more involved in goal-testing than in goal-achievement, appropriate methods will sound more like political science than environmental design.

17

Protecting Prime Farmland

"Between 1967 and 1975, there was about one million acres of prime farmland converted to non-farm uses each year...:

One of the problems in trying to promote land conservation in the 1970's, and particularly, the preservation of prime agricultural lands was that the amount of reliable information about the dimensions of the problem and its importance to national welfare was limited. The 1967 Conservation Needs Inventory (CNI) was the only attempt at seeking out state and national statistics, and it had not asked the same kind of questions that were bothering policymakers in the 1970s.

The farm problem that had long plagued U.S. agricultural policy – crop surpluses – was suddenly reversed in 1972, when a combination of bad weather worldwide and a huge outflow of U.S. grains combined to raise the specter of crop shortages. USDA was urging farmers to "produce, produce" and they were responding to the market signal. Marginal lands that had been in Soil Bank were being plowed up and, in the Great Plains old windbreaks from the 1930's were being torn out. Soil conservationists were alarmed, and significant wind erosion increases bore out their concerns.

By the time Neil arrived at the Washington Office in 1974, the concerns were rising and most of them related to the land use issues of the day. Could the ongoing conversion of prime farmlands to development be slowed? How could conservation systems be installed on these marginal lands that were being brought into cultivation? Was the Nation facing a shortage of cropland? How much more could be developed safely? How serious were these problems?

All there were for data were anecdotal stories and many assumptions. It was not a good basis for USDA or national policy. The USDA Land Use Committee was raising the concern, and SCS took action by launching what became known as the 1975 Potential Cropland Study. Coordinated in Washington by the Soil Survey Division, with Ray Didericksen, Al Hidlebaugh and Keith Schmude doing the work, the survey was designed in cooperation with the Iowa State University Statistical Laboratory. A sample of the old plots from the 1967 Conservation Needs Inventory was re-surveyed to see what changes had been made in land use during that time. SCS field people visited each plot and determined both the land use and any problems that might be involved if it were to be converted to cropland from grass or trees. The result was reliable data at the river basin and national levels about the current land use changes and the conservation problems inherent in expanding crop acres.

The results showed that, between 1967 and 1975, there was about one million acres of prime farmland converted to non-farm uses each year, along with about another million acres of lower quality farmland with the potential to economically produce crops. Neil was quickly involved in interpreting the data, drafting papers for the Land Use Committee, and making presentations to Washington groups and others. Speeches for SCS and USDA leaders began to include information on the cropland situation based on the 1975 PCS findings, and national policymakers began to take notice of the findings. The message was that agricultural land was being converted to other uses at the rate of some 1.9 million acres per year (much higher than had earlier been estimated) and that a disproportionate share of the land being lost was prime farmland. There was unused cropland available to replace the losses, but much of it was marginal and would take extensive conservation protection to produce sustainably. It was a sharp conservation and land use message that was in dramatic contrast to most of the situation in the preceding decades.

Neil's presentations of the findings from the Potential Cropland Study caught the attention of people on the Hill, and soon he was invited to come and discuss the issue with a staff briefing. The briefing was set up by Charles E. (Chuck) Little of the Congressional Research Service at the request of James M. Jeffords, the Republican Congressman from Vermont. Robert J. (Bob) Gray on Jeffords' staff was instrumental in getting the issue in front of Jeffords.

Jim Jeffords had been Vermont's Attorney General during the period when Vermont had enacted one of the very early pieces of State Land Use Legislation, so he was well versed in the issue. He was serving on the House Agriculture Committee, and was the ranking minority member on the Conservation and Credit Subcommittee, so he was in a very good position to take leadership on the agricultural land issue. Gray, raised on a dairy farm in upstate New York, was also very knowledgeable on farm and agricultural issues. He was skilled in maneuvering through the political thickets in the House, and had a strong concern over the loss of agricultural land. Little was a very creative and politically savvy land use policy expert, skilled at drafting legislation.

With Neil leading the data interpretation and Administration efforts, Bob Gray doing the political work in the House, and Chuck Little providing both innovative concepts and legislative drafting, it wasn't long before the team had a piece of draft legislation for Jeffords to review. It was pretty politically timid, avoiding the "land use regulation" charge that people regularly used to shout down any attempt at using public policy to guide rational land use by proposing that the federal government seek to reduce the federal subsidies that were pouring into projects that converted prime farmland to non-agricultural uses. The strategy was to say the federal government probably couldn't do a lot to prohibit needless farmland conversion, but it could stop paying for it. It also called for a national study of the loss of prime farmland and the role of the federal government in subsidizing it, as a basis for future policy and program actions.

Jeffords introduced the bill in 1977, but it did not make it out of the House Agriculture Committee. In spite of its cautious approach, opponents criticized its "land use" implications and voted it down. Despite that failure, the bill was bringing national attention to the issue. Within a year, the Environmental Protection Agency had issued new guidelines asking federal project planners to take account of farmland issues in siting projects and facilities. USDA issued a new land use policy, drafted by Neil at the direction of the Land Use Committee, committing the Department's agencies to "seek to avoid irreversible conversion" of prime and unique farmlands, or encroachment on flood plains, unless there were no viable alternatives.

As the work to bring attention to the issue continued, both in the Administration and Congress, USDA Secretary Bob Bergland and CEQ Chairman Charles Warren decided to go ahead with the study of agricultural land called for in the proposed legislation. The Study, named the National Agricultural Lands Study (NALS) was headed up by Bob Gray. As the NALS proceeded, there were a series of "interim reports," written on a variety of pertinent topics that were at the heart of the agricultural land issues.

Charles Little of ALF wrote a background paper published in one of the interim reports that suggested the idea of farmland conservancies. Little was impressed by the effectiveness of conservation easements in saving landscapes around the country. The report, reprinted in the Journal of Soil and Water Conservation, had a major impact on the thinking about farmland protection. It proposed that "somewhere between the extremes of zoning and purchase of development rights is an alternative means to control the loss of important farmland."[8]

Neil wrote a special report released as *Interim Report No.4—Soil Degradation: Effects on Agricultural Policy.* The full NALS study was released in 1980, and its findings ramped up the pressure on the farmland loss issue. Farmland was disappearing under asphalt at a significantly higher rate than earlier reported – some 3 million acres a year – and the federal role in subsidizing its conversion was a major factor. There was no longer much doubt about farmland protection being a major public policy concern.

---

[8] Little, Charles E. "Farmland conservancies: A middleground approach to agricultural land preservation," *Journal of Soil and Water Conservation*, Sept-Oct 1980, V. 35, No. 5, 204-211. Also reprinted in *American Land Forum Magazine*, Vol II, No 1, Winter, 1981, 8-29.

Jeffords continued to press the issue in the House Agriculture Committee, and Neil worked with the committee staff to provide background information that was emerging out of the 1977 National Resources Inventory (see Chapter 23). By this time, he was at NACD (see Chapter 22) and working with Congress on a variety of conservation issues, including farmland protection, which was strongly supported by NACD's leaders. This time, Jeffords' bill was passed by the Agriculture Committee, but was again rejected by the full House in February 1980, largely on the basis of opposition to anything that might smack of "back-door federal land use planning."

Work was beginning on the next Farm Bill, however, and Neil was working with the committee staffs in the House and Senate to press the farmland protection issue. The result, not just of his work, but that of many people and organizations, was the first-ever "Resource Conservation" title in the 1981 Farm Bill. One section was devoted to the creation of the "Farmland Protection Policy Act," which was the Jeffords Bill re-incarnated. By the time the Farm Bill was in process, the findings of the NALS were available and there was no longer much doubt that farmland losses were troublesome, and that the federal role in hastening their loss was significant.

While USDA did very little to implement the 1981 act, the issue did not go away. Several organizations emerged with farmland protection as a major goal. Chuck Little had established the American Land Forum in 1978. ALF was a non-profit conservation organization that operated for a while out of NACD's offices, with Neil as the Chairman of the Board of Directors. Chuck was an outstanding writer and editor, and his new quarterly magazine *American Land Forum* (soon changed to *American Land Forum Magazine*) attracted many of the Nation's leading authorities and leaders in conservation to its pages. It carried the conservation message, with a heavy emphasis on farmland protection, from its inception in 1980 until 1987.

In 1980, Patrick Noonan, formerly chief executive of The Nature Conservancy, and Douglas Wheeler of The Conservation Foundation, worked with the Rockefeller Brothers Fund to establish the American Farmland Trust, a national non-profit organization dedicated to the goal of preserving farmland and farming opportunity. It was dedicated to implementing the original ALF proposal, advocating the use of tools like conservation easements to prevent conversion instead of the more politically controversial zoning or the costly approach of purchasing development rights. AFT quickly attracted staffers like Bob Gray, who joined after his role with NALS ended and Norm Berg, who joined AFT after leaving his post as Chief of the Soil Conservation Service. It continues to this day as a powerful and influential voice for the conservation of farmland and support for farm families and communities.

Meanwhile, the information continued to flow. In 1982, the American Land Forum published *The American Cropland Crisis,* by W. Wendell Fletcher and Charles E. Little. While most economists and analysts were unwilling to use the term "crisis," these authors boldly defended it, saying "No, the crisis is not now one of acres or bushels. It is a crisis of *sense,* for our great body of farmland is being diminished at an increasing rate.... If we don't muster the political energy to save our farmland, who do we suppose will do it for us? And further, if we don't tend to it now, how is it to be accomplished later, after the land has already been converted? That is the crisis."[9]

With this kind of material building public support, and the continuing data provided by USDA about the trends on America's rural land base strengthening the case, even the Congress was unable to ignore the issue.

Taking ALF's ideas on easements, the 1996 Farm Bill created the Farmland Protection Program that authorized USDA to collaborate with local community organizations to purchase development rights and conservation easements to keep productive farmland in agricultural use. This time, the Department implemented the program, and began to help purchase easements. The program was changed in 2002 and re-named the Farm and Ranch Lands Protection Program. By 2003, USDA estimated that the program had protected over 300,000 acres in 42 states

---

[9] Fletcher, W. Wendell and Charles E. Little. 1982. *The American Cropland Crisis: How U.S. Farmland is Being Lost and How Citizens and Governments Are Trying to Save What is Left,* Bethesda, MD: American Land Forum, vii.

Like so many things in Washington, it's never easy to tell what is going to emerge from the policy work that one does. Spending several years on the farmland protection issue seems to have paid off. It may have taken 30 or 40 years, but the ideas that came out of those early talks between Neil, Chuck and Bob have snowballed into something far beyond their dreams. In commenting on Chuck's recent death, Wendell Fletcher called him "a wellspring of ideas and creativity." Amen.

"But what are two million acres? Let's get it down to smaller numbers. We've spent the morning looking at this fine dairy farm built up by three generations of the Hardesty family. Jack introduced us to the three families the farm employs and we've seen the dairy herd that produces 1,000 gallons of milk daily.

"If this farm is about half prime farmland and about half other land, which I suspect is fairly much the case, and today is a typical day, the farmland equivalent of three of these farms went out of production before we sat down to lunch and four more will go before nightfall.

That's what's happening. Over 5,000 acres of farmland going out of production every day.

R. Neil Sampson
Excerpts from speech at Virginia State Holstein Field
Day, Harvue Farms, Berryville, VA, July 8, 1977.

18

Land Use Legislation

"Land use planning and policy was the dominant political topic in the early 1970s"

The Jackson Land Use bill that had been passed by wide Senate margins in 1972 and 1973 had suffered a narrow defeat in the House of Representatives just before Neil arrived at SCS headquarters in July of 1974. The bill was meeting stiff political opposition, but the general assumption was that it would soon be revived and passed.

At USDA, some concerns with the legislation still were felt. Although it was based on the idea of having the states lead the direct action of land use planning and coordination with federal financial assistance, the federal leadership was to be the Department of the Interior (USDI).

In addition to the normal inter-agency competition for programs and money in the federal government, USDA had another concern: it feared that USDI would be more likely to assert strong federal control over the process. "We don't want them directing the process of affecting private land use in the same way they control parking on the Mall," was Norm Berg's way of expressing concern.

But USDA's reluctance was not enough to cause the department to oppose the bill. They wanted to get the USDI leadership role tempered, perhaps with an interagency Council in charge, but only if it could be done in a positive way. The problem with that was the bill was lodged firmly in the House Interior Committee under the tutelage of Morris Udall, and that administrative change was somewhere between unlikely and impossible. So SCS and outside organizations like the National Association of Conservation Districts were left with needing to understand and temper a bill while still supporting its general thrust.

Neil's role was to monitor the activities in the House Interior Committee, stay in touch with the Committee staff to assist if needed, and report back to Norm Berg and the USDA Land Use Committee. As time passed, however, it became apparent that the enthusiasm for a comprehensive national land use policy and planning approach had faded. Narrow legislation affecting specific issues such as surface mining were still in play, but the big push for comprehensive policy was dead and would not be revived.

The fate of the Jackson land use bill provides an interesting political lesson that relates to many current conditions. Land use planning and policy was the dominant political topic in the early 1970s and occupied many thousands of hours of work on the part of hundreds of people, both in Washington and in the States that were convinced they would soon be called upon by the federal government to accelerate their efforts.

A betting person could have made a lot of money had they bet against the inevitability of a federal bill, as it was thought to be virtually assured. But it was not, and in the near-30 years since its demise, there has been little or no political interest in reviving it again. Is that a lesson for some of today's "hot button" issues such as response to climate change? Perhaps.

The failure of national legislation did not, however, spell the end of the strong interest in land use policy. In 1973, passage of the Coastal Zone Management Act brought states and localities into a planning process that was virtually identical to what had been envisioned in the Jackson Bill. By 1977, Congress was grappling with major land use questions, including the settlement of the native land claims in Alaska, a new approach to surface mining, and new water quality programs aimed at reducing the runoff and pollution from land-using activities like farming and forestry.

19

The Surface Mining Act

"The law required the separation and separate storage of the topsoil and its replacement such that prior productivity was restored."

The harmful effects of surface mining became the focus of intense lobbying efforts from the environmental community that resulted in the passage of surface mine regulation legislation in 1974 and 1975. Both of those bills were vetoed by President Ford over concerns about harm to the coal industry. With Jimmy Carter's election in 1976, the prospects for legislation brightened and the Surface Mining Control and Regulation Act of 1977 was passed and signed by the President.

The legislation focused on regulating surface mining and reclamation of previously mined lands. While the program is housed in the Department of the Interior, Neil was closely involved with writing the section on reclaiming prime farmlands. This provision was fiercely fought by the coal industry, which saw it as driving up costs, but USDA had been successful in raising concerns over the loss of prime farmland and the role that government-funded programs played in it.

As a result, Neil worked with the legislators to show how prime farmland could be technically defined and identified in the field, and demonstrate that it could be restored to productivity if properly handled. Neil worked for weeks with legislative staff, negotiating the legal language for the bill. The final legislation contained provisions for special restoration of prime farmland soils, with guidance from USDA and SCS about the definition of prime farmlands and the methods used to restore productivity after the mining was finished. The law required the separation and separate storage of the topsoil and its replacement such that prior productivity was restored.

While the prime farmland provisions remain in the law, it is hard to tell what the actual results have been. There were many legal challenges to the provisions, and if there are data to suggest how effective the effort was in protecting some of the prime farmlands lying over coal fields in the Midwest, it is not readily available.

20

Conservation in Africa

"Sanyang, the Seyfo of Jarrol has problems that take a great toll - like hippos and such that muck up the huts, and spirits that he can't control." ---William M. Johnson

In 1976, the U.S. Agency for International Development (AID) came to the SCS national office to request help with a project in the West African country of The Gambia. A major concern with soil conservation and agricultural production needed to be addressed, and SCS was the logical technical leader in the effort. SCS assigned the leadership of the project to William M. "Bill" Johnson, who was the Associate Administrator for Soil Survey. Bill chose Neil as a member of the team and USDA added Charles McCants, Head of the Department of Soil Science at North Carolina State to make up a three-person team.

Bill Johnson, in addition to being the agency's top soil scientist, was a very experienced international traveler. He loved to work abroad and was diligently studying languages so that he could be more effective. A distinguished-looking man, he was a credible and well-received conservation ambassador. Neil had never travelled outside the U.S. so there was a fast scramble to get a passport as well as all the shots that West Africa required at the time. In the brief time before departure, Neil also needed to find out something about The Gambia and its issues.

The situation was fairly grim. The entire Sahelian region of Africa had been caught in the grips of a major drought in the early 1970s and recovery was beginning, but very slowly. Drought is a periodic visitor to this region, but this time was different. In previous decades, most of Africa was made up of European colonies and the borders were fairly loose. As drought threatened farming and grazing people, they simply moved South to where conditions were more favorable.

Land tenure in Africa was called *usufruct*, and it means that the land essentially is considered public and if the land is not being used, people can make use of it. So the displaced people could move to more favorable conditions, plant crops or graze livestock on vacant land for a year or two, then migrate back to their home territory when the normal monsoon rains returned.

In the 1960s, however, independence came to these former colonies, and many hardened their borders so that north-south migrations were discouraged or disallowed. As a result, many Sahelian villagers were forced to stay on their lands until they were destitute. When food supplies and seed stocks ran out for the farming groups, or when breeding stock began starving and dying for the pastoral groups, desperation set in. Unable to remain where they were or to move to better climates, people migrated toward the coasts and the cities where food aid from abroad could be found.

Dakar, Senegal, on the West African coast, became a city with millions of people crowded into newly-established slums. There, food aid could reach them, but when the drought emergency eased and the food aid began to dry up, many were unable to return to their historic villages. Without seed to plant new crops, or breeding stock to replenish family herds, they were stuck in the city's poverty. Helping to re-start and restore agricultural production was a major task, and AID was trying to help.

The Gambia had been an English colony, surrounded on all sides by French-speaking Senegal. It is a tiny country that runs up the Gambia River from the coast some 300 miles inland. Its history was one of slavery and war. Proceeding across the flat West African plains, the big river was navigable for over 200 miles inland. This made it an important access to interior Africa that was used by British slave ships to penetrate the Dark Continent in their search for slaves to capture and transport to Europe and the New World.

Using their naval might, the British established a border some 10 miles or so from the river on both sides, and beat off the French to establish the colony. On a map, the country looks like a snake entering West Africa, following a winding river in a strip about 15-30 miles wide, from the coastal port of Banjul, the capital, to the head of navigation.

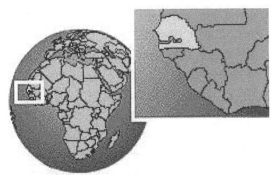

Map: The Gambia bordering the Gambia river, surrounded by Senegal

The largest farmer group was the Mandinka, who lived in settled villages and cultivated crops like sorghum, peanuts, rice and vegetables in the surrounding fields and gardens. It was subsistence farming, with most of the produce needed for family food. Peanuts (called groundnuts locally) were the major cash crop as well as a source of protein in the diet. Fields cleared out of the native savannah and forest were cultivated for a few years until the fertility declined, then allowed to revert back to native vegetation and re-build productivity

Pastoral groups such as the Fula lived close to the Mandinka villages and traded meat and milk for grains as well as the right to graze their cattle on nearby shrub lands, crop residues, and other un-cropped areas. After the crops were removed from the fields, Fula herdsmen staked their cattle in a pattern so that they could eat the crop residue and spread their waste across the field.

The ancient system worked as long as it was nourished by the annual monsoon rains that normally sweep the region and the population did not expand to the point where it exceeded the carrying capacity of the land. With the failure of the rains in 1968 coupled with rapid population growth, agriculture was overwhelmed and famine returned to the region. By 1976, the rains had returned to normal, but the population challenge remained.

As the SCS team met with local AID and Gambian officials, it became apparent that previous development efforts in The Gambia had not been hugely successful and there was much skepticism about the potential outcome of the current effort. Examples discussed included forestry projects that established plantations of fast-growing trees designed to produce saw-timber when what the Gambians needed were daily wood supplies of small stems that could be harvested by women wielding machetes. The plantation trees grew well, but didn't supply the local need.

Another example was the importation of tractors. The small-field pattern of Gambian agriculture (fields were seldom larger than 1 hectare (2.5 acres) was ill-suited for large machinery. Plus, the locals were not familiar with the needs of the machines, and when they ran out of oil and stopped running, they were simply abandoned where they failed.

The local AID official, Doug Broome, had organized orientation meetings and tours for the team as had been common with previous teams, so the round of meetings with national agricultural officials was followed by an aerial tour of the country. In a light plane, a reconnaissance flight covered the entire country in an afternoon. The flat topography was virtually indistinguishable everywhere. The pilot kept bearings with the river, road, and railroad, but there wasn't much variety to be seen. Villages surrounded by fields and scrub forest were everywhere. Few roads marked the land and most of the villages were connected by foot paths.

The aerial tour was followed by a driving tour that crossed the river from Banjul, took the only road up the southern side of the country, re-crossed the river at the lone ferry some miles upstream, and came back the main road down the northern side to Banjul. The drive was slow, as the roads were primitive and clogged with people on foot, cattle, and other traffic. The view was about the same—villages and fields, savannah and scrub forest. Large wildlife were virtually absent, unable to compete with the dense human population, but many species of birds could be seen.

Back in Banjul, the SCS team made a realistic (but apparently shocking) request: "We want to go visit a farming village and find out exactly what is going on at that level." There were mild protestations from the Gambian officials, who intimated that everything necessary could be learned in the capital, but the team persisted and Doug was able to make the necessary preparations.

The next day found us in a village 50 miles or so up the river from Banjul, where a meeting had been scheduled with the local officials. Here we had our first taste of real Gambian society and agricultural practices. The visit began with a formal reception at the *bantaba*— the local meeting center of the village. The team joined the village leaders, sitting on a raised platform in the shade of a great baobab tree in the center of the village. Team leader Bill sat with the *seyfo*, or local leader, and an educated imam who was able to translate between English and the local language.

The men at the *bantaba*—and all were men—were the eldest males in their respective families. By virtue of being oldest, they were the spokesman for the family. All families in the village were represented. The *seyfo* was the oldest of the assembled men, thus maintaining the age-related pecking order in the society. The meeting was fairly formal, but the atmosphere was cordial. Bill asked about the concerns of the villagers, and the speeches were soon forthcoming, with the imam doing his best to translate as fast as possible.

The concerns were universal. The village was growing and there were no job or marriage opportunities for the young men. Thus, they were leaving the village in droves, heading for the towns where jobs were more available, although still not plentiful. The elders worried about where those trends were heading, and how their children and grandchildren could find a place in Gambian society as they knew it. Food was always a concern, particularly at the end of the dry season when the year's stored supplies were lowest and the work of cultivating and planting the new crops imposed a heavy burden on the men and women in the fields.

Neil found the concerns familiar. He was reminded of being among his Native American friends at home during their annual pow-wows when they got together and talked about their plight, as well as his own farm community where there was no future for most of the young farm people who were forced to get an education and flee

109

the area for greener pastures as soon as they could. The issues were the same the world over, it appeared.

Bill was directing his efforts and questions to the *seyfo*: "We represent the United States and we are your friend. What do you need, and what can we do to help you?" Persistence on this approach eventually brought forth a specific request.

"Our women cultivate the rice paddies next to the river," the *seyfo* said. "They work hard to build levees and ditches that bring the water to grow the rice. There is a hippopotamus living in the river and he comes up and goes through the fields, where his heavy body destroys the ditches and levees and causes the women great stress and additional work to grow their rice. If you really want to help us, could you go kill that hippo?"

That put Bill back on his heels. It was the height of the environmental decade in the U.S., and there wasn't a lot of support for U.S. technical teams going into the world to kill rare hippos as a federal project! So a change of subject was in order! Bill asked about the dryland farming, and how the villagers were managing their croplands for production. After a discussion revealed that traditional knowledge of the land was used to decide where to grow which crops, we were taken on a walking tour in the surrounding fields.

Using the imam as interpreter, the farmers showed us how they evaluated very subtle changes in the soil, with one place best for growing sorghum and the other better for groundnuts. The family plots were divided up fairly equally, with each family sharing a portion of the better soils, as well as some of the poorer ones. The lesson for the SCS team: these people knew their soils far better than any formal soil survey could distinguish on a map, and a U.S.-style soil survey would be a waste of our money and their time. Having started with the American notion that a good soil survey was the beginning of any conservation planning effort, the team was confronted with the need to change strategy.

As the team talked with the villagers about their problems, it became obvious that there were two main issues to solve. The first was crop residues and animal manures. There was no way, cultivating with hand hoes and oxen-drawn plows, that residues and manures could be effectively incorporated into the topsoil. Therefore, they were burned, and the nutrients and organic matter largely lost. This contributed to the rapid decline in fertility of the cultivated fields.

Traditionally, this fertility could have been restored in a fallow period where the native vegetation would have had 20-30 years to re-build the soil. But the population pressure and the need for food demanded a shortening of that fallow period, and now it was only 5-10 years between cultivation periods. As a result, the soils were gradually declining, and the future of sufficient food production was very uncertain. With such a brief fallow period, a new way to incorporate organic matter and nutrients into the soil would have to be found.

The other problem was water control. During the rainy season, the soils became saturated, and the heavy rains would cause significant runoff. Even on relatively flat land, the topsoils were being seriously damaged. Those runoff waters could be fairly easily diverted into less harmful patterns but again, with only hoes, shovels and oxen plows, these structures weren't easy to design or build. Since the land use pattern was a complex mix of small family plots, one diversion terrace would have to protect everyone's plot and it would probably intrude on just about everyone's land in the construction process.

The local village organization that could agree on project designs and implementation was in place, but that meant that a project designer would need to work with and convince the village elders at the *bantaba* in order for a project to proceed. The elders would have to be universally agreed on the solution before anything could be done. The situation called for a combination conservation engineer and social scientist to get the job done.

Sending this type of person into the villages to help with problem-solving was not consistent with the Gambian methods which, after all, had been copied directly from their English mentors and fortified with European scientific educations. The Gambian agency specialists were very good at sitting in their offices in Banjul and writing excellent scientific reports, but not very well trained to go out in the villages and grapple with problems there.

The SCS team decided that what was needed was an SCS-trained person who knew both soil and water conservation practices and the approach needed to work with independent private decision-makers and communities. That recommendation was met with some reticence by the AID and Gambian officials, but it was what Neil wrote in the report to USDA and AID at the conclusion of the field work.

In 1977, SCS got the word that AID had approved the project, and that a new SCS team was needed in The Gambia to prepare the full project plan and budget. This time, Neil was chosen as the Team Leader, aided by Don McCormack, a soil scientist in the Washington headquarters office. The third team member was a sociologist from Kansas State who had studied and lived among the Mandinka and turned out to be a valuable member of the team. She could fill in the gaps of the social structure so that Neil and Don could tell what was going on under the surface activities they observed.

Particularly important was a more subtle understanding of the role of women in the rural society. While they were excluded from the official decision-making at the *bantaba*, and spent much of their time in women's groups doing laundry, group cooking, and other tasks, they were also the primary owners of the rice paddies and were incredibly important in the village decision process. An American male couldn't converse directly with them, due to social and religious beliefs, but there needed to be a strategy to make them aware of the conservation needs and supportive of the village actions or success was unlikely.

On the second trip, the first action was a return to the same village, where Neil was received with a great outpouring of joy and friendship. The Gambians had never expected the outsiders to return, as most such visits were a one-time affair; but here they were, still trying to find ways to solve problems. It was a welcome change and the Gambians responded with great hospitality and gratitude.

The project plan was worked out with the AID and Gambian officials, Neil prepared all the project documents, and the effort was ready for launch. An experienced SCS technician would be recruited and posted to Banjul for a period of several years. An office and support staff would be provided, along with a vehicle and other necessary tools. The Gambians would work to set up a soil conservation structure that could support the project.

Neil returned to Washington, where the project was taken over by the appropriate folks in AID and SCS, and proceeded apace. Although he had nothing more to do with any of the implementation work or decisions, an experienced SCS person was recruited and posted to The Gambia, and once in a while, Neil would hear a report that the project was proceeding smoothly. Project evaluations, of which he was not a part, reported that the project was becoming a poster child for development success within AID.

In 1987, Clarence Durban, then President of NACD, travelled to The Gambia to attend the commissioning of the Foni Jarrol Conservation District, the first to be organized in Africa. Newsletter stories from AID indicated that the project was among the most long-running and successful development efforts in the Agency's history.

Fula herders stake their cattle in harvested fields for the night so that they can eat crop residues and spread waste more evenly

A Gambian family uses an oxen-drawn plow to prepare a field for planting. Burying all this organic matter in the soil to build soil quality is not possible with their traditional tools, so the grass cover would be burned to open the land for crop planting, and the potential soil-building value would be lost.

21

Environmental Coordination

"Farmers were up in arms over their economic plight in the late 1970s, . . . making their anger known with pilgrimages and tractor-cades to Washington."

Neil's role in USDA broadened in 1977, when he was assigned to the Office of Environmental Coordination that had been established under Rupert Cutler, Assistant Secretary of Agriculture. In this role, Neil worked with Congressional committees on the major land use legislation as well as providing a coordinating role among the USDA agencies involved in complying with the new rules associated with the National Environmental Protection Act (NEPA) and representing USDA on inter-agency committees related to water quality pilot projects, coastal zone management, and other land use efforts.

He also chaired a Land Use Position Statement Task Force established by the Soil Conservation Society of America (now renamed the Soil and Water Conservation Society) that produced its own position statement.

Farmers were up in arms over their economic plight in the late 1970s, and were making their anger known with pilgrimages and tractor-cades to Washington. At USDA, there was some alarm within the staff over the influx of angry farmers demanding federal action. As one of the few USDA staff that had experience in dealing directly with farmers (including angry ones), Neil left instructions that he would be happy to meet with any farm groups who requested an appointment.

The result was many small sessions around the conference table in his office on the third floor of USDA's main building. The sessions were generally cordial, for while Neil couldn't do anything about their complaints over prices and markets, he could hear them out and promise to bring their views to USDA's leaders. For most of the people involved, that was what they sought—someone who would listen to them and try to understand their situation.

That all ended abruptly one day, however, when an angry, shouting group entered the USDA patio and created a ruckus. Loud reports that sounded like shots rang out, and the smell of cordite went throughout the building. On the third floor, Neil's secretary was under her desk in terror and people were fleeing down the hallways. It was reported that Secretary Bergland was whisked away by security forces through his private escape route to the basement. Later investigation revealed that the noises had come from some firecrackers that had been lit by someone in the crowd, but the damage to the farmer's protest had been done.

Security was tightened and farmer groups were no longer as welcome in the federal buildings. After running their tractors around town and plowing up part of the National Mall, most of them gave up and went home to plant their crops, having had little effect on the basic economic problems they faced.

22

The View from the Private Sector – NACD

"We cannot jam people full of numbers and statistics.
We must help them see what those numbers really mean."

In early 1978, David Unger left his position as the Executive Vice President of the National Association of Conservation Districts (NACD) to become a Deputy Assistant Secretary of USDA, working under Assistant Secretary Rupert Cutler. That left a vacancy at NACD and Neil began thinking about applying for the job. His situation at SCS had developed to the point that he knew his desire to return to an SCS state office was probably not going to be realized, and the idea of working at headquarters for another 20 years until retirement was not particularly appealing. He went to Norm Berg who, in addition to being a valued mentor, was intimately familiar with NACD and its needs. Berg was unhesitating. "Go for it," was his advice.

The result, following a series of interviews, was that Neil was selected by the NACD Board of Directors as the new EVP of the organization. Resigning from his position at SCS and taking up the new job was completed in March, 1978.

It didn't take long to discover the most important difference between working in the SCS bureaucracy and being the lead writer for NACD. In Neil's role as NACD Executive, he would write a weekly editorial for the *Tuesday Letter*, using Lyle Bauer's name as President of the organization. If there was a mistake, and Bauer didn't catch it in their phone consultations over the piece, it would immediately go into national circulation. Instead of spending 10% of his time writing something and 90% of the time getting it edited and approved by a chain of reviewers, he could now spend almost 100% of the time writing and virtually none getting it approved.

Clearly, from a political and technical point of view, this was working without a safety net and it required a far different approach. If you weren't your own quality control person, there might not be any!

Once again, Neil also needed to be at the forefront of modernizing an office. At NACD, the *Tuesday Letter* was written in Washington on Friday and mailed to the NACD Service Department in League City, Texas. At League City, it was received on Monday, typeset and printed, and mailed on Tuesday. If there was a glitch or an error in the process anywhere, the schedule was violated.

The speed-up involved purchasing two of the early fax machines— the kind that ran the paper around a spinning drum while a stylus traced the outlines on the paper and converted them to telephone signals. A second machine at the receiving end spun similarly, but "wrote" the transmitted image on a special heat-sensitive paper. That took out the uncertainty of postal delivery, but the material still had to be re-typed when it got to League City.

The next purchase was a word processor, no small thing. After shopping around, the best buy available was a Lanier that came in at around $22,000. That was a lot of money for a financially struggling organization, but the Board approved it, and soon the staff was learning the new technology.

By 1981, when everyone at NACD was "hooked" on the word processor, Neil was eager to get something like that for his personal use. The early personal computers were not very capable of doing professional work, and they were expensive. Finally, one came along that broke through those barriers, and Neil purchased his first home computer.

It was an Osborne 1, a suitcase-sized "luggable" machine with a removable keyboard that opened up to reveal a 4-inch screen flanked by two 5-1/4" floppy drives. It had something like a 64K com-computing capability and you could put about 90K of data on one of the floppies. It cost $2,500 and a 9-pin impact printer to go with it added another $900! But Neil was launching into the computer age, learning WordStar to do word processing and SuperCalc to do spreadsheets.

As he gained confidence in using the programs, he put NACD's annual budget into a SuperCalc spreadsheet and carried the computer to the Board's annual budget committee meeting in League City. There, he borrowed a television set and hooked up the Osborne to the TV so that the whole committee could view the spreadsheet as it developed. The annual budget review, which previously had taken the committee two days to complete, was essentially done by noon on the first day. The spreadsheet, calculating the bottom line as each decision was made, had simplified the process greatly.

After the meeting concluded, NACD Treasurer Sam Chinn of California took Neil aside. "You go buy one of those computers for the office," he said. "I don't want you to have to use your personal machine for NACD's benefit." So NACD entered the computer era as well, with another Osborne. As larger, better and cheaper machines entered the market, NACD continued to expand and improve the office equipment in all its offices. The computerization of the organization was complete within two years.

The timing for the change was important, because the old way of doing business in the League City, Texas Service Center was rapidly going obsolete. Printing and mailing thousands of copies of the *Tuesday Letter* each week, plus mailing district newsletters for many local conservation districts was a huge workload that required maintaining up-to-date addresses for as many as 25,000 potential recipients.

The job was done by an "Addressograph" machine, which used a small metal plate about the size of a business card that had the address on it. A drawer-full of these cards would be fed into the machine and it would grab them one at a time, ink them, and press the address onto the mailing piece as it went by on a belt. In operation, it sort of looked like a bottling machine, stamping addresses on the moving pieces instead of bottle caps. Keeping the addressograph plates up to date with address changes, etc., was done on a special machine like a typesetter. At the League City office a long wall was filled with tall filing cabinets that held hundreds of drawers of addressograph plates.

The technology was doomed, however. The company had stopped making the machines, and it was getting impossible to buy repair parts. Like it or not, it was time to change. Neil hired a com-. puter programmer in Washington, and set him to work building a membership management program using dBase II, one of the early database management programs. In the process, Neil was also being taught the rudiments of dBase programming, so that when the job was finished, he could take the program to League City and   help people there understand and use it. In spite of the limitations of the early personal computers, and the limits of the early dBase program, the staff at League City began to use the program and, before long, the old Addressograph files were a thing of history.

R. Neil Sampson
"Building a political commitment to conservation,"
Journal of Soil and Water Conservation, Vol. 37, No. 5, Sep-Oct, 1982, p. 252.

"It is with truth, reason, and integrity that we must build a political commitment to conservation. We must use the best facts we can find and tell them in the most honest and compelling ways we know how. We cannot jam people full of numbers and statistics. We must help them see what those numbers really mean.
"And we must speak in terms of ethics as well as economics. We must help people understand that when we inherited this earth from our forebears we were not accorded the God-given right to steal it from our children.
"But we can only do this successfully if we come together as professionals, in an organization such as SCSA, and reduce or eliminate intramural bickering over facts and trends. If we cannot accomplish that, then we can never hope to gain a valid political commitment to conservation, and we will continue to see case after case of Americans destroying the resource base upon which our people's future depends. Neither our profession nor the society at large can tolerate that folly for too long."

23

The RCA Program

"Giltmier wanted...a new national plan for soil conservation
programs, complete with budget recommendations."

In 1975, Jim Giltmier, a staffer on the Senate Agricultural Committee, had asked SCS for drafting assistance on a bill to create a new
approach to evaluating and budgeting soil conservation programs.
The past history of crop surpluses had led the economists at the Office of Management and Budget to resist higher conservation budgets. Their argument was that there was no need to spend money on
conservation which would, as one effect, maintain farm productivity
in an era when crop surpluses were the major problem.

Giltmier wanted a program similar to the one that had successfully focused attention on forestry programs and their needs in the
Forest Service. It would be based on a national resource assessment
that would lead to a new national plan for soil conservation programs, complete with budget recommendations.

While Neil was active in working with land use and water quality
legislation in USDA, he was not involved in the development of the
new program, named the Soil and Water Resources Conservation
Act, or RCA for short. Rich Duesterhaus was the staff leader, working
closely with Norm Berg and the other SCS leaders. The legislation
was passed by Congress, but vetoed by President Ford at   the urging
of OMB, who saw it as another means for USDA to plead for higher
budgets. In November of 1977, with the Carter Administration in
office, the bill was once again passed in Congress and the President
signed it.

USDA began work on the resource study called for in the bill and hastily conducted the first national resource inventory (NRI) in 1977 to provide the needed data. Work began on developing a national conservation program, which Congress had demanded by January, 1980. A series of regional meeting with agricultural, conservation, and other interests was held to gain public input, and the program development involved a huge amount of staff work in the USDA agencies. NACD's leaders were active in facilitating the public meetings and encouraging attendance. Neil authored a 4-part series in *Tuesday Letter* during May 1978 that explained the background of the RCA, outlined the public participation process envisioned by USDA, and explained the plan for developing the appraisal and program it required.

As the process continued, Neil monitored the work at USDA and spent many hours trying to understand and interpret the results from the 1977 national resource inventory. In May 1979, several hundred pages of technical reports were condensed into a 6-part series carried in *Tuesday Letter* to every conservation district official in America. While these officials were knowledgeable about their local conservation concerns and needs, they did not have the national understanding that would be needed to help mold the new national conservation program.

The analysis had significant weak points. The only prior studies available to compare the 1977 data against were the 1967 Conservation Needs Inventory and the 1975 Potential Cropland Study, neither of which were comparable enough to the 1977 NRI to provide reliable trend data. Thus, while the 1977 NRI pointed out that soil erosion levels were high, the prior studies were not adequate to say for sure whether that high rate of erosion had been increasing, decreasing or staying stable. Totally missing was any sound analysis of the costs imposed by soil erosion, farmland conversion, and other resource depletion.

In developing a conservation program for the nation, USDA faced a significant hurdle in trying to convince OMB and Congress that funding a new conservation program, or increasing an existing one, would produce the reductions in soil damage or farmland loss that were needed. And, again, the lack of economic data was cited. "Was there a real problem?" OMB asked. "If so, what does it cost the Nation so we can know whether it is worthwhile to try to solve it." Those questions had not been part of the resource inventories, and those answers didn't exist.

By the time the new RCA program was released for public review in January 1980, the political situation in the country had dramatically changed. Ronald Reagan had been elected and the new political leadership at USDA had two problems with the proposal. First, it was the product of the prior administration, so they didn't trust it. Second, if it proposed spending any federal funds, it was inconsistent with the Reagan goal of reducing federal domestic spending. So the RCA faced an uphill battle.

At NACD, Neil again presented a summary of the USDA draft program report. A special 12-page edition of *Tuesday Letter* (February 5, 1980) contained a condensation of the report and its recommendations, and encouraged conservation district officials to comment on the proposals during the public review period, which was slated to end on March 28, 1980. In addition to 18 major regional meetings hosted by USDA, conservation districts sponsored over 9,000 local meetings attended by over 100,000 people.

The first round of public comments on the RCA draft drew some 68,000 comments for USDA officials to review and catalogue. The opinions stated didn't, however, have much effect on the political leadership in USDA or OMB, and any proposals that suggested new funding were rejected out of hand.

Neil and the NACD leadership were not waiting, however. They worked with Congressmen Ed Jones of Tennessee and James Jeffords of Vermont to facilitate the introduction of the Soil Conservation Act of 1981. The bill contained all of the pieces that NACD was supporting, including a Special Areas Conservation Program, matching grants for local conservation activities, conservation loans, an Agricultural Land Resource Policy, and an organic act for the Resource Conservation and Development Program.

This bill was strongly opposed by the Administration, but Congress was flexing its muscle, and the entire bill was included as a new

Conservation Title in the 1981 Farm Bill. Thus, while Neil was working with Congress on NACD's behalf to achieve these new programs and policies, USDA was being handed a set of programs it had not requested, did not want, and, in the end, would not implement.

Interestingly, however, most of the ideas from the Conservation Title of the 1981 Farm Bill have in fact come into play over the intervening years. The Special Areas Conservation Program envisioned there was very similar to today's Conservation Reserve Enhancement Program and the special emphasis programs such as the Chesapeake Bay effort.

The Political Chief

It wasn't just the RCA program and the Farm Bill programs that were affected by the policies of the Reagan Administration. In March 1982, Secretary of Agriculture John Block announced that Norm Berg would be replaced as Chief of the Soil Conservation Service by Peter C. Myers, a Missouri farmer and conservation leader.

This wasn't a new idea, as the selection of a politically- appointed agency head had been discussed for many years. The history of SCS and Forest Service, in particular, had been marked by professional leadership, but there was never any certainty that this would continue. The idea of a professional leader was strongly supported by NACD and many other conservation organizations, particularly in regard to the natural resource agencies in USDA and the Department of the Interior. The reality, however, was that political appointments were always a possibility.

Norm Berg was well aware of that situation. During the early days of the Nixon Administration, he and Ken Grant had waited an uneasy several weeks while their resignation letters sat on the desk of USDA Secretary Earl Butz. The Secretary finally decided against moving the two men out of the agency's leadership and, in fact, eventually moved both jobs into the professional service where they would be less likely to be subjected to political pressure. This was largely at the urging of Assistant Secretary Bob Long, who felt strongly that the political leadership of the programs should come from the Secretary and Assistant Secretary, but that agency leadership was best done by someone familiar with the internal workings of the agency.

The pathway to political agency leadership had been strengthened during the Carter Administration with the Civil Service reforms that were carried out at that time. Under the new reforms, all agency heads and leaders above grade GS-16 were transferred into the newly-created Senior Executive Service, where they were open to transfer anywhere in the government that their skills were needed. This was the authority under which USDA Secretary Bob Bergland had transferred R. M. "Mel" Davis out of the SCS in 1979, opening the way to appoint Norm Berg into the job.

Block took the process one step further, going outside the professional SCS ranks to name Peter Myers as the new Chief. NACD was highly opposed to the move, and Neil called Secretary Block to make their case. That really didn't have any effect, however. Block was well within his authority and he explained to Neil that he really felt the agency would benefit from having someone who understood farming at the top. It was a typical conversation between the two – friendly, but with no change as a result.

It wasn't long until Neil met Pete Myers, and the two struck up a personal friendship that lasted over the years. Pete was a capable, likeable person and it was clear that he was dedicated to making the best out of his time at the helm of SCS. A chain of professional agency leadership that extended from Hugh Bennett had been broken, but it was not apparent that any real damage had been done. Like many policy changes in Washington, the impact might not be fully realized for a very long time, and even then, different people might make very different assessments of the impact. For Neil, it was a time to take a political defeat as quietly and gracefully as possible and move on to other issues.

For former SCS Chief Norm Berg, it was the beginning of another long and illustrious career. He became the Washington Representative for the Soil and Water Conservation Society and was named Chief Emeritus of the SCS and, later, NRCS. In those roles, and in working with the American Farmland Trust, he remained actively engaged in national soil conservation policy making until his death in 2008 at age 90.

In a book dedication after Norm's death, Neil wrote: "A modest man, Norm Berg's name will seldom be listed as highly on the list of contributors as it ought to be, but his many friends and co-workers realize that his name belongs alongside H.H. Bennett's as one of the most influential people shaping America's soil and water conservation program into the 21st century."

24

The Red and Green Ticket Ideas

"The political implications of the Red Ticket were too high and the potential budget impact of the Green Ticket was unacceptable."

As the RCA program proposals went through the public review and comment period in 1980, most of the comments on the idea of cross-compliance were negative. That proposal suggested that land users would need to have an approved conservation system in place before they could qualify for participation in USDA programs. It was informally called a "red ticket" program. It was initially rejected by nearly all farm organizations and NACD opposed it as well. Interestingly, after some initial negative reaction, public polling revealed that the approach was supported by a growing number of farmers.

NACD's support was centered on another type of incentive program that had been initially drafted by Neil and reviewed by the Board. It was informally labeled the "green ticket" approach and was, as well, one of the proposed approaches contained in the RCA program proposal. This approach focused on the need for farmers to develop and implement a conservation plan approved by the local soil conservation district. Neil worked with NACD officials and other conservation leaders to define and explain the idea.

Each farmer that carried out a satisfactory conservation program would earn an annual Green Ticket that could be used to qualify for participating federal and state programs. The conservation district would enter into an agreement with each participant based on his farm, ranch, or forest management plan. By voluntarily signing the agreement, the participant would certify their belief that the conservation system proposed was feasible and reasonable, and agree to carry it out. Periodic reviews by the conservation district or their agency partners would assure that the participant was keeping their end of the bargain.

> "Americans must turn their genius to the search for ways to work with nature, through science and the best technology; not to conquer or tame the land, but to understand it and use it wisely. With each bite of food, we must not consume a bite of the irreplaceable land that produced it." R. Neil Sampson, "Field, Forest and Mine," in Smithsonian Exposition Books, *The American Land,* New York: W. W. Norton & Company (1979). pp. 242-252.

NACD argued that there were many economic and social benefits that could accrue from the Green Ticket. In addition to farm support and incentive programs, it was possible to provide tax benefits similar to those available for people who installed energy conservation features in their homes. The Green Ticket could also certify that a land manager was meeting state and federal regulatory programs such as those required under the Clean Water Act, which might serve as a protection against regulatory hassles that might otherwise develop.

The inherent problem with the Green Ticket idea was that it promised to end up providing public financial incentives that might not otherwise be required, or reduce tax revenues if that aspect were included. Those features smacked of additional federal budget impacts, a politically unacceptable outcome. By contrast, the regulatory Red Ticket approach could shift the cost of conservation progress onto the private accounts of land managers, and, if they resisted, the result would be lower program outlays for the affected federal programs.

As the RCA program worked its way through the system, it became obvious that neither the Red Ticket nor Green Ticket program would be one of the preferred alternatives in the final RCA program proposed by the Reagan Administration's USDA. The political implications of the Red Ticket were too high and the potential budget impact of the Green Ticket was unacceptable.

Interestingly, both concepts eventually found their way into federal farm policy. Conservation compliance (the Red Ticket) became a centerpiece of the 1985 Farm Bill reforms, and a conservation incentives program very similar to the Green Ticket concept was contained in the Conservation Security Program enacted in the 2002 Farm Bill. Some ideas just take a while to mature!

25

Farmland or Wasteland

"The importance of topsoil to humans and to the quality of our life
is difficult to overstate." *--Farmland or Wasteland*

In 1980, there was a national conference on the "Decade of the Environment," held in Colorado. Neil spoke on the soil conservation situation that had gotten considerably worse with the great crop expansion of the 1970s. As Secretary Butz urged farmers to "plant fencerow to fencerow" in order to meet the commodity market demands that had sprung up overseas, conservation systems were abandoned, windbreaks removed, and fragile grasslands plowed out for crops. Soil erosion rates skyrocketed, and USDA had documented the problem with its first National Resource Inventory in 1978. That acceleration of agricultural intensity, coupled with the continued loss of prime farmlands to development, greatly concerned the conservation community.

Neil appeared on a panel with Robert Rodale, the owner of Rodale Press, who was promoting the virtues of organic farming. After the day's session, the two met for a beer to talk. "That's a powerful story you tell," Rodale said. "You should write a book. If you'll write it, we'll publish it." Bob was deadly serious. His company published mostly books on health prevention and organic agriculture, and was a well-run and respected publisher. Neil wasn't certain. He was an accomplished writer, well versed in the conservation subject, but a book? That sounded like an awful lot of work on top of his responsibilities at NACD.

After some thought, he made a counter-offer: "I will write a book, but not on NACD time, and not without a word processor."

Rodale came right back. "We've been wanting to test the new technology that converts word processor files directly into typesetting without needing to re-enter the text," he said. "If you will rent a word processor that can provide us with electronic files, I'll pay the lease fee." So the die was cast. Neil rented a second Lanier word processor and began to work on the book.

A meeting with the Rodale editors at their Emmaus, PA offices led to re-thinking and tightening the outline for the project, but after some work back and forth, the project was ready to go and a book contract was signed in June, 1980, with a proposed submission date at the end of the year

Neil had envisioned taking his previous speeches and issue papers that were all contained on Lanier disks and assembling them into a book quickly, but the process doesn't really work like that. Neil was stunned to learn that when he built a solid outline for what needed to be in the book, the story needed to be written virtually from scratch.

Months of effort followed, and the family dining room table was piled high with reference material surrounding the leased word processor. The work at NACD was intense, as well, with the 1980 fall election of Ronald Reagan promising to change many of the soil conservation programs that would be described in the book. So progress on the project, working evenings and weekends, was slow. It would be March, 1981, before the manuscript was finally delivered to Rodale, and publication was scheduled for September.

The first publication run of "Farmland or Wasteland: A Time to Choose" was 5,000 copies, and those were quickly sold, so a second run of 10,000 was printed. NACD sold something like 1,500 copies through the Service Center, and Neil dedicated all the royalties from those sales to the NACD Endowment Fund. Congressman Ed Jones sponsored a Capitol Hill reception, where Rodale Press provided copies to members of Congress, Administration officials, and leading environmental organizations. Rodale's staff also sent review copies to agricultural and conservation publications. Many favorable book reviews were received, and Jones put one of them in the Congressional Record on October 20, 1981.

Farmland or Wasteland was selected as the Outstanding Book of 1982 by the Natural Resources Council of America, a national umbrella group of conservation and environmental organizations. By the time the book went out of print in 1984, many of the ideas it contained had shown up in conservation legislative initiatives that were working their way through the Congressional process.

Congressman Ed Jones (D-TN) and Neil at the
Capitol Hill reception for *Farmland or Wasteland*

26

The Sodbuster Program

*"...conservation systems were being destroyed,
cultivated crops were being planted,
and soil erosion rates were escalating."*

One of the more frustrating conservation problems associated with the agricultural expansion of the 1970s was the plowing out of fragile grasslands in the Great Plains region. Many of these lands had been protected since the tragedy of the 1930s Dust Bowl through significant public expenditure and effort through programs like the Soil Bank Program, the Great Plains Conservation Program and the Agricultural Conservation Program. Now, those conservation systems were being destroyed, cultivated crops were being planted, and soil erosion rates were escalating. Conservation districts in Colorado were publicizing the problem and demanding solutions in Washington.

Neil worked with the staff of Senator William Armstrong (R-CO) to develop a legislative approach to the situation. The basic idea was to deny any type of federal price support, insurance, or other incentive programs to cropland that had not been in cultivation during the preceding 10 years. Armstrong was a great person to lead the political effort. He was a conservative who could not be accused of simply advocating added government spending. It was also his state that was being torn up terribly, and there were local conservation districts and counties in Colorado screaming for action.

"When government target prices and similar commodity programs yield a higher price to farmers than the market...the only way to increase production is to increase acreage by plowing erosion-prone lands," Armstrong said. "If the crops do not pan out and the land begins to blow away, the government subsidizes the farmers to reseed the land. In effect, we are providing incentives to plow up more land—and then the taxpayers pay again to retire the land after the damage has been done."[10]

Neil promoted that idea in papers and speeches, and the Sodbuster Program was incorporated into the 1985 Farm Bill. It is still a part of federal conservation programs, where it has been linked to a similar program limiting USDA benefits to farmers who have converted wetlands to crops (originally called the Swampbuster program in 1985) as the central features of the conservation compliance effort.

> "Many farmers today are seriously abusing their land, not because they want to, but because they are either unaware of the damage they are causing, or feel it is insignificant compared to the losses they might suffer if they changed their farming system. Often, they are being assured by scientists from agricultural industries, agencies and colleges that what they are doing is real progress. The criteria, too often, is that if it is profitable, it must be right."
>
> *Farmland or Wasteland p. 294*

---

[10] With One Voice, pp. 40-41, quoting from the *Tuesday Letter*, February 2, 1982.

27

The Conservation Coalition
and Swampbuster

"By the early 1980's, it was increasingly recognized that it was impossible to address many of the nation's serious environmental problems without solving the conservation problems on private lands."

As the 1985 Farm Bill was starting to be shaped in 1983, a "conservation coalition" was formed in Washington that brought together a wide array of environmental, conservation, and other groups to work on Farm Bill issues. In some regards this was a "first" for Farm Bill politics. Many of the environmental and conservation organizations had not previously been active in lobbying for or against the Farm Bill, which they saw as focused on commodity support programs that had little or nothing to do with environmental concerns.

By the early 1980's, however, it was increasingly recognized that 2/3 of the nation's land was in private hands, much of it was used for agriculture, and it was impossible to address many of the nation's serious environmental problems without solving the conservation problems on private lands. Trying to regulate water quality with the 1972 Clean Water Act was not going to do the entire job.

So the large environmental organizations became very active in the conservation coalition. Many of the staffers that came to the meetings to discuss and debate the issues were learning things completely new to them. Of the 25 or 30 people that regularly attended, only two—Neil and Norm Berg (who by then was retired from USDA and was representing the Soil and Water Conservation

Society)—had any field experience in administering these conservation programs.

They often found themselves trying to help others understand how that process worked – and needed to work – as it addressed private landowners.

Some of the conservation issues facing agriculture, such as the plowing out of grasslands, had been addressed in the earlier Sodbuster legislation, so they were quickly adopted by the coalition and supported by most of its individual members. The coalition continued to work on Farm Bill issues in 1984, as the legislative process worked through the complex and huge bill. Members of the coalition came to the meetings to gain information on issues, and were often briefed by USDA experts and Congressional staffers about different aspects of the bill.

The group members were not always full agreement, but cohesion was maintained since the coalition itself did not take political positions, but relied on every member to lobby from the perspective of their organization's policies. It was both unique and surprising to members of Congress to see some of these organizations appear side-by-side to press for improved conservation laws. It was also effective, as the coalition got virtually everything it requested in the Conservation Title of the 1985 Farm Bill.

One of the proposals that caused some differences in the coalition was brought into the process fairly late by some of the major environmental organizations. Taking a page out of the sodbuster approach, which had met broad support in Congress and seemed certain to become part of the Farm Bill, they came forward with a twin proposal aimed at fighting the conversion of wetlands to crops or other agricultural uses. If a landowner drained wetlands for conversion to agriculture, they would lose access to all USDA assistance or support programs.

When the proposal was presented to the conservation coalition, there was immediate and enthusiastic support. Neil, however, was troubled by it. He agreed that wetland conversion was a problem, and that addressing it was important. He couldn't see, however, just how the SCS could handle it in the field.

While he was in the environmental role at USDA, he had been involved in an effort between SCS scientists and their counterparts in the Department of the Interior and the Corps of Engineers to update the field handbooks and definitions of wetland. (This had been made necessary by the 1972 Clean Water Act, which initiated the federal regulation of wetlands through its "dredge and fill" provisions.) The definition had, however, proven very difficult and controversial.

The status of land that was wet for part of the year, but dried out at times, was not easy to agree upon or define, and could be very difficult to identify and categorize in the field. Two scientists could look at the same situation and come to different conclusions. That had to be remedied, but by 1984, it had not been.

So Neil and Norm voiced their concerns in the coalition. SCS field people would be faced with the prospect of going onto a farmer's land, putting a hard boundary around a piece of land that was a defined wetland, and on the basis of that decision, costing the farmer what could be a considerable amount of money. That was going to be both difficult and controversial, with the prospect of the decision being appealed to USDA or taken into court.

Without a solid scientific basis upon which the decision was made, the SCS people would be very vulnerable to losing those cases and, in the process, damaging or destroying the effort to protect wetlands. In the extreme, it could damage the entire conservation program by discrediting the lead agency. The problem wasn't with the effort to reduce wetland drainage—it was with the lack of a good scientific basis upon which to do it.

But those implementation concerns failed to sway the coalition, which saw an opportunity to address a critical national conservation problem. Support for the Swampbuster program, as it was called, was high, and it went into the Farm Bill and was enacted almost exactly as the coalition proposed. Linked with the Sodbuster program, the two eventually became a centerpiece in what has been labeled as the Conservation Compliance program in USDA. The technical difficulties in implementation were significant, and challenged SCS for many years, although the programs continue in USDA to this day.

As predicted, The Conservation Compliance program did run into significant implementation problems in subsequent years. It regularly attracted critics from the environmental community as USDA proved either unwilling or unable to pursue it diligently. One such criticism was documented in 2003 by the General Accounting Office in Congress:

"USDA's Natural Resources Conservation Service has not consistently implemented the 1985 Food Security Act's conservation provisions. Inconsistent implementation increases the possibility that some farmers receive federal farm payments although their soil erodes at higher rates than allowed or they convert wetlands to cropland....

According to GAO's nationwide survey, almost half of the Conservation Service's field offices do not implement the conservation provisions as required because they lack staff, management does not emphasize these provisions, or they are uncomfortable with their enforcement role....

Finally, the Farm Service Agency, the USDA agency responsible for withholding benefits for violations identified by the Conservation Service, often waives these noncompliance determinations without adequate justification. Without support from the Farm Service Agency, the Conservation Service's field staff has less incentive to issue violations."

—GAO-03-418, a report to Ranking Democratic Member,
Senate Committee on Agriculture, Nutrition, and Forestry

28

The Conservation Reserve Program

*"Too often, conservation requirements
are set to the easiest possible standard"*

In 1983 Bob Cashdollar, the staff director for the House Subcommittee on Conservation, Credit and Rural Development under the chairmanship of Ed Jones (D-TN), came to Neil informally and asked for help in drafting legislative language for a conservation reserve program. The program needed to be different than the Soil Bank program, but designed to address the problem of soil erosion on marginal croplands – land that should be taken out of cultivated crops and put into grass or trees that could provide a sustainable and economically sound system.

Neil dug out the old Cropland Conversion Program from the 1960's to see what could be salvaged from that effort. The idea was to encourage people to convert the cropland into another economic use, such as grazing or forestry so that there could be a way to intercept what had been a frustrating merry-go-round with the Soil Bank. When people rented their marginal cropland to the government for a few years and planted it to grass for erosion protection, they nearly always put it back into crops at the end of the rental period. That just started a new round of surplus production and erosion damage, and the public was faced with the damage and expense of getting it back out of cultivation and into another retirement program.

If the new program did what was hoped, it would be a transitional effort that would get those landowners into a different type of agriculture—one that was compatible with the land and water situation they faced. To begin the transition, the new program would have land-owners bid for conversion and rental payments, with the amount of the bid based on the remaining market opportunities within the contract. This was to be based on a plan that the landowner presented with their application, showing how they would make the transition to a new form of agriculture. The hope was that the more market income the landowner could achieve under their plan, the lower the cost would be to the government and the more likely that a successful transition could emerge.

Cashdollar and Jones liked the idea, and introduced it for sub-committee consideration, but it didn't last long in the original format. Cattlemen and Christmas tree growers both saw it as a potential source of new competition in their industries, fueled by government subsidies. So the economic transition idea was shelved, and the bill as it emerged from the sub-committee was for a straight set-aside program with conversion and rental payments, and with no economic use allowed on the land while it was under contract.

The other original idea that didn't survive was that the definition of marginal land would be based on the old Land Use Classification System that SCS had used for decades. There was significant pressure to replace that classification with a new one, labeled Highly Erodible Land (HEL), that SCS would develop based on the Revised Universal Soil Loss Equation (RUSLE).

With those two modifications, the early version of a Cropland Reserve Program began to move through the House Agricultural Committee.

In 1984, the Committee draft, along with several other important pieces of conservation legislation, was incorporated into what would eventually become the 1985 Farm Bill, formally known as the Food Security Act of 1985. In the Farm Bill, it was recognized that the marginal land in the CRP would need to be put back into economic use at the end of the rental contract, but that was tempered by the creation of a Conservation Compliance approach that would at least mean that an effective conservation system would be required if the land were put back into cultivation.

Whether or not that would be rigidly enforced by USDA was a remaining question, however. Both the politicians that develop the Farm

Bill and the Department are caught on the conflict between enforcing good conservation policies and being helpful to farmers and ranchers and friendly with their national farm associations. Too often, the latter wins out, and conservation requirements are set to the easiest possible standard—to the dismay of the conservation community that advocates for the conservation provisions of the legislation.

29

Rob Gets a Job

*"...the NACD crew was surprised to hear from Rob
that he had been accepted as an SCS Student Trainee in Idaho."*

In 1981, an SCS personnel specialist, Roger Montague, accepted a brief Intergovernmental Personnel Act (IPA) loan to NACD to help the organization develop more formal and consistent personnel policies for the use of state agencies and conservation districts. Districts had been increasingly successful in raising state and local funds that allowed them to hire managers and technicians, but there were few personnel guidelines or policies for them to readily adopt and NACD was committed to helping fill that void.

In the normal coffee conversations around the office, Neil brought up the fact that his son Rob, a freshman civil engineering student at the University of Idaho, was going to need a summer job soon and that staying in Idaho would be helpful in achieving resident status for tuition. Roger said, "Why don't you see if he can get on as an SCS Student Trainee? This year they are expanding that program significantly."

Neil was fairly cool to the idea, based on the fact that he had never been able to land a similar trainee position in Idaho because in the late 1950's, the funding for the positions was never assured until July 1 and by then he was always on another job somewhere. There was also the fact, as Roger noted, that freshman students weren't often taken as trainees. "Too many of them change their majors and go a different direction before graduating," he said, "and the agency loses its investment in their training."

Still, it seemed like a worthwhile effort, even if it was a long shot, so Roger ran down the application forms and Neil bundled them up and sent them to Rob, suggesting that here was one option if he wished to try it. Time went by, and the NACD crew was surprised to hear from Rob that he had been accepted as a Student Trainee in Idaho. Roger went behind the scenes and learned that Idaho had identified an engineering student as their top priority for the year, and Rob filled the bill in spite of being so young.

The situation was great for Rob, but Neil had to treat it carefully. Because his work at NACD was so closely tied to the Washington SCS headquarters, he had to be very certain not to do or say anything that would suggest that Rob's appointment was somehow a special favor of some kind. It wasn't, of course, but it was the appearance that mattered most.

30

The Conservation Tillage Information Center

"Jim Lake of NACD, Bruce Julian of SCS, and Jim Morrison of Purdue University completed the first national surveys of conservation tillage in American agriculture."

The idea of conservation tillage (or "no-till" as it is often called) had been around for a long time, but it needed a lot of development to move from idea to action. That development began to take off rapidly during the 1970's, as the concern with the "great plow-out" and the associated increase in soil erosion on cropland was documented and publicized.

The reasons for the emergence of conservation tillage systems were plain. Farmers found they could cut costs, maintain yields, and protect their lands at the same time. Where they could do that, it meant farm profits as well as conservation.

The challenges for successfully implementing conservation tillage were many—new machinery that could handle seeding through heavy crop residues on the soil surface, new crop varieties adapted to the cooler soils encountered at seeding time, and better herbicides that could safely control the weeds that would take advantage of the reduction in cultivation.

In fact, a great deal of research was needed to show where and how conservation tillage could be applied — what soil types, crops, and fertilizer combinations worked best—as well as what other management practices would have to be incorporated. It was not just a different type of cultivation; it was a whole new system of managing soils and growing crops.

NACD had been a strong supporter of conservation tillage for many years, and a series of special projects in Indiana, managed by Jim Lake and supported by the EPA, had been demonstrating its effectiveness in reducing erosion and preventing water pollution. But there were lots of questions remaining, and no good place to go find answers. Dick Foell of Chevron was proposing an idea for a national organization of no-till farmers, researchers and suppliers.

When a group of conservation, industry, and agency leaders met to discuss Foell's idea, however, they came out with a recommendation that there should be an "Information Center" that would focus on helping people adapt conservation tillage to their individual situations.

Neil and NACD's leaders liked the concept and agreed to host the center as the most ambitious special project the organization had ever undertaken. An executive committee was formed with the industry, agency, and organization sponsors to support and guide the effort. Foell was elected the first chair, and he immediately engaged Bob Rice of Gibbs and Soell Public Relations to help the group and serve as the organization's acting secretary. Lake was the project coordinator.

A $50,000 challenge grant from the Joyce Foundation in Chicago helped launch the program within NACD, with the industrial sponsors agreeing to match the funds. Technical staff was provided by NACD, EPA, SCS and the Extension Service, and the Conservation Tillage Information Center was born. The name has since been changed to the Conservation Technology Information Center, but CTIC still works as the best-known label.

The tensions within the partnership during the formation period were significant, and the leaders were challenged to keep things on track. Conservation tillage relied on chemicals for weed control, and there were several competing companies that had little prior experience in collaborating on a single information program. Equipment companies were not at all sure that they wanted to see a major increase in no-till, which meant a comparable reduction in the amount of tillage and, a reduced demand for their products. Many within NACD, the federal agencies and others in the conservation community were not accustomed to collaborating closely with industrial companies, and some expressed their discomfort to NACD's leaders. But gradually the focus on improving conservation agriculture, saving energy, and bolstering farm profits provided a mission that all could support.

In 1983, the CTIC staff, consisting of Jim Lake of NACD, Bruce Julian of SCS, and Jim Morrison of Purdue University completed the first national surveys of conservation tillage in American agriculture. Gathering data from conservation districts and SCS local offices across the country, they produced estimates of tillage practices in both 1982 and 1983, along with an opinion survey of local views and questions. The CTIC was instantly established as the primary source of sound information and data on tillage practices.

In the NACD Washington office, Dr. James Bauder of Montana, on loan from the Extension Service, led the effort to develop a national network of scientists and practitioners that could be a "referral service" to help answer the questions that were coming into the Center. In addition, he established the start of a library system for the Center.

Conservation tillage was definitely an idea for its time, and the Center was part of its success. With newsletters, information releases, field days and exhibits throughout farm country, CTIC kept the topic at the top of many rural agendas. The data and information provided by CTIC were carried by an enormous cadre of communicators, including the sales forces of the CTIC member companies, the conservation districts, and the USDA field people from SCS and Extension Service.

Annual reports from the CTIC-sponsored surveys showed steady and significant growth in the practice for many years, and subsequent soil erosion surveys done as part of the National Resource Inventories indicated the result was a marked decrease in soil erosion from cultivated cropland.

In 2012, as it celebrated its 30th anniversary, CTIC remained a vibrant force in American agriculture, promoting not just conservation tillage, but all forms of conservation technology aimed at maintaining sustainable agricultural production while protecting environmental values.

146

31

For Love of the Land

"The issues covered in *For Love of the Land* provide a track record of the accomplishments—and the unfinished agenda—of the conservation movement in the United States."

David Stewart, the NACD Service Department Manager in Texas, was not only one of the original NACD staffers but also a history buff. He maintained a huge and well-organized library of old NACD papers and photos at the League City office.

One such file was a start at a history of NACD's first days that had been a project of Hal Jenkins, who had retired after a long career as an information person at SCS. Jenkins had personally known the early SCS and NACD leaders and had been assigned to help them with their information work in the early days, so he was in a key position to write this story. He had, however, given up well before it was finished.

Gordon Zimmerman, in retirement, had also started to take a shot at the manuscript. He, too, had been a key figure in NACD's early days, so his expertise was exceptionally valuable. Gordon was stricken with cancer, however, before he had been able to do much with the project. David was still hoping someone would finish the book, and Neil decided to take it up. He rounded up all the original Jenkins and Zimmerman work and got it transferred to word processing disks on the Osborne. After editing and smoothing those parts, it was time to begin writing original manuscript. The book process was barely started in 1984 when Neil was fired from NACD by then-President Bud Mekelburg. [11]

---

[11] For the story of that firing, from Neil's viewpoint, see *With One Voice: The National Association of Conservation Districts,* Tucson: Wheatmark. (2008), pp. 82-83.

That left the manuscript up in the air again. But Neil and David Stewart agreed to finish the project, and Mekelburg approved. Neil would work on a contract basis, with NACD owning the copyright and book outright.

The manuscript of *For Love of the Land* took several months to complete, working with the Osborne as the word processing machine. Since the floppy disks on the machine could only hold about 100k of data, it took one or more of disks per chapter, and since those disks had a frightening history of failure, there were backups galore. But the job was finally finished, and Stewart's crew at the Service Department took over the task of typesetting and publishing the book.

The initial press run sold out fairly quickly, but no record of the total that finally were printed appears to exist. When the NACD Service Department was closed by the organization in 2005 there were no more copies of the book remaining in stock. In 2009, Neil worked with NACD to get the book republished by an on-demand publisher, where it remains currently available.

32

Neil Goes Forward

"Neil was active in the Intergovernmental Panel on Climate Change, serving as Lead Author or Convening Lead Author on several projects."

In 1984, Neil was working on *For Love of the Land* and doing some public relations work for a New York PR firm when he was approached to interview for the job of Executive Vice President at the American Forestry Association. Once again, he sought Norm Berg's counsel and, at Norm's urging, applied for the position, which he held until 1995. During that time, he remained active with NACD, where he worked with the Soil and Water Stewardship Committee to prepare the annual study material for NACD's Stewardship campaign from 1989 until 2005.

Exciting things happen in a conservation organization like American Forests, and it's impossible to tell what might be coming next. Recently, to honor the death of singer/songwriter Pete Seeger, my son Christopher recalled a story that involved AFA. Chris is now a Vice-Dean of the Music School at the University of Southern California where, among other things, he teaches songwriting. The following is his telling of the story, which he posted on Facebook and tells his classes:

"OK - here is my Pete Seeger story. I frequently share this story with my students as a cautionary tale even though it is personally embarrassing. The experience taught me quite a few life lessons that I try to keep in mind every day.

Back in the late '80's, my father, Neil Sampson, was the Executive VP of American Forests, a wonderful organization dedicated to helping the environment through forest health. At the time, I was a very earnest classical guitar student at USC - fighting my way through Bach Suites and other masterpieces of Western classical art music.

One of Dad's employees reached out to Pete and asked if he would write a song for the organization, knowing his love for the environment. In response, Pete generously sent complete, hand written lyrics for an original song with the directions "do whatever you'd like with the song!" His notes also said "maybe you could include some dancers – maybe a little choir!" and I remember he had drawn little birds in the margins.

Upon receiving the lyrics, however, none of Dad's employees knew what to do with them because they were not musicians. My father suggested sending the lyrics to me since I was a musician. And, this is how I received a FAX'd copy of handwritten lyrics by Pete Seeger.

At the time, I wasn't mature or aware enough to understand the significance of Pete Seeger. I was shamefully unaware that the original lyrics that I held in my hand were uniquely special – and that the opportunity to write music to them was truly a "once in a life time" kind of thing. Even worse, I was too lazy / ignorant to actually do a little research to discover that I had something amazing in my possession. But, worst of all (and I mean, really worst of all)....I remember thinking that these "folk" lyrics were somewhat beneath me – because, after all, I was a "classical" musician.

So, I put the lyrics in a drawer and mostly forgot about them. And, with a couple of moves to different apartments over the years they were probably thrown out and were never seen again.

It hurts me still to think that I was given the OPPORTUNITY TO CO-WRITE A SONG WITH PETE SEEGER!!!!! – and I squandered it through a wicked combination of arrogance, ignorance, and intellectual laziness. As the years went by and I learned of Pete Seeger and fully realized the mistake I had made – I promised that I would do everything I could not to repeat such stupid behavior.

Pete's generosity of spirit in immediately writing down some lyrics in response to an out-of-the-blue request is amazing. I only wished I would have matched that generosity by putting a few chords behind his words. Without knowing it, Pete taught me an incredible lesson that I try to live by today.

So, the lesson here, kids? Don't be a snooty, arrogant, ignorant jerk that thinks something is beneath you or so intellectually lazy that you can't even bother to find out more. Otherwise, you might miss out on something remarkable....like writing a song with Pete Seeger."

Neil, too, lost the original song lyrics, so the story ends there. Except—maybe the experience has done more as a lesson for Chris and generations of students than a finished song might have done. If so, "Thanks, Pete."

In 1993, at the early stages of the Clinton Administration, Neil's name was proposed as a candidate for the position of SCS Chief. Although there were many nice letters of recommendation, the candidacy was never, so far as Neil knows, given serious consideration. Paul Johnson, a widely respected conservationist and administrator from Iowa, was chosen for the position and led the transition in the agency from SCS to NRCS.

During that time, Neil was also active in the Intergovernmental Panel on Climate Change, serving as Lead Author or Convening Lead Author (CLA) on several IPCC projects. For that service, he and the other IPCC participants were recognized by the Nobel Committee in 2007. As CLA of the chapter on implementing the agricultural and forestry components of the Kyoto Protocol, he was sponsored as a U.S. participant by the Natural Resource Conservation Service.

In 2005, at the request of the NACD Past Presidents, he agreed to write a sequel to *For Love of the Land,* designed to bring NACD and the national conservation program's history forward from 1980 into the 21st Century. This turned out to be a different and far more difficult task than the first book. With David Stewart's retirement from NACD in 1987, and many personnel changes in the organization, the history interest had been largely lost, and there were very few files and photos available in any kind of organized fashion to assist in the research. As a result, it was not until late 2008 that *With One Voice: The National Association of Conservation Districts* was published by Wheatmark.

With One Voice covers a tumultuous period in the national soil conservation program, with five Farm Bills making dramatic program changes – none more dramatic than that of the 1985 Farm Bill which introduced conservation compliance, sodbuster, swampbuster, and the new Conservation Reserve. Those programs, significantly influenced by concepts developed through Neil's work at NACD in the early 1980's, remain important factors in today's soil and water conservation effort.

From 1995 until the present, Neil has been active with the External Review Panel of the Sustainable Forestry Initiative, serving as Panelist and Executive Secretary. This group provides oversight and external review of the SFI program, which is the largest forest certification program in North America and is recognized internationally.

Since 1999, Neil has been an adjunct professor at the Northern Virginia Campus of Virginia Tech, where he has taught graduate classes in land use policy as it affects private agricultural and forest landowners. He spent a semester in 2000 as a visiting lecturer at the Yale School of Forestry and Environmental Services, where he taught a graduate class in forest policy as it affects private landowners.

In 2000, Neil and partner Larry Walton established Vision Forestry LLC, a forest management consulting firm headquartered in Salisbury, Maryland. As President, Neil prepares long-term forest management plans for large public and private forest landowners, oversees data and information management, and coordinates efforts to achieve and maintain forest certification on client's lands under the Sustainable Forestry Initiative and the Forest Stewardship Council certification programs.

Vision Forestry has also provided a late-career opportunity to return to the land and help carry out the same types of actual land conservation and management work that was the mark of his early career. Seeing the results of good land management is a reward of its own, seldom matched by the paper (and often pyrrhic!) victories in the Washington scene!

Part II

by Robert W. Sampson

33

Rob: Student Trainee

*"Everyone in the Boise area office pitched in to help
with training and explanation."*

Home on winter break from his first semester studying Agricultural Engineering at the University of Idaho, Rob was helping Neil at NACD, providing some database input on an address database of conservation districts. Neil mentioned that Idaho Soil Conservation Service (SCS) might be hiring summer help, and that Rob might want to check into applying. The first semester had been a shaky start for the new engineering student, and one semester had hardly sold him on engineering as a career. However, summer options around Moscow, Idaho were limited, so going back to help on the family farm was the only other offer on the table at the time.

Rob's knowledge of the work done at the SCS, particularly by engineers at the field office level, was very limited. His view of the SCS was filtered through his teenage viewpoint when Neil had worked at the Idaho State House, at Harvard and at SCS National Headquarters, and these were obviously not field engineering positions. A job at the SCS for the summer seemed like a good alternative to farming, so Rob started the application process.

The application form in 1980 for a Federal student trainee position was the venerable Standard Form 171, or in the federal parlance, SF-171. The form asked a series of questions to determine your eligibility for Federal Service. Some of the questions, such as when you were born and your Social Security number, would be outright illegal today, but were requested and provided. There was space to note which languages you spoke, any awards you had received and your education and job history. Typically, following all of this base data were five questions -- the KSAs, an abbreviation for Knowledge, Skills and Abilities, and these questions were to be answered in essay form. The questions often seemed cryptic, particularly to someone outside of federal service. A question Rob once encountered while filling out the SF-171 read like this:

KSA 1 – *Ability to organize, analyze, evaluate and coordinate a variety of services, procedures, and dissimilar functions and activities and to manage various activities and projects simultaneously.*

How do you answer something like that? It wasn't clear to Rob then, and it isn't much clearer now!

Although filling out the form seemed unnecessarily complicated, Rob did fill it out and sent it in. There wasn't much self-aggrandizing that could occur; he had only been at college for one semester, and his earned GPA was low. He could tout his farming experience, but beyond that, working at Taco Bueno in the Springfield, Virginia mall didn't provide much support for a position as an Agricultural Engineer.

Rob heard very little after the application was submitted. A gentleman named Stanley Eugene Barker called in March and scheduled an interview with Rob at the Moscow, Idaho SCS field office. Barker was the Personnel Officer for Idaho SCS, and a very nice man. He stood about 5 foot 5 inches, and dressed in the snappy polyester leisure suits of the era. Topping off the ensemble were white patent leather shoes. After the interview, Rob felt he had done okay, but the shoes stuck in his head. Dad had always done field work during the early part of his career, and he was always dust from head to toe. Was this job the same? Or perhaps he had just signed up with the wrong agency, as the white shoes certainly would be out of place on a wheat farm.

April turned to May and Rob assumed he had not made the cut. He needed to commit to farming for another summer in order to make college tuition money if there was no SCS job. A quick call to Barker at the Boise, Idaho headquarters contained a surprise. "We had the paperwork to hire you completed when we interviewed" Barker said. "Your reporting date is May 20th, 1981 in Boise." What a shock! Rob had been worrying about a job for two months, and the decision to hire him had been made in March!

Boise, however, was 300 miles away. If he stayed in Moscow, there was free room rent and little travel cost. "No," Barker said, "we encourage people to move around." "Even people with nine dollars to their name?" thought Rob. The last of the money went for gasoline for the truck, and Rob lurched south on Highway 95 to Boise.

The first day Rob met his supervisor, Area Engineer Mark Jensen. Mark had been raised on an Iowa farm, and had graduated from Iowa State University in Agricultural Engineering. He was very familiar with all types of SCS practices such as terraces, pipelines and concrete structures, and was a good designer in his own right. In fact, as Rob would later learn, Area Engineer is one of the hardest, yet most rewarding jobs in the SCS engineering job ladder. Responsibility for quality control of all engineering projects, training for the field office staff and answering to the State Conservation Engineer regarding policy, technical standards, design, construction and certification made for a full-time balancing act even when there wasn't a trainee that needed attention.

Needless to say, trainee Sampson did not get the personal attention from Jensen he had expected. It turned out he got something better. Everyone in the Boise area office pitched in to help with training and explanation. But first, Jensen provided an assignment in an attempt to help the trainee learn some of the SCS technical policy and guidance.

Sitting at a drafting table in the middle of a large open room, Rob read books like the *SCS General Manual* and the *National Engineering Manual*. The first had policy for all of SCS while the latter contained policy specific to the practice of engineering. Technical information filled the *Engineering Field Manual* and SCS Technical Releases, as well as the *Field Office Technical Guide* (FOTG). The FOTG was particularly intimidating. The set of three binders contained some 160 conservation practices such as "Water Well" and "Irrigation Conveyance Pipeline, Steel Pipe." Some of the practices were very unfamiliar. "What in blazes is a 'Mole Drain'?" Rob thought to himself. He obviously didn't know that at one later point in his career, he would be the National leader for that particular practice standard and others.

In those first few weeks, Rob got a small taste of engineering field work checking a concrete ditch with Floyd Praegitzer, the Area Civil Engineering Technician. Water slope, ditch elevation, and compaction of the earth berm around the concrete were investigated and documented. Getting out to the field and talking about engineering was more along the lines of what Rob expected. Unfortunately, when Rob asked Floyd when their next trip to the field would occur, Floyd explained that he was working in another county the rest of the summer and that Rob would probably go back to reading manuals. With a less than an enthusiastic attitude, Rob went home hardly looking forward to work on Monday.

Monday came, and Mark Jenson explained that reading manuals was over and the next phase of training was starting. Jensen had been talking to disciplines outside of the engineering arena, and those other professions would play a large role the rest of the summer. In fact Mark had most of the summer scheduled with training in other areas, so Rob ended up doing an entire summer's worth of work that had little to do with engineering.

The first task was rangeland inventory with Jerry Lumm, a tall, rail-thin Texan who served as the Area Range Conservationist. He often drawled how he would "rather do anything else than train engineers," but in retrospect he provided the content and speed of the training in a very thoughtful pattern.

Ralph Fisher, Area Agronomist and Jim Smollinger, Soil Conservationist, took Rob to the field in Boise County to measure plots for the National Resource Inventory or NRI. In each PSU or Primary Sampling Unit, there were three plot locations. Depending on the land use, the forest was measured for stocking density or the cropland was measured for erosion rates. These data were sent up the SCS chain of command, eventually landing at the statistical laboratory at Iowa State University.

Examining these data provided the NRI with estimates of site productivity and erosion rates as well as crop yield, and these were aggregated at the county level. Land use and conditions on a PSU could be compared with the same facts gathered during earlier surveys to measure what had changed over time. The NRI continues today and the time spans and changes between samplings provide USDA and policy folks with analyses that show trends. NRI continues to be amazingly useful data. Rob had been taught about NRI from the ground up and how to use a 'tree stick' among other things.

Joe Icenhower was the Area Conservationist, in charge of supervising all the Area staff as well as the 16 District Conservationists that made up Idaho SCS's Area II in the southwest corner of the state. Joe spent several sessions with the engineer trainee explaining some simple management techniques and some philosophy. Joe was trained as a Soil Scientist, a profession into which gregarious people didn't tend to gravitate, yet Joe's management style boiled down to "care about your people and listen to them".

Aquaculture was booming in the Hagerman Valley in the early 1980's. Cold springs from the discharge of the Eastern Snake River Plain aquifer gushed from the side of the Snake River canyon walls. The purity and temperature of this provided for very rapid, high quality fish production. Rob followed Area Biologist Dan LaPlant around as he tested water chemistry and made recommendations to the fish farmers about raceway construction and plumbing. Some of the fish farmers also had access to natural hot springs, and could mix custom water temperatures and chemistry. This allowed them to grow catfish, tilapia and even alligators!

All of these activities, although interesting, were a pretty far cry from the trainee's background in engineering, but the knowledge gained about conservation planning and the activities of other disciplines in SCS would serve him well in the future. Wandering around new areas of Idaho and learning from such a diverse team of trainers was fun and invigorating. "I can't believe I'm getting paid for this, but I hope the engineering comes soon," was Rob's primary thought.

The best part of the student training from Rob's standpoint was provided by Gene Koozer. The junior civil engineer at the area office was fascinated by computers - so much so that he would eventually end up as an Information Technology specialist with the agency.

SCS engineers in Idaho had all been issued a Texas Instruments model 59 calculator. The machines had some programmable memory and used a proprietary programming language. A small magnetic card reader snapped on top of the calculator that could load prewritten programs into memory. The State and Area office engineers were busy trying to write routines that could answer some fairly complex engineering questions very quickly in the field or at their desks. How big did a settling basin have to be to allow all of the sediment to drop out of the water column? What were the pressures in a pipeline? How much concrete and steel were needed in a retaining wall? In addition, the calculator could be hooked to a small thermal printer that provided output of the solution and the calculations.

Having been exposed to computers and programming languages by his father, Rob took to the programming assignments with gusto. It was a fun but challenging task as the programs needed to be fairly robust, given the variety of people who would use them. In order to release a program to the technicians and engineers at the field office the code was put through rigorous testing. Documentation of the code, along with user instructions and several solved example problems were needed, and had to be approved by State Conservation Engineer LeRoy Zollinger. LeRoy wasn't particularly sold on the technology, and could foil most programmers by breaking almost any of the programs that came across his desk. It was frustrating to have to submit the same program multiple times for approval. Little did Rob know he would eventually occupy Zollinger's position, and would have a heightened appreciation for these quality control efforts.

The second summer Rob was again assigned to Boise. This summer saw him complete several original engineering designs, and deliver them to the landowner. A couple of sessions sitting around the kitchen table at the landowner's house were the best on-the-job training a young engineer could receive. Completing a design at an office desk from some survey notes and some practice specifications was one thing. Explaining to a landowner what the final project should look like, and what the wood stakes driven out in the field portrayed, was entirely another matter.

Similarly, it was sobering to learn that intricately drawn blueprints didn't mean nearly as much to the farmer as they did to the engineer. Ultimately, to be successful, an SCS engineer had to be very good at speaking in clear language, and finding several different ways to portray conservation practices and their specifications. Given Rob's lack of experience, these farmers and ranchers were very gracious to take their time and allow a rookie to learn the ropes, step and misstep at a time.

The summer of 1983 found Rob assigned as a trainee to the Pocatello area office, covering the eastern half of the state. He was finally figuring out how to learn at the college level and had made it past most of the sophomore engineering science classes that usually generated the largest number of students changing to a different major. More importantly, those classes helped to show students how to think in engineering terms. Rather than reducing problems to equations, engineering students headed into their junior year were learning to critically dissect complex problems into the different domains of physics that dictated why things break or why they move.

Once again Rob made an even longer drive on borrowed gas money in a vehicle of questionable operating condition, only to land in new surroundings. Significantly higher in elevation and colder in temperature, southeastern Idaho has a large part of the agricultural acreage and production in the state. That summer, tutored by Ken Hasfurther, the junior Civil Engineer in the area and Dale Schlader, the Area Engineer, was marked by a steep learning curve.

Installing dryland erosion control terraces on large wheat fields with 18% slopes was very different from planning a small sediment basin below a 40-acre irrigated field in the Boise area. Farms and ranches in eastern Idaho are measured in thousands of acres rather than hundreds. Being at almost the top of the river system, small concrete ditches were replaced by canals that were 6 feet deep and 30 or more feet wide.

Rob Sampson's first assignment was to inspect a large irrigation conveyance pipeline with a concrete inlet structure on Glenn Turner's place near Soda Springs, Idaho. The twin 15 inch PVC pipes had to be placed at a very precise constant grade, with each 20 foot section of pipe dropping two one-hundredths of a foot.

The primary lesson learned on the Turner job? If the pipe installers tell you they can use a carpenter's level to lay the pipe in the absence of the engineer and his surveying level, don't believe them.

161

The second lesson was that if the pipe was installed at the wrong grade due to using a carpenter's level, and the engineer tells the crew to remove the last 200 feet of pipe they had installed, the engineer is not very popular. The third lesson was that if the construction crew has to blast part of the pipe trench due to bedrock, be sure to move the government pickup very far away from the blast. Luckily there was no damage to any vehicles while learning that particular lesson.

Dale Schlader, the Area Engineer for SCS Area III, received his education from the University of Idaho. A farm boy from Nez Perce, Idaho, Schlader had no tolerance for technical mediocrity. A very large engineering workload in the eastern part of the state didn't allow time to rework designs and drawings several times, so getting it right first was important. Schlader could review work very quickly and his years of experience allowed him to discern between designs that had a high chance of success, and these were returned to the designer quickly with few comments. Similarly, if a design used questionable lines of logic, it often was returned to the sender with a very brief and unambiguous note and no approval signature.

When it came to training, Schlader was just as direct. Assignments were given with a deadline and a description of the expected project. This training style had a couple of results. First and foremost, the learning was quick, and if the assignment was executed properly, the training was imprinted in the work habits of the trainee. A similar, but opposite imprint was left if the design was not correct. Dale and Rob got along very well, and the trainee's respect for the Area Engineer increased daily.

Schlader was slightly skeptical when Rob brought a computer and a printer to the Area office. After watching the beginnings of a land leveling program emerge, however, the time-saving benefits were obvious to him. Land leveling of irrigated fields saved water and soil. The leveled field got uniformly wet during irrigation, so the application time, and hence the amount of water used were minimized. Uniformly graded furrows eroded less that those with uneven grades.

As Neil had learned in the first part of his career in Burley, land leveling design consisted of laying out a 100-foot square grid on the field and surveying every grid point. These elevations were trans=

ferred to a large sheet of graph paper where the trial uniform grade was plotted against the existing grade, and the difference between the elevations was either a cut or a fill. Cut stations were recorded in red pencil and fill stations were recorded in blue. After these calculations, the cuts and fills were summed up and compared with the goal of getting about 25% more cut than fill. This number was rarely correct on the first trial, so the starting elevation was adjusted up or down, and all calculations were repeated. The simple act of recording the trial results in red and blue pencil allowed the designer to examine patterns across the field. If one corner of the field showed all cuts, perhaps the grade in that region could be flattened.

The computer program could iterate these trials and move the planned elevation up or down with speed and ease. Unfortunately, at that time, the computer screen had only one color, as did the printer. Using the computer made it harder to visualize the distribution of cuts and fills, as there were no red and blue numbers. When Rob brought the final printout of the program to Schlader, the lead engineer suggested that taking the computer printout and circling the cuts and fills in red and blue pencil would help regain the larger picture of earthwork distribution.

Rob initially thought the manual labor ruined the speed and advantage of the computer program, but in order to get Dale's approval of the program, he dutifully circled the elevations on the printout with the correct color pencil. Although the lesson was subtle, eventually Rob understood that the act of engineering design was not just completing the calculations. Rather, engineering design involved a disciplined process of examining the calculations and deciding if they made sense.

While the computer did the calculations quickly, the act of design was the same whether it was automated or not. As it turned out, it was often more difficult to rationalize the overall design if a computer output was not carefully constructed to show all the thoughts and assumptions behind the very fast calculations.

Rob Sampson's fourth summer was also spent at Pocatello. More excellent training was provided by Billy McMurtry, the Area Civil Engineering Technician, Clay Erickson, the Soil Conservation Technician in American Falls, and Glade Moser, the Soil Conservation Technician in Preston. Rob learned to design many conservation practices as well as check their installation to decide if they 'met Standards and Specs', the SCS jargon for saying the project was installed according to the designs and the rules. He still had a long way to go in learning the skills to convince a farmer or rancher why installing a conservation practice the correct way was necessary, but he was beginning to be able to tell a good installation from a bad one.

These early experiences informed the rest of Rob's career. In general, designing and installing a single engineering practice is relatively easy. Making sure the practice was the right thing in the correct location, and describing the desired outcome to a contractor or a landowner is much harder—and more important.

The Student Trainee program that Rob had applied for four years prior turned out to be an amazing experience in ways that are arguably rare to find in any professional internship program. SCS employees in Idaho took their role as mentors very seriously. The cross discipline training prized by SCS helped put the role of engineering in context of the larger effort of improving soil and water resources on private agricultural land. Without this context, a Bachelors of Science degree in engineering would produce a young professional who might solve well-defined problems quickly, but would not have any idea how that solution fit into the bigger scheme of natural resource conservation.

Having four summers of experience with actual application of engineering and how it interacts with other professional disciplines made college classes richer and more relevant for Rob. Without the SCS experience, engineering probably would not have been the degree he ultimately acquired. The most valuable aspect of the Student Trainee program was that it led to a noncompetitive offer of full time employment. The letter that arrived documenting a full time position for him was a welcome sight that was not terribly common among graduating seniors in the recession of the mid-1980's.

34

At Work, Full Time

*"Rob went out with technicians, soil scientists,
range conservationists and soil conservationists
to see how they plied their trade."*

After graduation from the University of Idaho in 1985 with a degree in Agricultural Engineering. Rob's duty station with SCS turned out to be Rexburg, a small town in eastern Idaho where he would work under the tutelage of Civil Engineer Bob Lehman. Rob had never been to Rexburg, and had only met Lehman a couple of times, but he had heard good things about his boss-to-be and SCS had treated him right in the past.

The drive to Rexburg was about eight hours from Moscow. Having just sat through 18 credits of senior finals as well as the eight hour 'Engineer in Training' (now called the Fundamentals of Engineering) exam, the drive provided the first time for reflection. His fiscal situation was as dismal as the past four summers, but the letter offering full time employment with SCS suggested his annual salary was over $23,000. Driving a brand new truck, obtained with little more than that letter, Rob had a reliable vehicle for the first time.

Thinking about finding a place to live was daunting given the lack of liquid assets, but the excitement of being done with college and entering a full time job made for a chronically positive attitude. On that May drive through Montana Rob felt like the world was his for the taking.

Arriving in Rexburg, and securing a hotel room with a newly obtained credit card, Rob began to look around. Rexburg was famous for two immediately obvious reasons: It had nearly been wiped off the map when Teton Dam had failed catastrophically in 1976, and it was home to Ricks College, a two-year college run by the Church of Jesus Christ of Latter-Day Saints, the Mormons. Rexburg's population was reported to be about 8,000, of which, conservatively, 6,000 were active in 'the Church'.

Having worked in Pocatello, a town with strong Mormon influence, Rob had no problem with living in a Mormon community. Rexburg was a different city than Pocatello, however. Rental units were hard to come by even though school had dismissed its students for the summer. Rental rates were high and many units owned by the Church were reserved for students only or required adherence to the Church's code of behavior. Looking outside of Rexburg proper landed Rob in nearby St. Anthony, a small lumber mill town with a mix of people, religions and interests. After renting a small house for $175 a month, everything seemed in place to start his new career.

Bob Lehman had moved from southwest Colorado to Rexburg the year after the Teton Dam failure and the ensuing flood. He had trained many young engineers, and was an excellent designer of conservation practices. Courtesy of four years of summer training, Rob was pretty sure of himself and his design skills, but Lehman was quick to disabuse him of this confidence. "Designs done in school just are not practical for the average landowner to install," Lehman explained. "You have to have experience to get the feel of whether you need to design something large and complicated or something simpler that meets the landowner's needs."

It seemed to Rob that Bob was rewriting the rules. He had done his training; it was time to get out there and be an engineer! Bob had other ideas and scheduled the young engineer to meet with other SCS employees, and shadow them as they went about their jobs for the first six months of his career.

Rob went out with technicians, soil scientists, range conservationists and soil conservationists to see how they plied their trade. District Conservationist Steve Smart from the Driggs office, Soil Conservation Technicians Dave Steube from Idaho Falls and Ken Beckmann from St. Anthony provided the bulk of the training. In retrospect, Rob realized that his training was provided in an almost surreptitious manner. He was still pretty sure he was leading the efforts when meeting with landowners or laying conservation practices out on the land. But, without realizing it, he was getting his training as a conservation planner.

The SCS way of using undeclared mentors from a wide variety of disciplines was in the agency's cultural foundations, and evolved in part to provide guidance to employees that were very good at their discipline. None of this investment was to specifically make Rob a better engineer, but a better employee, and more effective at protecting agrarian natural resources. Engineering was only useful if the correct questions were asked and the conservation practices were designed to complement the other farm operations.

While Rob was being unknowingly trained by this cadre of top professionals, several events were taking place that would shape SCS for the better part of his career. The 1985 farm bill was passed in December of that year and it contained provisions that SCS had never experienced. A triumvirate of conservation provisions would change how SCS dealt with their customers (the landowners and farmers) as well as the Conservation Districts that SCS worked with in partnership. Rob saw Swampbuster, Sodbuster, and Conservation Compliance at the field office, while Neil's view of these laws was from a policy standpoint described earlier.

The new Conservation Reserve Program (CRP) allowed landowners to retire fields that had the potential to erode at a high rate. In return for seeding these lands to grass or planting them to trees, the landowners received a rental payment of $20 to $40 per acre. Erosion rates were calculated using the Universal Soil Loss Equation (USLE), and these calculations needed to withstand scrutiny. Imagine having to explain to a landowner why their neighbor was eligible for a 10- to 15-year rental payment from the Federal Government while they were not.

SCS was not used to their 'in-house' calculations being dissected and questioned so severely. That scrutiny caused SCS to refine their measurements, and document them more thoroughly. Still, this minor upheaval paled when compared to the impact of the other two conservation provisions.

Sodbuster and Swampbuster were the 1985 Farm Bill provisions that would change SCS's relationship with landowners for decades to come. Both of these new rules instructed farmers that if they broke out new grasslands or drained wetlands for the purpose of growing an agricultural commodity, they would be ineligible for Department of Agriculture benefits, including loans, price-supports and insurance, as well as SCS assistance and subsidies for installing conservation practices.

This caused SCS's good guy image and reputation of wearing the 'white hat' to fracture and become not-so-white, particularly in the Swampbuster program where SCS was responsible for making the technical determination about which areas counted as wetlands. There are significant differences between wet areas, and whether a spot was just a "wet place" or a "wetland" was not easy to tell. Infact, the field guidance that SCS had at the time was not always up to that task. For the first time in their existence, SCS might go to a farm to provide a simple act of technical assistance, and possibly be forced to report a landowner for drainage or tillage activities that violated Swampbuster or Sodbuster. Each year, when the landowner signed up for conservation programs or commodity subsidies, they had to self-certify that no grassland tillage or wetland drainage had been done on their properties. While SCS didn't go to each farm to ascertain the truth of these self-certifications, what would a technician do if they observed something contrary to the self-certification when visiting a farm?

The third and final piece of legislation from the 1985 farm bill dealt with was labeled 'Conservation Compliance'. Farmers growing crops on highly erodible land were required to farm according to a conservation plan that reduced erosion to an acceptable rate. Plans for farming this erodible land were dubbed with the ironically revealing acronym of 'HEL' Plans, which stood for 'Highly Erodible Land'. All of a sudden, SCS would be 'telling' farmers how to farm. This was a remarkable shift in authority for the small agency that was very proud of their record of promoting 'voluntary conservation' over the prior decades.

For Rob, the new conservation provisions provided a different way he could help the Field Offices and the planners. While still designing and installing conservation practices, all of a sudden he had to learn more about the Universal Soil Loss Equation (USLE), and

168

its partner, the Wind Erosion Equation (WEQ) than he ever thought possible. Once again, a computer showed up in an SCS office where none had been before. Using simple spreadsheets, the USLE and the WEQ were automated. Perhaps more importantly, the printed output used as supporting documentation in the farmers case file was uniform, easily understood, and the math was replicable and consistent.

While very few SCS conservationists had ever heard computer jargon such as *'supercalc* running on a CPM operating system', having the paperwork automated was a benefit they truly understood. The Rexburg office would process over 100 applications for the CRP, and write over 200 conservation compliance plans in the next 18 months.

Tri-State Training

A serendipitous turn of events gave Rob an opportunity that undoubtedly shaped his career and the trajectory it would assume. Tony Allen, a soil conservationist in the American Falls field office, resigned to go back to graduate school. Tony had been slated to attend Tri-State Training, a comprehensive school lasting four weeks, providing training in everything from conservation planning to good communication skills, and Rob was named to go in his place.

Tri-State was the replacement for the nationally-run SCS school held in San Luis Obispo that Neil had attended in 1960. The 1985 Tri-State training was Idaho, Washington, and Oregon's first attempt to replicate and customize the San Luis Obispo effort. The leader and coordinator for this training was Sharon Norris, Idaho's Public Affairs Specialist, who had followed Neil into that Idaho SCS position.

Each of the three states was allowed to send 10 people to the four-week training. After living in his rental house for all of two months, Rob found himself in La Grande, Oregon housed in the dormitories of Eastern Oregon State College. His roommate was Mike Combs, a Soil Conservation Technician from Malad, Idaho. Classes ran for eight hours each day. As many as six speakers a day would provide training on a wide variety of topics such as Agronomy, Range Management, Soil Science and Engineering. Many days had a field component where the students went to a ranch on the upper Grande

Ronde River to practice their new found skills at identifying and diagnosing natural resource concerns.

Ultimately, at the end of four weeks, each team would produce a conservation plan for the ranch to suggest how the land owner might use their resources in an optimum and sustainable manner. Sharon guided the young conservationists through the effort while coordinating speakers and logistics. The local details were handled by Jan Anderson, the District Conservationist in La Grande.

Given the overarching goal of providing young conservationists with a technically sound, uniform platform on which to build their career, the training was an excellent success. Although Rob had no idea at the time, he would end up working closely with many of the trainers and students at the 1985 Tri-State training. Some of the other 29 students would also form the core of his professional network and the Grand Ronde River would play a pivotal role in his career.

To suggest there was strong *esprit de corps* amongst the participants doesn't provide an adequately robust description. The dormitories were not air conditioned, and the mattresses had plastic covering. This combination guaranteed waking up in the middle of the night bathed in sweat, hardly befitting a good night's sleep. Surviving the physical conditions and meals provided on-going fodder for group discussion.

While all of the instructors at the training were technically top notch, none had been chosen for their training ability. It was not unusual for a trainer to show up with two dozen overhead acetates from their discipline's policy manual and proceed to read each agonizing word for the class. These naturally provided more grist for after-hours discussion and bonding. Volleyball, softball, hiking and fishing, as well as some beer-fueled discussion and debate passed the off-work hours.

Most students opted to stay in LaGrande on the two weekends included in the training rather than travel back and forth to their duty stations. A backpacking trip into the Eagle Cap wilderness was certainly a highlight for Rob. Kip Yasumiishi, Nicola Lui-Qwan, Mike Gondek, Rich Edlund, Tom Clark, and Glenn Hoffman became closer friends and colleagues than any ever intended to become. The other result, possibly correlated to the training and that backpacking trip, is that each person named here worked for SCS for the rest of their conservation career. Of the group of 30, at least 19 worked for SCS for all their conservation careers. Since a statistic to prove a negative doesn't exist, we can't answer the question regarding whether the training provided the agency with higher retention, but the camaraderie of that shared experience remains today.

That same year, Rob found himself signed up for 'NPEG'. New Professional Engineers and Geologists was a four-week course run by the SCS training center in Ft. Worth. At NPEG upper level techniques of engineering held sacrosanct in SCS were demonstrated and explained to young engineers. Many of the trainees were like Rob: they had two to four years of service and had recently completed an engineering degree. Given this demographic, some were pretty sure they didn't need any more engineering training. What an an eye opener it was for Rob! The science behind the construction of earth dams, the erodibility of the spillways and the hydrologic calculation to size the spillways was something he had never seen.

Most of the students did not know that SCS and several of the teachers were viewed as world leaders in soil mechanics, hydrology and engineering geology. Through the efforts of the agency and the 1954 Public Law 83-566 (PL-566) program SCS constructed some 11,800 dams. Many of these dams had auxiliary spillways constructed of the native soil or rock, and some had the earth core designed with very complicated soil and sand filters. Knowing how to construct a dam of earthfill, and how to build relatively stable spillways in the native material were skills not many engineers were taught in school.

SCS had sent engineers to Harvard to study in a program founded by Karl Terzaghi, the master of modern soil mechanics. Many of SCS's hydrologic calculations were copied by agencies and engineering firms around the world. And SCS's published work in sedimentation and sediment transport had been pioneered by none other than Hans Albert Einstein, the more famous Albert's son. Here again, a high proportion of engineers attending NPEG proved to be lifers with

SCS. The training roster for that class in Ft. Worth shows at least 16 who worked for SCS for the rest of their careers.

1985 Tri-State Training class

Sharon Norris, coordinator, front left. Kneeling or sitting from left. Terry Hicks, ID, Vern McMaster, ID, Norris, Phil Giles, WA, Mike Combs (back), ID, Fred Smith, OR, Joyce Scheyer, WA, Oscar Tobias, WA, Shawn Woodard, WA, Tom Clark, OR, Bobbette Parsons, ID, Kahle Jennings, WA, Nicola Lui-Kwan, OR, Kip Yasumiishi, OR. Back row: Dean Moore, ID, Rich Edlund, ID, Mike Gondek, ID, Doug Allen, WA, Dean Moberg, OR, Ron Myrhum, OR, Barry Nord, OR, Glenn Hoffman, ID, Rob Sampson, ID, Ken Mills, WA, John Tunberg, OR, Bob Ryan, WA, Steve Rhychetsky, OR, Fabian Fogerson, WA, Joanne Tomlin, WA.

SCS's lineage of technical expertise has been unusually high, given the relatively few people who have worked for the agency. However, some of the expertise is only two or three employees wide while the degree of separation between SCS employees is very low. Jack Stevenson, a nationally recognized Soil Mechanics Engineer, was one of the first SCS employees to study at Harvard. Jack's daughter Terril Stevenson was one of the agency's strongest Engineering Geologists, and a coworker of Rob's for 12 years. Jack passed away in 1995, but not before he passed much of the soils mechanics technical torch to Danny McCook, who taught Rob in NPEG, and was one of Terril's mentors. Danny passed away in 2013 while this book was being written, having shared much of his skill and expertise with Ben

Doerge, a Design Engineer at the Fort Worth, Texas technical center, who was a co-worker of Rob's in Oregon.

After working under Bob Lehman's tutelage in Idaho for three years, it became apparent to Rob that he needed to move on. The agency placed a premium on 'multi-state' experience. While not necessarily looking to leave Rexburg, and while valuing Lehman's extensive knowledge, Rob wanted to increase his engineering responsibility. Diving once again into the world of job applications, KSA'a and the venerable SF-171 was a bit daunting.

To suggest that communication around job hiring was imperfect is kind, since SCS employees were very seldom aware of what part of the hiring process was in play. Job announcements showed up on 'Green Sheets', a duplicated piece of green paper that was passed around the office. Without calling the hiring office, which was discouraged due to 'line and staff' concerns, the 'green sheet' provided the agency's only clues about how to apply for the job.

An application Rob sent to the Challis National Forest for the job of assistant district engineer went entirely unacknowledged. An application to Greeley Colorado SCS to be the Area Engineer elicited a cryptic note about being 'qualified - but not best qualified', and an application for the Boise Idaho SCS Area Engineer job brought a letter that he was qualified, but not referred to the selecting official.

Getting frustrated with the whole process and lack of feedback, Rob applied for the Area Engineer's job in Baker, Oregon only to get a letter that he had forgotten to directly answer one of the KSA questions, and his application was discarded. Then, the job mysteriously reappeared on the green sheets a couple of months later. Without much hope, Rob dusted off the SF-171 and reinitiated the application process.

Without so much as an acknowledgement letter, the next thing Rob received was a phone call from Gary Yeoumans, the Area Conservationist in Baker. After some pleasantries, Yeoumans stated that he was offering the job to Rob. And that was it. The next thing he knew, Rob received a flurry of communications from the administrative staff in Oregon. Did he own a home? How would he transfer his household goods?

The reporting-to-work date was set as September 6, 1988 and the 27-year old was off on a new adventure. Rob later learned that Yeoumans was soundly rebuked for not going through the 'line and staff' chain of command with the job offer. Yeoumans' call and offer of employment was the first time in the whole process that Rob knew where he stood.

St. Anthony, where Rob and his wife Dianna owned their home, was a timber mill town. The contract the mill had with the Forest Service to turn bark-beetle killed lodgepole pine into two by fours was winding down. Needless to say, real estate in St. Anthony wasn't a top commodity. But 1988 was also the SCS's first year of participating in the 'buy-back' program run by the General Services Administration (GSA). The Sampsons were thrilled to hear that they didn't have to sell their house on their own. The Government would 'buy it back'.

Three real estate appraisers showed up. The idea was that each would assign a value to the home and this would form the amount of the offer to purchase. While two of the appraisers submitted a purchase price to the GSA contractor, Better Homes and Garden Real Estate, the third appraiser, didn't provide a number. This appraiser had found some asbestos insulation on the oil furnace in the basement of the old house, and declared that the house was not financeable through the Federal Housing Agency (FHA), and thus ineligible for the 'buy back'.

In all the turmoil of moving Rob found himself researching the FHA rules, and how they related to GSA's contract with the realtor. A call to the SCS administrative staff in Oregon produced little. They were not involved in the GSA contract and had no desire to learn the byzantine process. So the Sampson's became landlords and would soon learn the joys of taking care of a lower-end rental from 400 miles away.

The start to the Sampson's great adventure was similar to the moves Rob had made as a student trainee: Full of uncertainty and, in general, poverty. But the move to Baker turned out to be an excellent step for Rob's career, and Baker remains one of the Sampson's favorite places.

35

Baker Area Engineer

"Supervising people always involves challenges, but supervising good people is easier, and luckily Rob's staff was very good."

On an organizational chart the job of area engineer is a simple step up from that of field engineer. The difference was fairly simple: you covered more counties, supervised a small staff, and reported directly to the area conservationist. What's more, eastern Oregon was somewhat similar to eastern Idaho: A diverse agricultural area, but primarily large ranches and forage crops. There were row crops like potatoes and sugar beets grown around Ontario in Malheur County, and some truck crops like green beans grown around Milton-Freewater in Umatilla County. Most of the agriculture was irrigated, with some dryland wheat in the western counties of Gilliam and Morrow around Heppner. Additionally, Oregon and Idaho were next to each other and Tri-State training had been given in a consistent manner for staff in the three states. How different could SCS be in adjoining states?

The area staff in Baker was one of high technical caliber. Rob was to supervise a civil engineering technician, and two GS-11 engineers, one dedicated to the North Powder PL-566 project, and the other based in Pendleton. An agronomist, soil scientist, and range conservationist rounded out the staff supervised by Area Conservationist Yeoumans. The area covered the 11 counties in the eastern half of the state from Nevada to Washington, and from Idaho west to the Deschutes River.

Simply getting a handle on the day to day work seemed like an impossible task to Rob. The 11 district conservationists were all very different personalities and that brought some people-skills challenges.

The biggest hurdles were learning how to be a supervisor and learning about the large PL-566 project he had inherited.

Supervising people always involves challenges, but supervising good people is easier, and luckily Rob's staff was very good. Several of them were twice his age, and that was strange for the new supervisor. What did they want to hear from some punk kid barely out of school? Greg Smith, the Project Engineer on the North Powder Project was closer to Rob's age, and had a closely defined job description: Make the construction happen on the project. Supervising Greg was more of an effort in getting up to speed on the project. Luckily, the words of Joe Icenhower from seven years before rang in Rob's ears as the only piece of management advice he always remembered: "Listen to your people."

Doubly lucky, Gary Yeouman's management style was centered around this tenet also. He undoubtedly spotted how terrified the young engineer was in the new position and attempted to provide gentle guidance. It took skill for Gary to tell a 20-something male how to do things, and not have Rob notice he was being directed! Gary embodied the type of person working for SCS in east Oregon. No flash or ego, just a genuine love of conservation and agriculture, with a priority placed on technical quality. He was focused on 'Getting Conservation on the Land.'

The other members of the area staff were also instructive to the new area engineer. The position itself, however, had some legacy since Dave Edwards had held this spot for more than 20 years prior to his retirement in 1986. Pat Willey took the position in 1987, but left in early 1988 for a job as the State Irrigation Engineer in Oregon State Office.

When Rob showed up, most of the staff were simply curious: Could he do the same things Dave and Pat had done? Though this legacy weighed heavily on the position, Rob was sure he knew the answer to the staff's question. He was not half the engineer Dave and Pat had been, nor would he ever be. Never one lacking in self-confidence, Rob was in a frustrating state of mind: questioning his own basic capabilities.

North Powder PL-566

The overall North Powder project was under the sponsorship of the Powder Valley Water Control District based in North Powder Oregon. In the fall of 1988, construction had started on the North Powder Rock Creek pipeline, NPRC for short. Alan Bahn was the area range conservationist and had been part of the North Powder watershed planning team.

Despite his title as the range specialist, Bahn knew irrigation inside and out, and took the time to show Rob the project area and provide the history. The project was made up of two reservoirs. One was Wolf Creek, built in 1978. Water stored here fed the W-1 gravity pipeline that irrigated some 9,000 acres without a single electric motor and pump. Pressure was provided by the slope of the land. The other was Pilcher Creek Reservoir, constructed in 1984, which pressurized the P-1 and P-2 pipelines serving 4,500 acres of crops with gravity pressure.

The current project work plan described three more pipelines to be constructed and one large dam to be built on the main stem of the North Powder River. One of the pipelines, North Powder-Rock Creek (NPRC) South was in construction when Rob arrived in Baker. Miles of welded steel pipe, some as large as two and a half feet in diameter, were rapidly being buried in the ground. Rob was thankful for engineer Smith, who kept track of construction, because the new area engineer could barely remember all of the names of the pipelines, let alone keep a clear pictures of what pipes went where. Smith took Rob to his first meeting with the Powder Valley Water Control District (PVWCD). The meetings were held in North Powder in a small, two room house that had once been the headquarters of the SCS team planning the improvement works for the federal project. Chairs were lined up in the larger room of the house, and the meeting commenced at 7:00 pm.

Harry Bigler was the PVWCD Manager and all-around fix-it man. Fred Colton, Don Dodson, Pete Schoening, Gerald Maxwell and Lyle Umplby were the elected board of directors. These men ran large ranches that were served in some way by the project's pipelines.

Rob was terrified they might ask him a question that would reveal his overall lack of experience and expertise. Instead, they warmly welcomed the new SCS engineer.

As the meeting progressed, Rob was impressed by the decision making and fiscal responsibility the PVWCD board had to shoulder. Loans for millions of dollars provided the financial match that the District was required to contribute to earn the Federal funds promised to the project. The Board was also responsible for securing the land rights where the pipeline was located so they could obtain maintenance on the pipeline. Occasionally, the Board had to cross private land with the pipelines where the owner was not keen on the pipeline, or simply not interested in having a trench dug across the family's pasture. In a community the size of North Powder, invoking eminent domain in order to install a pipeline was not a popular decision. Rob had never worked with a group of private landowners that had this level of organization, and it made the weight of the new job seem that much more. When the meeting ended at 10 pm, each Board member told Rob how much they looked forward to working together in the future.

Not more than six months into the new job, Rob was called to Fred Colton's ranch, where the water users needed to show him something. Arriving at the ranch shop, Rob saw a piece of one foot diameter steel pipe sitting on the welding table. Harry Bigler had been supervising repairs on the seven year old W-1 pipeline and this piece of pipe was removed because it had a hole in it. It also had silver-dollar sized pockets of severe corrosion on the *inside* of the pipe. The outside of the pipe was wrapped in a coal tar tape and looked brand new.

SCS prided itself on putting steel pipe in the ground protected from the corrosive forces of the soil. The protection specified in the SCS design standard for steel pipe was one of the strictest in the industry. Not only was the pipe painted with coal-tar enamel and wrapped with the heavy tape, but measures were taken to prevent corrosion from electrolysis. All of these protections appeared to be working well, but none of them protected from corrosion on the inside of the pipe.

Harry explained that many of the landowners on the W-1 pipeline had been removing flakes of rusty metal from their pipeline outlets. Rob's head was spinning. The pipelines SCS had installed had been planned to last fifty years and the PVWCD's loans had similar lengths. Now the W-1 pipeline was failing in its first decade. Standing in Colton's shop, no one voiced the obvious questions: What would SCS do to solve this problem? Who would pay for any solution? Rob wondered the same thing.

Pipeline corrosion receives no more than a passing mention in most undergraduate engineering curricula and everything Rob knew of this subject had come from the steel pipe design standard in the SCS Field Office Technical Guide, the same standard that guided the design of W-1. Corrosion of the exterior of steel pipe by acid soils is well known, and the corrosion susceptibility is documented in all SCS published soil surveys. Corrosion from electrolysis was less well understood outside of the oil and gas industry, but once again SCS was a leader in documenting and understanding the corrosive force of electrolysis on the outside of the pipe.

Depending on the electrical conductivity of the soil, a long steel pipeline can act like a battery when buried in the soil. The pipe itself behaves like the anode (negative) and the electrons flow away from the pipe to the soil which acts as the cathode (positive) part of the battery. A zinc or magnesium bar buried in the soil, and wired to the pipe will preferentially corrode before the steel pipeline, protecting the pipeline as the sacrificial anode corrodes.

Why was the pipe corroding from the inside? Inferior steel? Poor installation? The fact that SCS made the District drain all the water out during the winter? The problem seemed overwhelming, and more than 100 miles of steel pipe in the Powder Valley had been designed by the SCS. How could a brand new Area Engineer possibly fix this daunting problem?

The State Conservation Engineer in Oregon was Roy Bright, a good engineer and manager. Roy wrote a report describing the situation to the Director of Engineering, Gerald Seinwell, in Washington DC. Bright then appointed an Engineering Investigation team led by Art Shoemaker of Idaho and Mark Opitz of Wyoming. A contract was awarded to dig the pipe up in spots and remove sections for analysis. These were tested at a lab for steel quality, weld quality, and how much thickness of the pipe was remaining. When the report was returned, the conclusions were cause for concern. Only 60 to 70 percent of the original pipe material remained, and at the areas of the worst corrosion, only half of the pipe's original wall thickness remained. The steel used to manufacture the pipe was of high quality, as were the welds on the pipe. So what had caused the internal corrosion?

The problem turned out to be the water. The fresh, pure water flowing out of the granitic Elkhorn Mountains and coursing through the Powder River certainly didn't look corrosive. The pH level was normal. Powder River water was so pure that Baker City, Oregon had one of the last untreated municipal water supplies in Oregon. In fact, the water turned out to be too pure. Lacking in calcium carbonate and other dissolved solids, Powder River water attempted to come into electrical balance by picking up cations (a positively charged ion), which in this case were provided by the iron in the steel pipeline. After some testing around eastern Oregon, it was found that most of the water in the region would cause internal corrosion of steel pipelines to some extent.

Rob was glad to have another piece of the puzzle put in place, and he had learned more about corrosion than most folks, but what could the SCS do about it? He still felt dwarfed and inadequate in the face of this conundrum. And what about the Powder Valley Water Control District? These ranchers and farmers had put faith in SCS to provide them a long lived product.

There was also a concern about funding. The PL-566 program was under funded, and all of the money apportioned nationally was spoken for. There just wasn't any extra money to fix the pipe. Design engineers at the State Office in Portland began to research solutions. The West National Technical Center engineers provided review and advice. The PL-566 program manager in Washington DC was notified of the findings in the Engineering Deficiency report, and a cost to fix the pipe was determined.

Being stuck in the tactical trenches Rob didn't see any of these machinations. He worked with the ranchers to continue to identify trouble areas of the pipelines. He listened to landowners and the Water Control District people describe areas of the pipeline that could be configured differently to optimize water distribution. Several of the meters that measured total flow to the individual water turnouts didn't work, so that information was delivered to the engineering section in Portland. Rob travelled back to Idaho to observe the cement lining of a large pipe near the Utah state line. In fact, Idaho had been having trouble with steel pipelines too, and the cement lining was their selected solution. Oregon would also select this solution.

The next several years were a blur of construction contracts and amendments to the basic agreements between SCS and the Powder Valley Water Control District that had to be negotiated and signed. Construction contracts had to be bid, marked for construction and inspected, all while trying to keep the engineering program in 11 other Counties running. Rob had never been the government official on a contract before, but the invisible web of support structure in SCS had prepared him better than he realized.

Site showings for bidders? Well there had been that time in Rexburg where he had watched Bob Lehman skillfully describe a project for a dozen contractors in a way that let the contractors know what was expected of them and what the risks were. Rob knew that a sense of organization and protocol were required to let the bidders know they would be treated firmly but fairly so the project could be bid comparing 'apples' to 'apples'. He pointed out the parts in the large book of project specifications that really mattered and that would be inspected rigorously by the government inspectors. Dealing with contractors who tried to get an unfair advantage or cut corners? Lehman had shown Rob how to dissect the bids after they were open to determine which contractors really understood the work, and which ones had the correct equipment to complete the task.

Construction Inspection on formal contracts? Looking back Rob realized he had been taught how to inspect concrete structures, pipelines and all sorts of other works of engineering. He knew how to keep the official project Job Diary, how to process payment applications and how to write up proposals to modify the contract. He himself didn't realize how multi-faceted his training and coaching had been in nine short years of a career.

"Government contracts are full of red tape." "An elephant is a mouse designed to government specifications." "Government inspectors often take work breaks between cups of coffee." "The low bidder always gets the government job." All of these old saws are repeated a hundred times a day by the collective wisdom gathered at the local coffee shop. None of them are wholly true.

With an Engineering staff of five locally, and only 15 statewide, the SCS designed and successfully installed the retrofit of these huge steel pipelines, in 1990 to 1993. Some 20 years later, the projects are still working successfully. Could the SCS have been more efficient? Undoubtedly. Was there a reason for all of the paperwork, process and attention to detail? That process was one that had been honed in the SCS for 50 years and there was a reason for almost every single part of the very intricate procedure. Having the level of care and documentation for design and contracting was how SCS convinced Congress and other political leaders that they knew how to fix those pipes, and that they would get it right this time.

SCS completed lining of the larger diameter steel W-1, P-1 and P-2 pipelines and the newly constructed NPRC-South line. The smaller steel pipe had been replaced with PVC, which was more cost effective than cement lining.

Faulty water meters were replaced, and some additional acreage was added on several of the lines. Today the Powder Valley Water Control District operates Wolf Creek and Pilcher Creek Dams and five gravity pressurized pipelines. Over 18,000 acres grow irrigated corn, alfalfa and hay, with very few pumps and very little energy required.

36

Practicing the Profession

"The first streambank stabilization projects Rob encountered were on the Salmon and Lemhi rivers in Idaho."

When Rob learned surveying at college, the tools of the trade had not changed much from the late 1800's. Level line surveying was done with a 'dumpy level.' The machine was made level with four screws and a bubble of air in a glass tube. To survey angles and areas, a transit with a similar leveling mechanism was employed. Distances were measured with a steel tape known as a chain, a holdover name from the days when this tape was made of actual links that subdivided the measured distances.

A typical badge of surveying honor was to be able to wind the steel tape in a coil, then fold it into a figure-eight making two loops that folded in on each other. 'Throwing' the tape on the first try was how the experienced surveyors were distinguished, so the technicians that had mentored Rob made sure he could do this trick with ease. Little did anyone know how dramatically the technology would change in the 20 years after Rob learned how to 'throw the chain.'

As area engineer, the job was all about taking care of the day-to-day production engineering. Level terraces were a staple in the dry farm land, used both as a gulley control mechanism and a moisture conservation measure. Buried pipelines for stock water and irrigation were designed and installed regularly by SCS, as were ponds, troughs and concrete water control structures. Although each of these designs can become complicated, the recurring work mostly boiled down to one or two rote techniques that covered most of the situations. The area engineer's job was to make sure the quality of the installations remained high, and that the technicians and young engineers and soil conservationists learned the methods of SCS design.

The first streambank stabilization projects Rob encountered were on the Salmon and Lemhi rivers in Idaho. Typically the brush and trees near the streambank had been cleared to make room for more pasture and hay land. Without those deeper rooted plants the streambank soil didn't have the strength to resist the forces of flowing water and ice jams, so they often eroded.

The stock solution to this problem was to shape the bank back to a flatter angle, dig a trench below the bed of the stream and place a blanket of rock 'rip rap' on top of the sloped streambank and down into the trench. The weight and locking tendencies of the angular rock resisted the forces from the flowing water. This blanket of riprap used about one to three cubic yards of rock for every foot of streambank. At the time, rock riprap could be installed for about $25 per cubic yard.

As Rob designed his first job of blanket riprap, something didn't make sense. Even if the streambank eroded at the rate of 10 feet every year, 10 years of erosion would only lose an acre of ground for every 450 feet of streambank length. The ranchers and SCS were spending $11,000 at a minimum to protect that length of streambank. Since an acre of irrigated pasture was worth less than $1,000 dollars at the time, this did not seem rational.

Rob noticed that much of the planning prior to SCS agreeing to the rock work seemed less than rigorous. Often it seemed as if the only SCS input was to ask the rancher where the erosion started and stopped, mark those areas with flagging, and then survey the site to get elevations and complete a design for the rock riprap.

Rob had not been taught anything about river mechanics in his undergraduate studies. Water flow was always portrayed mathematically in a trapezoidal shape, all flowing at the same uniform velocity. Just standing on the banks of the Salmon River, it was easy to see the cross-currents, eddies, upwellings and surges in the flow. It also seemed to Rob a little disconnected to simply treat the erosion on one landowner's streambank. Much of the river shape and form indicated that if you changed the stream pattern in one spot, the stream would simply adjust somewhere else.

Rob's assignment was also taking place in a larger context. The SCS in eastern Oregon, along with the ranchers who owned this 'riparlan land ', were starting to feel other pressures when working around streams. In the late 1980s and early 1990s it was becoming obvious that salmon and steelhead would be listed under the Threatened and Endangered Species Act. In the cacophony leading up to the listing for Chinook in 1992, there were great discussions regarding who or what was responsible for the decline of the iconic Northwest species. Many argued the Federal dams on the Columbia and Snake Rivers were the root cause of population decline. Proponents of the dams pointed to the upstream habitat that had been degraded by years of agriculture, animal grazing, and forestry land management practices. Since these fish spent part of their life in fresh water, and part of it in the ocean, the problem seemed very complex, and there was enough finger-pointing that everyone could get some of the blame.

SCS's history of working around streams in the Northwest was uneven. Old engineering manuals from the 1940's showed how to use plants and plant materials to rebuild the streambank, but that approach fell out of favor as more and more machinery and machine operators returned from World War II. Society as a whole was entering an era where technological and manipulative fixes for environmental problems were demanded and valued. If a stream was eroding on the outside of bends, then removing the bends and straightening the stream might seem like a logical approach to minimizing the erosion.

The simplistic, uniform equations Rob had learned in school had only land slope, channel roughness, and channel geometry for inputs. Increasing slope increased a stream channel's capacity for water flow. Looking solely at the simple equations, the conclusion might be that straightening a stream and increasing the slope could only help the landowner, as it minimized flooding. SCS straightened many miles of stream in the Northwest from the 1950s to the 1980s. The North Powder River was already planned for straightening in the Powder Valley Watershed work plan that Rob inherited when he became the area engineer.

In 1990, the Northwest Power Planning Council (NPPC) began funding salmon habitat rehabilitation efforts in the John Day and Grande Ronde watersheds. The Soil and Water Conservation Districts and by extension, SCS, were natural partners for the NPPC. The Districts and SCS contacted landowners and asked them to help improve river and stream habitat for salmon and steelhead.

Most private landowners, however, did not feel that they should bear the entire blame for the declining salmon and steelhead population. The landowners also could not understand how their relatively small amount of stream channel and streamside vegetation could be changed to positively help the fish.

Quite honestly, SCS and the Conservation Districts did not know how changing the agricultural practices along private land impacted fish habitat either. But since some landowners were willing to change their grazing and farming practices, and there was a great deal of money to subsidize these actions, SCS, the Districts and the landowners proceeded to apply the conservation practices like fencing, streambank stabilization, and tree planting. In 1992, when the salmon were listed as endangered, SCS did not have a single practice in the Field Office Technical Guide that had 'fish habitat' as its intended purpose.

At this point in Rob's career, the intersection of surveying equipment, SCS's better understanding of stream complexity and the public concern over fisheries habitat, combined to change the arc of his future professional path. A course taught in Reno in 1994 turned out to be the catalyst. The members of the 'stream team' came from the SCS West National Technical Center (WNTC); Gary Conaway taught hydrology, and Leland Saele taught the streambank stability portions of the class. Carolyn Adams, a landscape architect, taught about the stream and its interaction with vegetation.

The highlight of the one week class was Frank Reckendorf, a fluvial geomorphologist. Frank's PhD from Oregon State focused on how streams interact with their floodplains. Frank was very animated, with wild white hair, and a deliberate yet introspective way of lecturing. It was not unusual for him to pause mid paragraph, and mutter "No, that isn't right either," as he mulled the topic in his head.

The first order of business was to explain what a 'fluvial geomorphologist' did, thought and was. The over-long title seemed intimidating just from its sound, but was a little less complex when broken down to the root terms of 'river,' 'earth' and 'change.' Fluvial geomorphology was about how rivers change on the landscape, and how the rivers themselves modify the land. Specifically, it is the science and art of predicting ahead of time what a stream might do, as well as describing the sequence of events that had led to the current river's form and function.

This intimidating job title was appealing to Rob as he thought back about hours he'd spent staring at streams to gain some understanding of streambank erosion. Attendees at this very first SCS training in stream science turned into many of the leaders in that field for the agency. Once again SCS had provided a unique opportunity through its training and mentoring efforts.

In order to start to understand the complexities of the interactions of water, sediment and vegetation in a stream or river, it is necessary to look at a significant length of the channel. Typical engineering practice would dictate surveying a cross section of the stream channel and floodplain. The cross section survey was repeated at some interval up and down the channel until the entire stream reach had been characterized. But these cross section surveys were no trivial pursuit. It was easy enough to survey a single cross section if the streamside vegetation was not too thick, but linking a series of cross sections together spatially required line-of-sight surveying, which often meant setting the instrument up multiple times. As the cross sections got closer together, the surveying took more and more time. To understand an entire stream reach could require weeks and weeks of careful surveying to portray the stream in three dimensions.

SCS had learned the pitfalls of just looking at a small section of a river, and the technical consensus was the more you surveyed and measured, the better your understanding of the stream hydraulics and sediment transport would be. Surveying a long section of stream was not a trivial task. Very seldom could you see all of the stream from one spot. Moving the surveying transit required a complex set of actions that had to be done carefully or the entire survey could be useless. So, although it was well know that surveying a long section of stream improved understanding, it was not always practiced in the field.

SCS in Baker received their first electronic total station in 1992. This machine used a laser beam that when properly aimed, was reflected by a pole-mounted mirrored prism serving as the surveying rod. Using electronic measurements of horizontal and vertical angles measured by the machine, coupled with a distance measurement obtained from the laser reflection, the three dimensional coordinates of the prism pole could be calculated. As the technician moved the prism pole across the stream channel, not only was the channel cross section charted, but the cross section's distance and position relative to the next cross section were described very precisely. Each survey shot with the electronic 'total station' took about 30 seconds, and the information about that shot was recorded electronically in a data collector.

Compared to the tried and true conventional transit, this change was revolutionary. Using the traditional transit, a technician occupied the point of interest, holding a graduated pole, a surveying rod. The traditional transit operator had to assure that the machine was level, focus the machine's telescope on the rod, read the elevation number and meticulously record it in a notebook. As well, the transit provided two other numbers to record, 'stadia' readings that would be used later to calculate the distance between the transit and the surveying rod. Two very fine angles representing the tilt of the telescope and the compass bearing from the transit to the rod were also observed and recorded. A typical transit reading took between two and five minutes to complete by an experienced surveyor, and the possibility of error could be significant.

Back at the office, the readings from the traditional transit notebook were painstakingly plotted on a piece of paper. With all of the stream survey points plotted at the appropriate relative position to each other, the engineer could then manually draw topographic lines of equal elevation, and portray how the stream moves down the valley.

Compared to the electronic total station, the hand drawn method is tedious and cumbersome. With the total station, the data collector is taken to the office and the raw data file, with the computed coordinates of all the survey points, is downloaded into a computer. Each point is 'plotted' on the computer screen and three lines are drawn between three adjacent points in a process called triangulation. These triangles are then interpolated to electronically draw the topographic lines. An experienced computer operator can obtain a completed map of a stream project in under an hour.

Now SCS, and the employee trying to understand the stream, could move beyond the calculation of stream velocity at single cross sections. With the electronic topographic map, a stream cross section could be 'cut' across the channel anywhere there was an interest. More importantly, the cross sections could be linked together by an energy-and -momentum balance and the forces in the channel could be examined over a wide range of flows.

The basic principles and techniques had been known in the engineering community since the 1940s and 1950s. But the combination of the computer and electronically portrayed stream could be queried repeatedly, and the graphic portrayal of the stream could be easily interpreted. This linking of surveying and computer technology allowed a small, interdisciplinary team to truly understand the marriage of hydrology, hydraulics and the interrelationship of water and sediment movement that made up fish habitat.

When were the forces on the channel the greatest? When did the sand and gravel in the channel bed start to move? What low-flow condition caused pools to start to diminish? Examining questions like these brought a richer understanding of basic stream behavior.

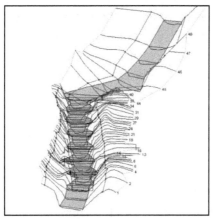

A simple model of a stream generated with electronic survey data
Model image courtesy of Sean Welch

37

History of Computers in SCS

"Wild-west programming continued in SCS Idaho
until a field in Eastern Idaho got land-leveled backwards
using Rob's software."

Rob started working for SCS full time in 1985. Later that year SCS got its first computer system at the field office level, an AT&T Unix server called a 3B2. The terminals were AT&T personal computers with 5 MB hard drives. The system used the UNIX operating system and spreadsheets, databases and word processors bundled in a suite called Prelude, software that was supplied to USDA by Ross Perot's company, Electronic Data Systems.

Suffice to say, very few SCS employees were knowledgeable about computers, let alone well versed in UNIX or Prelude. If they did know that typing *DIR:* into a DOS computer would result in a directory listing, they probably didn't know that typing *ls–l* in UNIX was equivalent. Programmers and UNIX aficionados knew right away you were asking for a 'long list'-- a directory with all the details.

Helpfully, even prior to 1985, the Sampson household was more up to date on the latest technology than most of the neighbors. Neil bought their first electronic calculator in 1972 for around $100. The red LED lights intrigued all the kids. The calculator was about 8 inches square, and had a single memory bin. It could add, subtract, multiply and divide.

Neil purchased the first computer for the Sampson household in 1982. It was an Osborn 1, the first commercially successful portable computer. The Osborn had a 5 inch screen, two 5-1/4 inch floppy disk drives, and the case looked like a large beige suitcase. 'Portable' was a relative word as the whole thing weighed about 35 pounds.

The kids played with the computer a little, but mostly Neil used it to program databases and spreadsheets. Thus NACD had its first automated label printing program to distribute the weekly newsletter, among several other database applications. Self taught, Neil was writing complicated databases in an era where ATMs were a novelty, and most cash registers still printed their audit information on paper tape.

An ad for Osborne computers, about 1982.

SCS at that time was writing some computer programs, mostly in FORTRAN and running the punch cards on a mainframe in Ft. Worth, Texas. Most of the available programs were for engineering solutions. Coded forms were sent to the programmers in Ft. Worth, who generated the cards for that project, ran the program, and the results were mailed back to the State Office. If another alternative solution was needed, the process was repeated. The local conservation technician wasn't very interested in presenting an alternative design to a landowner, then waiting four weeks to receive the second alternative, so many avoided this system, or accepted the fact that analyzing several alternatives was agonizingly slow.

The SCS State Office in Idaho began to test technology with a large Harris word processor beginning in the mid 70's. The machine used 8-inch floppy drives and provided output on a printer that used a 'wheel' that had all of the letters and symbols. The wheel spun to the correct symbol and the wheel was struck, forcing it onto a ribbon that inked the symbol on the paper exactly like a mechanical typewriter, but much faster. The entire unit was about 6 feet square and was mostly used by the administrative assistants.

At about the same time Neil installed a similar word processor at the National Association of Conservation Districts (NACD) as well the first facsimile machine the Association acquired. This FAX used a thermal imaging process to read the image, as well a similar process to 'burn' the copy at the receiving machine.

In 1981 SCS Engineering was using Texas Instruments (TI) programmable calculators. The TI 57 and 59 could accept code written in a proprietary language. The TI-59 could read and record programs from small magnetic cards run through a detachable reader and could provide output through a small thermal printer. Using these tools, the SCS engineer or technician could run simple routines while they visited with a farmer. The amount of excavation for a pond or the size of pipe for a drain could be quickly shown.

Many SCS engineers and technicians used this programmable calculator technology as late as 2005. Most of the programs have been currently converted to spreadsheets, but some of the code that helped with difficult engineering tasks has been lost to posterity as technology rolled ahead.

Neil gave Rob the original Osborn computer along with an Epson 9-pin dot matrix printer in 1983. This computer served well for writing college papers, and also became the first personal computer at an Idaho SCS office when Rob took it to the Pocatello area office.

A program was being developed to calculate land-leveling designs. Idaho SCS had received the BASIC code from Arizona SCS. Rob and Gene Koozer, one of Rob's first engineering trainers, worked to modify it for use in Idaho. Land leveling is particularly difficult as the final solution is achieved through trail-and-error and many variations of a design could be conceived. Ultimately, Rob's version of the code and the alternatives it could generate got very large.

Senior engineering management was intrigued, but wary of the generated output. Still, they loved the speed with which designs could be completed. Instead of a hand drawn map with elevations calculated every 100 feet across the field, the printed computer output shows the starting elevations, the final elevations, and the cuts or fills at all the grid points. The total cubic yards of cut and fill could be optimized so there was enough soil to be redistributed around the field. All the data entry and calculations could be done in about 20 minutes for an average field. Compared to about two or three hours to do the first alternative by hand, the technicians really liked the computer program, while still being slightly wary of the technology.

SCS was following a similar trend nationwide. Personal computers began showing up at work, and ad-hoc programming was the norm. Computers were still mostly the domain of the Soil Scientists and the Engineers, and there were very few trained programmers. A Government Accounting Office report contained the following observation in 1987:

> According to the inventory, 22 of SCS's 50 state offices and two of its four national technical centers have collectively developed or were developing about 300 software applications as of April 1986. But in January and February 1986 we communicated with each of these organizations and found that 28 state offices and three national technical centers had collectively developed or were developing about 700 software applications.

Wild-west programming continued in SCS Idaho until a field in Eastern Idaho got land-leveled backwards using Rob's software. The slope flowed towards the supply ditch rather than away from it. After using SCS funds to slope the field the correct way, a policy came out that all 'standardized' computer programs would be approved at the state office level, and only those approved by the Boise office would be allowed for use in design.

Currently there are file drawers in the Boise NRCS state office filled with documentation of the testing that went into these approved programs. This collection served Rob well in his position as State Conservation Engineer, but the role his program played in compelling the development of the 'approved policies' was ironic. Later, after Rob became the National Water Management Engineer, he found the letter from Idaho SCS that requested additional funding to fix the backwards field.

Surveying technology and the designs generated from those surveys developed along the same trajectory as the computing hardware. The hand-held programmable calculator had a routine that calculated the area of a surveyed cross-section after the coordinates were input manually to the program. In Idaho SCS this evolved to a computer program that could calculate cut and fill from before-and after-project surveys, and these were printed out graphically.

Today the NRCS collects a great deal of survey data using satellite Global Positioning System (GPS) technology. Randomly acquired 'before' and 'after' survey shots can be electronically stored and transferred to Computer Aided Design (CAD) software. Using these electronic coordinates and elevations, the computer can subtract the two surfaces and provide a very detailed map with cut and fill volumes shown.

Similarly, the pre-project topography can be used to calculate where a pond or a pipeline might be located. These surface elevations and locations can be placed back into the GPS data collection unit (a hand-held computer) and the GPS survey rod will be directed where to locate different points in the design. These points are flagged to show the landowner and contractor where to construct the conservation practice.

NRCS now uses desktop and laptop computers wired together in a Local Area Network for almost all of their communications and day-to-day tasks. All of the local networks are connected together through the internet into a very efficient wide-area network. Several private computer specialists have commented that the USDA network is a leader in that technologic field.

NRCS's Conservation Delivery Streamlining Initiative (CDSI) is another effort that plans to provide conservation planners and engineers with data delivered through a cellular network that they can map in the field while doing conservation planning with an agricultural producer. CDSI envisions all of NRCS's corporate datasets such as soils, rainfall, and crop growth to be housed in one location and universally accessible, so that all programs ask for data in a similar manner and receive data from a single source.

In July of 2012, NRCS released an application for a mobile 'smart' phone that maps the soil where you are standing, providing information about texture and layers, as well as suitability for conservation practices, such as ponds. The agency has come quite a long way since 1985!

In fact, technology of any kind is always a double edged sword. Students often consider anything not done on the computer to not be worthwhile, so the groans when an instructor suggests using a pencil, paper and calculator are audible. But a magic black box that does calculations quickly does not know how to determine a landowners needs and desires. Without the right questions asked and answered, input into the black box has no context, and the calculated answer has no meaning.

38

Mid-Career Decisions

"The important part of the experience at Graduate School was in reloading the firepower in the technical skills and in rekindling the passion for learning."

In 1994, Rob was at a cross roads. As a member of the Grande Ronde model watershed technical team, he regularly listened to other disciplines speak in terms he didn't fully understand. Engineering was frequently disparaged as the profession that had ruined much of the fish habitat in the first place by simplifying and armoring river channels. Although that assessment was probably an overreaction, it didn't appear that engineers had a role in the restoration of salmon and steelhead populations.

Overlaid on the model watershed experience was the fact that SCS was in the throes of reorganization. The new SCS State Conservationist in Oregon was Bob Graham, who moved to Oregon after a much ballyhooed reorganization of SCS in Montana. Graham was convinced that middle management, the area conservationists and their staff, were inefficient, adding work that kept SCS from engaging farmers and ranchers. Then the area conservationist and Rob's mentor, Gary Yeoumans, retired, and Rob became the acting area conservationist.

At that time Rob was already engaged in some study of management and leadership, and some of the theories piqued his interest. He had watched his father provide vision and leadership at NACD and American Forests. Rob had (admittedly under protest) participated in and studied the 'Total Quality Management' trainings Graham and his management team had provided for the slightly bewildered Oregon field staff.

SCS itself was struggling hard to understand its role after major farm legislation had been passed by Congress and a reorganization craze was sweeping the Federal Government. In the face of change, it seemed important that the agency try and 'do the right thing' for its employees, its clients and the tax payers. If he transitioned into management, even part time, Rob could help.

There were also some distinct disincentives. State Conservationist Graham seemed determined to eliminate both the position of area conservationist and that of area engineer, positions that Rob had seen make a real difference. With the state leadership squarely at odds with Rob's observations and values, it seemed a good time for professional soul searching. Would he continue down a path of management or that of being a technical specialist?

Graduate Studies

When Neil went to Harvard, Rob was 11. To be a boy from Idaho transplanted to Boston, Massachusetts was unsettling to say the least. But the memories from Boston persisted as happy ones for Rob and all of the family. Dad had seemed excited by the new challenges, and adapted to the reentry into colligate rigors with passion. Rob and Neil watched Boston Bruins hockey games together and the entire family had great fun visiting the historic places of Boston and the northeast.

To Rob the Boston lifestyle seemed almost vagabond. It was a place where each passing week brought adventures such as tasting lobster for the first time, visiting the houses of witches in Salem, and wandering through the pushcarts and their screaming hawkers in Haymarket Square. Demonstrators like Gloria Steinem or LSD trippers in Harvard Square exercising their Constitutional rights and Dad getting lost driving in Chelsea at dusk one night all rolled into a memory that was largely positive.

When the job announcement for the SCS Graduate Studies program crossed his desk in 1994 as it had sporadically throughout his career, he did what he hadn't done in previous years, and read it with interest. Baker, Oregon was a long way from any Universities of note, and Rob had not put any effort into keeping in touch with academia.

Having escaped from the University of Idaho with no money and under a 3.0 grade point average, Rob figured he had closed the door on that part of life. A phone call to Neil changed his career path once again. Neil called some of his colleagues and several schools continued to come up in the discussion.

Rob didn't know exactly what he wanted to do in further study; he just knew he wanted something to change. He didn't want to be confused when fish biologists described the habitats that a myriad of fish needed. He didn't want to have to accept people's discussion of statistics at face value, without understanding the inner workings of that field of logic. And he wanted to know the seemingly magic science of predicting the behavior of rivers and streams. The intersection of ecology, earth science, and rigorous statistics came in the form of a field then unknown to Rob called 'watershed science.'

Watershed science embodied different things at different universities and in the various colleges and the departments that made up those institutions. Yet one thing was universal: the study of watershed science depended on different departments and colleges collaborating together. While this is touted at many different institutions, Neil's inquires kept coming up with the University of Washington, Utah State University and Colorado State University as the places where watershed science was a rigorous, robust program.

At Washington it was primarily taught in the department of forestry and geology, while it was led from the fisheries science, range and geology areas at Utah. CSU's watershed science degree was taught from the Earth Resources Department housed in the College of Natural Resources, on the same floor as the geosciences. First glance suggested a good interaction with the College of Engineering, as well as the fisheries program in the College.

Rob and his wife Dianna talked about leaving Baker, their home for seven years, and the place where all their friends lived. Having been detached from academia for almost 10 years, Rob didn't think he had much of a chance since the program would only select five SCS employees nationwide. In order to be successful in the graduate studies application, Rob would need Bob Graham's endorsement, and it was evident to both of them that they had a difference of opinion about how SCS in Oregon should be organized.

Was it Rob's positive thoughts about watching his dad go to school in Boston that were in play, or was it was just a seven-year itch to do something different? Rob and Dianna made a decision and he proposed a course of study in watershed science to SCS in his graduate studies application.

Next came studying for the Graduate Record Examination. Then, after digging out of snowdrifts at the ranch where he lived, Rob drove to Boise, Idaho through a snow and ice storm and took the day-long test. He applied to both the Utah State and the Colorado State graduate schools and was conditionally accepted into both.

He and Dianna took a two week road trip to look at Logan, Utah and Ft. Collins, Colorado and to meet with professors. On the face of it, USU and CSU offered different but equivalent programs of watershed science studies. The tipping point was at Fort Collins. The town had an excellent system of bike paths and it was very close to outdoor recreation opportunities for backpacking and mountain biking. The small downtown area seemed laid back and inviting. Ft. Collins boasted the largest number of microbreweries per capita and some of the craft brews were quite tasty. Coming from Oregon, the self-appointed home of the microbrew, Rob doubted Ft. Collins' claim, but as a brewer himself, the large number of breweries was not to be ignored.

To Rob's surprise and probably everyone else's in SCS, he was accepted into the SCS graduate studies program. The program would pay for tuition and books, and Rob would continue to receive his GS-12 salary while attending school.

So, in July 1995 the Sampson's loaded up a U-Haul moving truck, as moving costs in the Graduate program were paid by the student. With the help of friends from Baker, Rob and the family moved to their newly purchased house in Ft. Collins. The graduate school adventures over the next two and a half years were memorable. Rob finished 61 graduate credits and conducted research in the Virgin Islands about how the sediment from roads impacted coral reefs around Virgin Islands National Park. He also assisted with research in Rocky Mountain National Park to determine the impact of irrigation withdrawals on wetlands at the headwaters of the Colorado River.

He coauthored a report about how the urbanization and population growth in Colorado Springs were changing the shape and form of Fountain Creek as it ran through town and to the farms below.

Other research projects included the occurrence of rain-on-snow generated floods in Montana, the impact of wildfires on erosion and sediment transport in the Front Range of the Rockies, and how water withdrawal for urban use might impact the wetlands and farms of the San Luis Valley.

The important part of the experience at Graduate School was in reloading the firepower in the technical skills and in rekindling the passion for learning. The passion came from the field work, the camaraderie and the challenge. Rob helped with graduate field work wherever he could, as it came easily to him and was where he felt the heart of the science lay.

His graduate advisor, Lee MacDonald, challenged him at every turn to be better and better. Fifteen credits of statistics and nine credits of ecology and aquatic science at the graduate level had plugged a few gaps in Rob's scientific portfolio. Kindred souls in all things hydrology, Kevin Reid and Scott Woods, made Rob as a 35 year old graduate student feel young. Kevin and Scott became lifelong friends.

Obviously, the fun and freedom of going to college while earning a salary had to come to an end at some point. While Neil had spent nine months at Harvard, Rob had managed to spend almost 27 months at CSU. He did owe a significant amount of indentured time to the Federal Government as a result of his sponsored education, but the path of technical study was the best thing Rob had ever done.

School had improved his proficiency in writing, logic and research, a fact that would serve NRCS very well over the next 20 years of Rob's career. The experience gained by stepping out of direct service to farmers and ranchers and being able to immerse himself in research and learning was profound for Rob. In addition to taking many new engineering classes, he learned a good deal of the science behind watershed runoff, nutrient movement, river shape and form, and wetland function. Statistics could be discussed and understood, and classes in ecology and aquatic biology added to the mix of cross-discipline training.

As well, the university culture was a place to stretch technical boundaries and foster curiosity. The opportunity for this rich suite of training was a once-in-a-lifetime experience. Being able to use field skills cultivated in the SCS and have the collected data be informed from technical first principles was a mix Rob wouldn't have gotten working 40 hours a week at SCS positions requiring constant production.

Rob was accepted into the PhD program and had completed negotiations with Bob Graham to stay an extra nine months in Colorado, but the administrative rules finally broke from the constant bending. Rob had applied for a two year position in graduate studies, and the decision-makers determined that extending that period was outside of the personnel rules. So Bob Graham called Rob home to Oregon SCS.

Although both Rob and Dianna wanted to go back to east Oregon, that was not to be either. SCS in Oregon was now called the Natural Resources Conservation Service (NRCS), and the area offices in Oregon had been eliminated. Bob Graham wanted Rob to work in southwest Oregon, and the Sampson's ended up in Roseburg.

39

Organization
and Reorganization

"The biggest changes in Rob's career occurred in 1993 and 1997. Reorganization fever hit SCS in the early 90's."

NRCS in Oregon and nationwide was a different organization from the SCS Rob had left. Being in western Oregon was change enough from the high deserts of the eastern half of the state, but the agency felt different also. SCS had a history of organizational changes and putting the change from SCS to NRCS in context with the organization's past shows it to be part of a long history.

The organization that rose out of the Dust Bowl era prided itself in assisting locally elected Soil Conservation Districts (SCDs). A locally elected board of landowners works with a local district conservationist (DC) employed by the agency to prioritize work and resources concerns. The DC is the leader of that field office, and interacts directly with the Conservation District board of directors. This Federal-Local partnership was authorized nationally in 1935 and authorized in Idaho in 1939. The SCS office and the SCD are typically defined by County boundaries, although geographic factors, and occasionally politics or feuds, sometimes split counties into multiple SCDs.

The operative generic model for the agency is that the DC answers to an area conservationist (AC), who answers to the state conservationist (STC). The state conservationist is selected by the Chief working at National Headquarters (NHQ) in Washington DC. This fairly direct line of authority is referred to internally as 'line and staff'

Technical leadership is split into three major areas: Soils, Engineering, and Ecological Sciences, with subdivisions such as Agronomy,

Range and Biology. These three major divisions are mirrored at the same four levels as the 'line officers' described above, although at the field office level, the DC's staff would generally be a planner and possibly a technician.

Neil and Rob Sampson have both been assigned to all four levels of the organization. As in many organizations, the changes have occurred at the middle management level of the area office. Prior to 1960, SCS in Idaho was divided into six areas headquartered in Boise, Idaho Falls, Pocatello, Twin Falls, Moscow, and Lewiston. The Lewiston area office was closed in 1960. Since then, Idaho has been structured to have five, four, three, zero and currently two area offices.

The Idaho offices have consisted of a base staff of as high as 12 to 14 technical people such as the area agronomist, range conservationist, engineer, soil scientist, resource conservationist, biologist and administrative positions. Currently, the two areas in Idaho are headquartered at Moscow and Pocatello, attempting to divide the State into eastern and western portions.

Technically, the current area staff consists of an engineer, resource conservationist, biologist, and soil scientist. In the case of the western Idaho area, these technical specialists cover the almost 600 miles from Canada to Nevada, encompassing elevations from 11,000 to 700 feet and annual precipitation totals of over 100 inches to less than 8.

The quality of the technical work of the agency seems to vary in direct proportion with how many technical leaders are deployed at the Area and Field levels. The Area specialists do the heavy lifting of writing complex habitat plans, completing engineering designs and making the call when inevitable grey areas are encountered. When these specialists are closer to the resource conditions they live and work with, their technical analyses and solutions are more robust and rich, so it seems instructive to look at the numerical changes through the years.

In 1960, SCS in Idaho employed about 200 people. About 35 (18%) of these worked at the state office. The remainder worked at the area (about 30 or 15%) and field levels (the remaining 67%). There were 50 field offices working in 44 counties serving 54 SCDs. In 1985, Idaho SCS employed 200 people with 35 (18%) working at the state level. There were 40 field offices servicing 50 SCDs and the State was divided into three areas served from Pocatello, Boise and Moscow, with 35 employees (18%). The remainder, 64%, were in the field.

Today, Idaho NRCS has about 170 full time people in 36 field offices serving the 50 SCDs. Thirty-eight people work at the State office (22%) and 16 people work at the area office level (9%). The remaining 69% work at field offices.

So the changes have been a trend of fewer employees, reflecting the agency number across the nation. In Idaho's case the overall number of employees has dropped by about 15%, but the relative proportions of people at the State Office have remained steady with a slight increase at present. Below the State Office level, there has been a loss of bodies working at the Area office level, from a high of 22% of the workforce down to 9%. Idaho has maintained the level of people working at the Field Office level, and this has helped the State deliver program contracts and money.

But someone has to plan and design all those conservation practices. The lack of people at the Area Office level means that a great deal of the complex work is not done as thoroughly as it once was, and the managers are left to triage strategy. And while efficiencies have improved, the lack of strong technical leadership at the Area level had degraded the quality of the delivered product. Under Rob's seven years as State Engineer in Idaho watershed-wide, holistic planning had evaporated from the State technical team's repertoire. Designs were being completed by third parties, dealers and power companies. In and of itself this is not bad, but there needed to be a commensurate effort by NRCS in quality control and oversight.

The SCS Rob joined in 1981 seemed to be remarkably talented in a technical sense. An engineering design contained a thorough, thoughtful set of calculations and documentation. A high level of critical thought in the documentation was the norm. The area office provided a well-measured function of quality control, and in examining the old 'quality assurance' reports Rob found them thorough and clear.

Although it highlights some personnel issues as well as technical capacity, a look in the rear-view mirror is instructive. When Rob joined an area quality assurance review at a field office in 1982, it became obvious early in the review that the DC was writing conservation plans that did not have any input from the farmer. In several cases, interviews with some landowners revealed they had never seen their farm conservation plan. Work had up until then been pretty light-hearted in Rob's eyes, but the quality review quickly turned sober and serious. It was quickly apparent to all involved that the DC's position, if not his job, was on the line. That quality review did result in a reassignment of the DC to a different office and a lower-paid position.

Watching his area office colleagues agonize over the serious problem they had found and the difficult decisions they would have to make was enlightening. This job and the duties were played for keeps.

If there is truth in the old saw 'the only constant thing is change,' it has certainly been the case for SCS/NRCS in Oregon; but the biggest changes in Rob's career occurred in 1993 and 1997. Reorganization fever hit SCS in the early 90's. In the West this charge was led by Montana SCS. Then state conservationist Richard 'Dick' Gooby, and deputy state conservationist Robert 'Bob' Graham led the effort under the rationale that eliminating area offices would place more technical assistance at the field office level. Areas were abolished and eight 'self-directed teams' were formed. The process of 'Total Quality Management (TQM) pioneered by the 3M Corporation was employed to assist the teams in reinventing their management to match the new structure.

Graham was selected to be State Conservationist in Oregon in 1993 when Rob was the area engineer in Baker City, covering the eastern half of the State. Graham brought his ideas of organizational structure and TQM in Montana west with him. He immediately toured the State meeting with the local SCDs, posing the question: "Would you want more technical staff assistance to your District?"

Needless to say, the Districts generally responded in the positive. Area offices and the line officer position were abolished and eight 'Basin Teams' were formed, mostly along watershed boundaries. District conservationist positions were abolished, and those in that position were to assume the title of resource conservationist. This change, in theory, allowed more time for the ex-district conservationist to provide direct assistance to the farmers and ranchers.

Thus the Baker City area office was no more and the Snake River, John Day/Umatilla, and High Desert Basins were created, each having a Basin Team Leader (BTL) who answered to the state conservationist. Technical leaders at the state office found their positions renamed also. The position of state conservation engineer, obviously enough named, became the 'Leader for Implementation'. Only in 2011 did that title revert back to the earlier and clearer one.

Under the National Partnership for Reinventing Government (NPR) led by Vice-President Al Gore in the Clinton administration, SCS went through some remarkably spasmodic changes. The most obvious was the name change to the Natural Resources Conservation Service (NRCS). Reorganization was the watchword for the day, and most states participated in one way or another. Oregon won an award from Vice President Gore, and each employee was given a small lapel pin shaped like a hammer.

With the arrival of State Conservationist Luana Kiger in 1995, Idaho went through changes similar to those in Oregon. Areas were abolished and many different organizational structures were described and tested. One named 'hub and spoke' envisioned a group of technical specialists responsible for a certain geographic region, with each specialist in charge of some group of spokes out to the field offices dictated by their technical skills; those with broader skill sets serviced more 'spokes'. The organization settled upon involved 'Divisions' replicating the six geographic regions used by SCD's in Idaho. Each Division had a rotating position of 'Coach' among the district conservationists (DCs). The Coach interacted with management at the state office and attempted to provide guidance to the fellow DCs in the Division.

States that retained a mid-level management position and technical specialists at an area office, however named, seemed to fare the storm of change the best in terms of technical quality and capacity. in both Oregon and Idaho, many of the functions that the area office performed, particularly those of quality assurance, simply disappeared. After all, who would willingly have the procedures and quality assurance functions of their office assessed if no one was charged with that function? And no technical specialist in their right mind would assume that responsibility if they did not have a supervisor to report the findings to whoever was authorized to enforce suggested reforms.

40

Roseburg

"Father and son wandered through the second growth on the Roseburg hillside with endless new technical things to discuss."

Rob's first exposure to Roseburg, Oregon had come in 1993 when the NRCS Oregon Engineering staff had a week-long meeting at that location. Watching TV in a rather dumpy motel, Rob witnessed the local zeitgeist in the form of a TV commercial paid for by local logging interests. The commercial started out with a picture of a great-horned owl flying through the air, ready to flare its wings and land in a tree. With a very loud sound the owl exploded in a pile of feathers. The commercial cut to a guy in logging clothes with a shotgun who explained: "That's what I think of Spotted Owls".

Given that Rob had grown up with raptors of all sort living in the back yard of the house in Boise, the inference that someone would kill an owl, spotted or great-horned or any kind, was shocking, bordering on tragic. Add to this the fact that one of the longest tenured denizens in the Boise backyard was a great-horned owl named Bubo, easily Rob's favorite. The TV commercial provoked some rather visceral feelings.

Little did Rob know then that Roseburg, Oregon would play a bigger role in his professional trajectory than just the memories of a dumpy motel and a rather backward approach to raptor management.

Rob and Dianna Sampson's move to Roseburg was uneventful as far as relocating households go. Rob had to get used to the crops that were grown, the limitations of the soils, the steep slopes and very different hydrologic patterns. But these factors paled in comparison to learning the new culture the NRCS in Oregon had assumed.

Some of the differences in southwest Oregon had always existed compared to his experience in east Oregon, but some elements were new.

Rob's job title was now 'basin engineer' and the southwest corner of Oregon for which he provided technical services was called the Southwest basin. This area was comprised of Douglas, Curry, Coos, Jackson, and Josephine counties with the communities of Roseburg, Coquille, Grants Pass and Medford.

The basin team leader (BTL) at the time was Ed Peterson, based in Coquille. Ed was old school SCS, a range conservationist by training. He applied for, and got the BTL, mostly as an act of defense. The SCS reorganization itself was disconcerting enough for staff and landowners, and Ed figured the boss should be a local person with field experience. Rob reported to the BTL, but much of his work was working on stream and wetland restoration statewide. The skills he had gained at graduate school in river and wetland science, coupled with field data collection experience served these efforts well, and gave his work a new depth.

The reorganized NRCS seemed much more poorly organized and difficult to navigate. Rob didn't report to the State conservation engineer or lead project planner, but nonetheless they gave him assignments. The BTL gave very few assignments and, for the most part, seemed detached from day to day conservation planning and field office operations.

Because there were no other multi-county specialists stationed in Roseburg, interdisciplinary planning occurred less frequently than it had in the Rob's former post as Area Engineer. In order to assemble a team of technical specialists with skills adequate to look at a catchment as a whole, Rob would have to talk to two or more BTLs and get their blessing for their employee's participation. There was no particular advantage for BTLs to give up the staff time, no overarching technical team to provide review of a large-scale plan, and no incentive for them to do so.

This lack of ability to look at the complicated inter-relationship of physical and biologic processes happening at a watershed scale was in direct opposition to local demand. The Threatened and Endangered Species listing of Coho and Chinook salmon and steelhead trout demanded a comprehensive look at watersheds, and the recently formed watershed councils knew that without a bigger picture view, their actions would lack impact and consistency.

To add to the confusion, the 1996 Farm Bill had created the Environmental Quality Incentive Program, or EQIP. On the face of it, this was simply an extension of the old Agriculture Conservation Program (ACP). In general, the landowner applied for supplemental funding to complete a conservation practice on their farm. NRCS employees went to the farm and helped the farmer plan a strategy to deal with the problem.

If NRCS and the landowner came to agreement, a conservation plan was written that described the order and the combination of conservation practices to be implemented. This plan was approved by the Soil and Water Conservation District (SWCD)[12], then the District Conservationist developed a contract that outlined the federal money set aside for that landowners conservation practices. The producer entered into the contract, and design and installation of the conservation practices began.

EQIP had a few new wrinkles, however. The landowner's application to the program was ranked, with point scoring based on which resource concerns were being treated. That landowner then competed against other applicants in the County. The highest-ranked projects were funded and the remainder had to wait another year to try again. For a brief period, the landowner could 'buy-down' to get a higher ranking by agreeing to take less Federal money.

All EQIP contracts were required to be a Resource Management System or RMS. This is NRCS jargon for a plan that treats every resource concern on that operator's land. Hence many EQIP plans contained practices that the landowner was not particularly concerned with. The landowners had to add things like wildlife habitat practices and nutrient management to complete an RMS when they were mostly concerned about switching to sprinkler irrigation.

---

[12] All of Oregon's conservation districts included the word 'water' in their title.

While the ACP program had specifically been designed to put in a single practice, the EQIP required landowners and NRCS personnel to plan for all of the resource concerns. That resulted in many half-finished contracts. If a farmer wanted a sprinkler system, it was most likely installed first. Wildlife habitat and nutrient management fell off of the landowner's radar screen pretty fast, leaving NRCS with quite a few partially complete contracts and a farmer that was no longer interested in their contract.

Rob would travel to the different field offices and help the staff at that office design the practices in the EQIP contracts and try to convince farmers to finish all the practices in their contract, not just the ones they favored.

With only one engineer serving the five counties of southwest Oregon, efficiency was important. While none of the offices were very far away, it took two hours or so to drive to Cave Junction from Roseburg. Being efficient generally meant meeting with the land operator, and this often resulted in scenarios where practices that were different from the ones in the EQIP contract would be more effective on a certain farm.

Had the resource concern changed, and was this driving contract revisions? Sometimes. But most likely the practice had been promoted by the resident conservation planner, who didn't have engineering background or experience. Additionally, most likely there was not a senior supervisory planner in the office training the junior soil conservationist, or if there was, that was not part of their assignment under the new NRCS structure.

Such oversight and guidance had been present in most of the pre-reorganization offices in the form of a District Conservationist. In the new structure, no one in the local office was seen as the boss. The Basin Team Leader would come around to each office as they could, but day-to-day there wasn't a presence of staff leadership.

Similarly, there was no direct liaison in that office to the Soil and Water Conservation District. Without the communication bridge between the SWCD and NRCS, there was no one to articulate the District's priorities for the office, or to describe NRCS priorities to the District. No overarching message or theme resulted in a potpourri of conservation planning and a broad range of rigor in the conservation plans and EQIP contracts.

One result of these bureaucratic changes was that the travelling technical specialist would often be looked to for resolution of a dispute or to enunciate a clear message of direction. While that was possible, it provided less consistency of message rather than more. Most technical specialists did not achieve their rank by being good visionaries or big-picture thinkers. Moreover, the technical specialists had no person in the line and staff organization to go to if there was a problem or a success.

With all of the forces acting on NRCS, Rob often encountered poor planning, poor design or poor behavior. This was foreign to him and there was not an obvious person to hold accountable for the repair or training that was needed. Since almost all of the supervision resided with the Basin Team Leader (BTL), Rob would dutifully report to that person. However in many of the field offices, there was no day to day supervision, so any dedicated slackers were allowed to increase their slacking skills. Those who liked to get things done, and done correctly, had more work than they could handle, but no authority to help prioritize work.

Rob had been very proud of the product and process delivered by the area and field offices in eastern Oregon. He was proud of the technical rigor and the reputation of NRCS. Now, reorganization had changed the structure in which he worked, and the satisfaction of getting good conservation 'on the ground' was less.

A problem similar to Rob's was encountered by the SWCD Board of Directors. Prior to the Oregon reorganization, a District Conservationist attended all of the District meetings, provided an NRCS activities report, and brought any message or emphasis the board needed delivered back to the 'line and staff' hierarchy of the agency. In the two years Rob had been away, many of the SWCD's had grown weary of the reorganized structure, and felt ignored by NRCS. Several of the SWCD board meetings Rob attended resulted in his having to defend NRCS and their priorities. Instead of an SWCD welcoming the description of the latest engineering project for one of their farmers, the SWCDs were less trusting of the NRCS. They didn't always feel they were a full partner in concert with the Federal agency. With that strength lost, any project that didn't go perfectly became "NRCS's project."

To be fair, not all of the chaos was related to the local or national reorganization efforts in NRCS. Many things were changing quickly on the Oregon natural resources scene. President Clinton's forest plan was enacted in 1992, and as it became fully implemented, logging on public land essentially ceased. Since the removal of logs from public land both employed citizens and brought money to the County from the Federal Government, local governments in timber communities suffered financially.

In 1997 Rob and Dianna had bought a manufactured home plopped down on 20 acres of second-growth firs on the north slope of a steep hillside overlooking the confusingly named Parrot Creek, outside Roseburg's city limits. The sun didn't hit the house on clear winter days and given the 40 inches plus of annual precipitation in the area, there were not that many clear days. The poison oak grew at least as fast as the firs and alder, and the heavy clay soil stuck to everything when it was wet, which was most of the time. The ongoing family joke was that walking to the house across the bare soil that made up the front yard provided you the extra benefit of being six inches taller when you reached the garage.

The hillside was a marvelous laboratory for studying hydrology, landslides, and the impact of roads and houses on runoff processes. Similarly, vegetation patterns changed rapidly in the Roseburg climate, unlike the deserts of eastern Oregon. From a technical and scholarly standpoint, Rob was in heaven. Many weekends were spent wandering through the trees and brush watching how soil and water moved around. Similarly the gravel roads of the subdivision distinctly changed the runoff patterns, and Rob being fresh from writing a thesis on this very topic, the questions came at a rate that far outstripped the answers.

The hill-slope hydrology and forest succession journal articles that he had read in school finally connected with real events, as most of that research had been conducted west of the Cascade Mountains

213

in Washington and Oregon. The apex of the advantages to this steep north hillside laboratory came when Rob's parents visited. Neil was completely immersed in the issues and politics of sustainable forestry practices in context of forest health and the endangered species act. Father and son wandered through the second growth on the Roseburg hillside with endless new technical things to discuss. Both father and son were natural resource professionals who were dealing with similar issues, arguably from opposite ends of the same telescope—national and local.

At the time, Rob just enjoyed debating everything from big-picture politics to the mechanics of soil erosion with his Dad. But maybe the intersection of Rob and Neil's profession wasn't as unlikely under examination as it seemed on the surface. The combination of destiny, nurture and serendipity that makes up anyone's professional life is certainly unseen and not understood in the moment. Even in retrospect the unseen forces that buffet someone's career choices cannot be completely understood or articulated.

There was no possibility that rainy Roseburg was a long-term stop; both Rob and Dianna Sampson thought of themselves as desert people by nature. Yet even Rob's scientific playpen on the hill could not reverse the decline in his family's morale. The climate of no sun and lots of rain were one problem. The politics of a timber economy in drastic decline was another. The local government's regressive stance on almost every type of conservation or sustainable management added a third factor. Rob's low level of job satisfaction added to the overall notion that Roseburg and maybe even NRCS didn't play into his long term plans.

41

Listed Fish and Watershed Councils

"Oregon knew the potential power of the SWCD's. . . but felt a broader coalition would be needed to solve the seemingly intractable salmon recovery problem."

Almost simultaneously, the Columbia River Chinook and Coastal Coho Salmon were listed as Endangered under the Endangered Species Act (ESA), joining the Spotted Owl. Many small timber and fishing communities of west Oregon were devastated, and felt disproportionately singled out. Often, Federal officials got an earful of opinions when they ventured out to engage the public.

The salmon were a special case. They lived part of their life in the fresh waters of inland streams, then swam to the ocean, only to return to those streams at the end of their life to spawn the next generation of fish. Little did the salmon know that when they crossed from fresh to salt water, they changed jurisdiction from the US Fish and Wildlife Service (USFWS) under the Department of Interior, to the Department of Commerce and their National Marine Fisheries Service (NMFS) under the National Oceanic and Atmospheric Agency, NOAA.

While this distinction made no difference to the fish, it was not missed by the citizens of western Oregon. Early on, the federal government had decided that NOAA-NMFS would lead the effort to protect the endangered salmon, but the two agencies would still have to interact despite the fact that they came from very different institutional cultures. NMFS enforced the Endangered Species Act for fishes, shellfish and corals, as well as marine mammals under the

Marine Mammal Protection Act. The USFWS managed ESA-listed birds, plants, amphibians and mammals. NMFS had a long history of dealing with international treaties and the powerful US commercial fishing lobby, so the agency kept in close touch with in-house and Department of Justice lawyers. This skill showed when they were confronted at meetings with the public.

By contrast, the USFWS biologists were very good at dealing with ESA and determining critical habitat for a variety of plant and animal species. USFWS was arguably better than NMFS in looking for the 'art of the possible' when dealing with private landowners. Suffice to say that private landowners, local governments, and other Federal agencies who witnessed the two very different agencies administer the ESA saw two very different styles. The local citizens were often given multiple interpretations of the laws and rules, and that frustrated groups like the SWCDs that saw themselves as the bridge between environmental protection and private property rights.

As if the SWCDs in Oregon were not already feeling buffeted by all the changes in laws, rules, regulations and Federal stances, the state of Oregon was moving very quickly to participate in the management of streams and rivers to assist with the ESA listed species, as well as to somehow fix the rift between the general public, the timber industry and the Federal land management agencies. Governor John Kitzhaber didn't feel like there were high levels of collaboration or leadership at the local level, and the state had invested a great deal of effort in the Oregon Salmon Plan to help manage streams and rivers to increase the number of Chinook and Coho.

Oregon knew the potential power of the SWCD's and supported them in significant ways, but felt a broader coalition would be needed to solve the seemingly intractable salmon recovery problem In the 1993-1995 biennial budget, Oregon provided $10 Million to the Governor's Watershed Enhancement Board (GWEB) to support local Watershed Councils modeled after the Northwest Power Planning Council's efforts with the Grande Ronde Model Watershed. [13]

---

[13] From the Oregon Association of Conservation Districts, accessed 3/6/13: http://www.oacd.org/partnersoweb.shtml

GWEB funding had been a major input into SWCD programs and projects. To them it felt like the Watershed Councils were a duplication of effort.

Watershed Councils were authorized in Oregon in 1995 by HB 2441. That law was clear that the legitimacy of the Council was bestowed by local, county level officials. These groups of local citizens and agency representatives that made up the new Watershed Council were eager to provide a local influence and leadership to untie the Gordian knot that was endangered species.

Their enthusiasm was not enough to sustain forward motion, however. Local landowners were leery of the inclusion of environmental advocates on the watershed councils, as well as some of complex theories of ecology, biology and functional watersheds brought by some to the Council

Some SWCD's tried to become recognized as the local Watershed Council, and this worked to some extent in the eastern part of Oregon where most of the population was rural and ESA species concerns did not dominate the agenda quite as heavily as in western Oregon. For the most part however, the Oregon Districts could not bring a diversified enough group to the watershed council. Without representation of advocacy groups as well as user and consumer groups, most 'collaborative solutions' were doomed to failure.

If the Councils were divorced from the SWCD, they had no method to talk to private land managers and hear what was broke, what was not, and what was working in the form of local watershed management. Similarly, who would these Councils tap for technical advice that had enough local flavor to be palatable by the citizens?

As Rob had seen at many junctures in his career, strong technical assistance in the form of advice, designs and technical resources such as specifications for conservation practices, were often limiting factors in the conservation planning and delivery system. There simply were not that many people trained to assist private land managers making complex decisions about natural resources.

NRCS training, both the formal kind and the unspoken mentoring, provided several generations of agency personnel trained in the art of communicating technical ideas in ways that allowed people to envision what they were talking about. Similarly, an NRCS employee is trained in helping land managers hear about what is in it for them. Though most Oregon farmers and ranchers have a strong respect and even love for salmon, it doesn't do anyone any good if the management practice proposed to them is sold simply with the benefits of good intentions.

If the management proposal is untenable or obviously proposed by someone who doesn't understand the lifestyle in that particular region, there is no incentive for landowners to cast about trying things that come from a dubious source. What good would it do to financially break the ranch and have it sold to a corporation somewhere if the goal is good stewardship, local control and local partnerships?

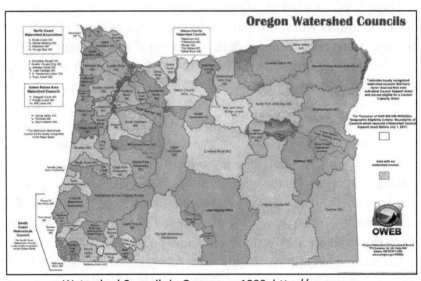

Watershed Councils in Oregon, c. 1999. http://www.oregon.gov/oweb/pages/watershed_council_contacts.aspx#Map_Disclaimer

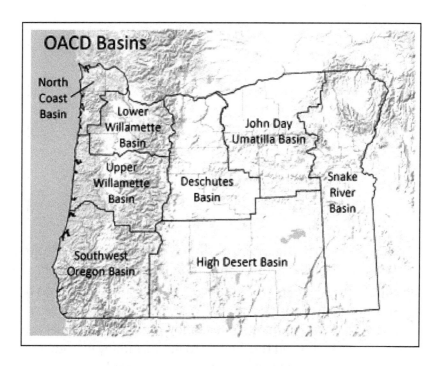

Groups of Conservation Districts in Oregon organized along the same basins as NRCS. Note each basin has multiple, individual soil conservation districts within its boundaries.

42

Wetlands Reserve Program

*"That WRP limitation on production presented NRCS
a very different type of interaction with the landowner."*

The 1990 Farm Bill authorized the Wetlands Reserve Program (WRP). In essence, WRP paid for the wetland and development rights in perpetuity on a wetland that had been converted to grow an agricultural commodity. The easement was held by the NRCS. This was a very appealing proposition to some landowners and to Conservation groups because it allowed the agency to put its money into good projects that were forward thinking rather than a simply a 'remedy' for a problem or poor management that already existed.

However, the notion and mechanics of a conservation easement that NRCS controlled was foreign to the agency. Conservation Reserve Program (CRP) had paid a landowner to remove acreage from production and plant those acres to trees or grass. But that contract was only for 10 years, with the landowner receiving an annual payment on a per-acre basis. And the landowner was responsible for maintenance on the field. NRCS visited the land each year to see if reseeding, or weed control or burning was necessary, and if work needed to be done on a CRP field, NRCS could hold up the rental payment if they needed to provide more 'incentive' to a landowner.

In contrast, WRP paid a lump sum at the beginning of the perpetual easement. WRP also paid 100% of the costs of rehabilitation efforts designed to reverse the drainage of the wetland. Drainage ditches were blocked off or obliterated, wetland plants were planted and dikes and levees were removed or breached. The title to the land remained with the landowner, but no activities were allowed that would produce an agricultural commodity.

That WRP limitation on production presented NRCS with a very different type of interaction with the landowner. Rather than deciding on conservation practices that fit into an agricultural operation, WRP restoration practices were conceived by the NRCS, and presented to the landowner for approval. Since NRCS was paying the entire cost of the restoration practices AND paying for the land, the landowner had little incentive to actively participate. Often the landowner had very little interest in how the wetland was restored or what form the wetland ultimately took.

By contrast, partner agencies such as US Fish and Wildlife Service, the State Fish and Game and local conservancy groups like Trout Unlimited or the Nature Conservancy took great interest in the type of practices proposed for wetland restoration. The decision on the best practices lay with NRCS, with a host of special-interest groups trying to influence the outcome in their constituencies' favor. So NRCS was left with a balancing act of listening to outside groups, trying to do the right thing for the wetland, and using the WRP restoration funds effectively.

So WRP became the proving grounds for NRCS technical people to conceive and defend restoration plans--one of NRCS's brightest spots of interagency coordination, as well as partnering with resource groups like Trout Unlimited. The relationships with the State Fish and Game Department and the Federal biological agencies built trust amongst the players from all sides. This trust could ideally be parlayed into some good will with the SWCD, and in a perfect world between the local Watershed Council, the SWCD, NRCS and conservation advocacy groups. It is only slightly ironic that this strong collaborative program for NRCS isolated their one constituent they were most proud of: the landowner. Particularly on perpetual easements, most landowners cashed the check, and headed off for their next career.

Some Counties and user groups like the Cattleman's Association did not think turning farmlands or pasturelands back into wetlands was a great idea. That was particularly true for Counties in northern Idaho where farming perpetually wet ground was a struggle. Boundary County adjacent to the Canadian border in Idaho even passed a resolution limiting the size and extent of a WRP easement on a single farm. The irony of a County that espoused freedom and land-rights at every turn limiting a private landowner's right to sell their property was not lost on some. In some ways the tone and tenor of the argument was similar to Neil's experience documenting conversion of prime farmland in southwest Idaho.

43

Boise, Part I

"Because of his interest in the physical science that shaped streams, rivers and wetlands, Rob was assigned many of the more difficult stream restoration or streambank stabilization projects."

Oregon NRCS had paid for Rob to go to school and he felt both gratitude and debt to them. Then, similar to the Graduate Studies program announcement that turned into over two years in graduate school, an unforeseen announcement for the job of NRCS State Design Engineer in Boise, Idaho arrived. This presented Rob with a serious professional conundrum. He had worked at the Roseburg job for the one year required by the service agreement he had signed with Oregon NRCS, but leaving the state after 14 months was hardly a great display of gratitude. He was still indebted to the Department of Agriculture to work for them for seven years to pay back the time taken for graduate school. So if he did want to escape Oregon and Roseburg, he had to take a job within USDA, and if he wanted to select that job on his own terms, the Idaho job was a Godsend.

Idaho had moved all of the State Office engineers out to field offices under the theory of providing more localized service. Unfortunately this left only the State Conservation Engineer to administer policy, quality control, and to be responsible for the difficult projects that were designed by field engineers. Seeing that technical quality and oversight could suffer, Luana Kiger, Idaho State Conservationist and Art Shoemaker, State Conservation Engineer, decided that the State Design Engineer position should be reestablished in the Boise State Office.

The Idaho state design engineer had been long held (about 30 years) by Karl Larson, who retired in 1993. A tall and gangly 'engineer's engineer,' Karl had always been an icon to Rob. Karl's designs were elegant. There were never any false leads or dead ends. The calculations flowed from beginning to end just as surely as a symphony. Sketches drawn in the margins to assist in visualizing the math in the main body of the sheets were clear and almost art-like.

Whenever Rob had called the Idaho state office in a panic, most often it was Karl that talked him through the answer. How could Rob have the unbridled temerity to step into Karl's shoes? Karl had been the face of engineering design in Idaho NRCS for a couple of generations.

Art Shoemaker had grown up on a farming and ranching operation out of Weiser, Idaho, studied engineering at the University of Idaho and was a lifelong SCS-er. Art had been the assistant state engineer when Rob started as a student trainee, and thus was firmly cemented in the young engineers mind as the source of authority and technical knowledge. But there was more than that. Shoemaker was technically oriented. He saw the lead engineer position as providing technical oversight first and foremost. Art thought that if you got the project technically correct, the administrative and political issues would resolve themselves.

This priority was almost opposite of the reorganized Oregon NRCS where emphasis was placed on using the buzz words of 'partnerships,' 'coalition,' 'teamwork' and 'leveraging alliances' at every turn.

Idaho, although reorganized to some extent, still had a 'get it done' attitude that put a higher priority on good technical planning. Art Shoemaker embodied this attitude, and so did the most of the state office technical specialists. These technical staff were highly educated as well as experienced—and they understood that the grandest idea, if presented with complex words and nuance, would never become a reality, because few landowners would accept the concept and it wouldn't be obvious what the next, tactical step would be.

The newly established State Design Engineer position would provide the majority of engineering input to this team of an agronomist, geologist, soil scientist, range conservationist, water quality specialist, biologist and an economist.

Rob had a great respect for these technical specialists and even greater respect for Art Shoemaker. The career choice he faced was pretty clear: continue to struggle as a one-person technical specialist in an atmosphere of mistrust and low teamwork levels, or join a cadre of specialists who prided their technical skills over all else. That second choice also meant he could work under a technically superior boss, instead of people intent on marketing, buzz words, and constantly shifting priorities.

Rob and Dianna Sampson moved to Boise, Idaho at the end of 1998. The house on the hill at Roseburg had not sold, but they were ready to get on with another phase of their lives. Cresting the Cascade mountains headed east had always provided a stark contrast, as the cedar and hemlock and steep streams and waterfalls give way to drier fir and pine forests. Clouds and mist give way to a brighter, sunnier continental interior climate. And the high desert allows vistas that go on forever. No more claustrophobic, moss covered, wet, confining landscapes—just the Rocky Mountains, the Great Basin and dry desert.

The professional parallels to the climate and geography, particularly when described with as much bias and poetic license as done above, were obvious. Rob and Dianna's spirits were good and getting better as they crested the Cascades, and headed east to Boise.

Rob reported to NRCS in Boise the first part of January, 1999. NRCS Idaho in 1999 was a complex and exciting place to work. The multidisciplinary technical team was working on the Wetland Reserve Program (WRP), as well as several State Agricultural Water Quality Projects (SAWQP). This State of Idaho program was instituted to provide a state-funded parallel to PL-566, federally funded watershed projects. Both of the programs had a focus on large-scale land treatment measures such as conservation tillage, terraces, and irrigation water management, rather than relying on larger structural measures to address water quality and quantity problems.

These projects were administered through the State Soil Conservation Commission, with assistance from the Idaho Association of Conservation Districts, and were planned to blend Federal and State cost share and incentive payments to farmers in a seamless manner.

NRCS and State employees used the PL-566 framework, in which the ultimate planning document was thorough enough to be used as an Environmental Assessment that met the regulations of the National Environmental Policy Act, or NEPA. This document included sections on all the natural resources of the planning area, such as soils and hydrology. There was also a significant inventory of the natural resource concerns that agriculture faced, such as water shortages or unsustainable crop rotations. It also included a significant public comment and input section.

These planning efforts had changed little from when Neil was working as the dryland erosion control specialist in Idaho Falls in the mid 1960's. The planning process was exhaustive, and detail oriented. The ideal result was robust planning that led to implementation of the correct conservation practices on individual farms and ranches. Rather than a random batch of practices, it provided a targeted solution to some of the resource problems.

Good conservation planning, after all, is getting the right practices in the right place to positively impact a larger outcome, such as less erosion that leads to less sedimentation, that leads to overall improved water quality. Much of this is detailed, one-on-one discussions with the land managers. No shortcuts worked, the time had to be invested to get the trust, so you got the whole story.

The planning process, particularly at a watershed-scale is not flashy, and leads to rather dull headlines. Implementing plans that attempted to target entire sub-watersheds was a labor of persistence at the field office level. If the plan had the correct analysis and conclusions, real change happened on the landscape. Almost every farm plan and large group plan that Rob saw fall apart could be traced back to either not following the planning process or focusing too hard on a single issue.

Contrast this to Rob's experience in Oregon during the infancy of the formation of watershed councils and planning for the endangered salmon and steelhead. The community councils that formed in response to Oregon's legislation understood their charge: improve conditions in the watersheds for salmon and steelhead by improving the overall function of the watershed. Improve agricultural practices so that they complimented salmon recovery or the often bandied-about term of 'watershed health'. The State had a state-wide recovery plan for endangered species, which was a good solid effort at the statewide policy level. Yet, comprehensive plans that were conceived at a correct scale—so the plans were both functional enough to implement at the individual farm and far-reaching enough to have an impact over a larger drainage—were lacking.

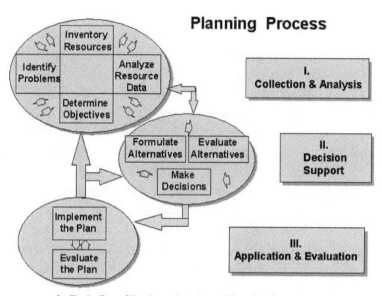

Planning Process

An illustration of the dynamic nature of the planning process.

The newly formed watershed councils did *not* have experience in planning and analysis or in comprehending and synthesizing input from a variety of technical specialists. Put simply, the Councils had no institutional knowledge, just a mandate from the state to make things better, be inclusive of all resource user groups, and do this at a scale that included multiple land ownerships, different land uses, and a cacophony of environmental organizations and regulatory agencies that each had a very narrow focus of interest and expertise.

The difference that Rob experienced seemed to be rooted in basic philosophy: Was good natural resource stewardship and positive outcome grounded in grandiose and complex conceptual thought or was it the product of basic technical efforts and thorough, consistent on-the-ground planning working one-on-one with the land managers?

Given Rob's love of field work, his tilt towards the latter is obvious. But it is also the method that was observed to work much more frequently.

Arriving at Boise inevitably felt like old-home week to Rob. Working with Art Shoemaker again was stimulating and refreshing, since the project assignments delegated to the new State Design Engineer were difficult and high-profile. But they were also mostly well-defined and achievable.

The caliber of the technical staff was high and many of the faces were familiar. The Agronomist, Ralph Fisher, had been one of Rob's trainers during his student trainee time in Boise. The Engineering Geologist, Terril Stevenson, was also a second-generation NRCS employee, and technically as good as they come at watershed-scale planning. Jim Cornwell, the Range Conservationist, Biologist Frank Fink, and Denis Feichtinger, the Economist, had top notch technical skills. Neil Peterson, Soil Scientist, Ron Abramovich, snow survey Hydrologist, and project planner John Kendrick rounded out the talented crowd. Chris Hoag, a Wetland Plant Ecologist was one of the few specialists Rob didn't know, but soon came to like and immensely respect. All of these NRCS employees, with the exception of Terril's 10 years with the Bureau of Reclamation, had worked their entire career with the SCS and NRCS.

The technical staff still did watershed-scale planning, and a majority of the staff was very talented at the art. Idaho NRCS partnered with State partners and blended the PL-566 program and the State-funded Agricultural Water Quality Program (SAWQP). The Environmental Quality Enhancement Program (EQIP) was also used to implementing the plans that were written.

Plans were motivated and ordered by local Soil Conservation District priorities and the newly-active phases of the Federal Clean Water Act (CWA) to allocate non-point source pollution loading and write a corrective action plan that proposed methods of achieving these pollution levels, called Total Daily Maximum Loads (TMDLs). Although these efforts at planning were mostly harmonious, they were not perfect; but the procedure was very familiar to Rob, and it made sense to him.

Because of his interest in the physical science that shaped streams, rivers and wetlands, Rob was assigned many of the more difficult stream restoration or streambank stabilization projects. Idaho, like Oregon, had experienced flooding of historic proportions in late 1996 and 1997. Many rivers in Idaho, such as the Potlatch, St. Maries and Little Salmon were completely rearranged, along with any houses or buildings that were close. Thanks to Terril's and Art's efforts, as well as the rest of Idaho NRCS, most of the emergency situations were dealt with by the time Rob arrived. But several projects had moved along more slowly and these became the province of the new Design Engineer.

44

Lawyer Creek

"...without some predictive capability, the argument about
how to stop the floods and damage in Kamiah
is left to coffee shop rhetoric."

Lawyer Creek drains a large portion of the Camas Prairie in central Idaho near the town of Grangeville. This 215-square mile drainage empties into the South Fork of the Clearwater River at the town of Kamiah (kam-ee-eye). Kamiah itself is a little over 20 miles upriver from Orofino, where Neil worked in the 1960s. The town is perched on the alluvial fan of Lawyer Creek, the domed pile of gravel, cobble and other sediment that comes out of the steep canyons and deposits on the flatter land near the confluence with another stream.

Alluvial fans are a mounded landform. As the stream deposits sediment around the channel the fan builds up, making the grade of the valley and the stream flatter and flatter. At some point the stream fills up its primary channel with rocks and soil and moves to a lower, steeper part of the fan and starts the process anew. In this way, the channel shifts back and forth across the fan building different parts at different times.

In the South Fork Clearwater canyon flat spots are at a premium, so the fact that the town is built on the fan is not surprising. Similarly, the fact that the town gets damaged by floodwater and erosion occasionally should not surprise too many people. Shifting channels are how the flat spot got there in the first place.

None of this esoteric talk of fans and shifting channels is of any comfort if it was your house that got washed away. The experience is terrifying, and most people would look for the town, county, state or Federal Government to try and help them, and possibly to keep the event from happening again. A popular outcry from the Kamiah citizens and others was that farming practices on the Camas Prairie, several thousand feet in elevation above them, had increased the runoff, causing more sediment to come down with the flood and making things much worse.

Many of the folks living at the mouth of Lawyer Creek suggested that the farmers above should start to farm in a way that kept the water up on the higher ground. To a certain extent this was a logical argument. The local NRCS technical guide is full of practice descriptions that minimize surface runoff and erosion. Planting the correct sequence of crops, and leaving the crop residue on the surface of the ground are well known practices to minimize erosion and runoff. Similarly, long level ditches, called terraces, can be built on the contours of the farm field to detain surface runoff, and small dams can be installed across gullies to have a similar effect.

Rob's cursory glance at the farm fields on the higher ground of the Prairie suggested there were some things that could be improved. A popular practice on this higher farm ground was to dig small ditches in the field's low spots to remove the surface water faster and to dry the field earlier in the spring so that it could be planted. This practice increases the speed of runoff delivery to the streams and could increase peak flows in Lawyer Creek, leaving the town of Kamiah to possibly bear the burden of higher floods.

Moreover, there was no consistent practice of leaving wheat stubble or other crop residues on the surface of the fields over the winter. Some farmers burned the stubble in the fall and let the field sit bare over the winter. A crop such as winter wheat can be planted in the fall if there is adequate soil moisture and this crop sprouts prior to winter providing some erosion protection. The more crop residue left on a field, the longer the moisture is retained in the soil the next spring. But this creates both good and bad results. If it was a wet spring this delayed planting of spring grains. The added residue acts as an insulator, keeping soil temperature cool, and delaying seed sprout which limits yield.

Some farmers applied conservation tillage and some contour terraces had been built and these were helpful at delaying runoff. Similarly, some small dams had been built across gullies to retain runoff.

The conservation challenges on Camas Prairie were well known to the Conservation District and NRCS. Along with the farmers, all had been working on improving conservation for the last 50 to 75 years, but the floods kept happening. A conservation practice installation is voluntary. NRCS and the Conservation District write a farm conservation plan at the request of a landowner, who then implements the plan as he or she can. A farm sale to a new owner, a shift in commodity prices or even a change in national crop insurance rules can force a change in farming practices that resets the efforts at soil and water conservation. So it isn't surprising that in the effort to keep a farm profitable in a complicated mix of economic factors, a farmer may not allow soil and water conservation to drive every decision.

Short of an immense experiment to implement all of the conservation practices across a vast region of the farm ground around Grangeville and Nez Perce, it was impossible to argue what the correct solution to Kamiah's flooding should be. There was very little way to quantitatively prove who was right or wrong about the sources of the flooding and how future damage to Kamiah could be minimized. Also, without some predictive capability, the argument about how to stop the floods and damage in Kamiah is left to coffee shop rhetoric.

NRCS, working through the Idaho and Lewis Soil Conservation Districts as well as local non-governmental organizations and groups like Clearwater Focus, offered their assistance. Using a hydrologic model and Geographic Information Systems (GIS, a computer database of maps and data), NRCS simulated different storms occurring on a wide variety of plant cover types including the imaginary, modeled installation of conservation practices over a large percentage of the Prairie cropland.

The range of answers and the results of the modeling effort were surprising. Lawyer Creek is a long, narrow catchment with steep, short tributaries. Although the soils on the Prairie are relatively deep, they have substantial clay content, and in many cases a harder, less permeable layer at two to four feet below the surface.

It turned out that almost nothing could be done on the farmland to change the peak flows that arrive at Kamiah. Changing the cropping pattern, adding conservation tillage, installing terraces and constructing small dams across gullies reduced the peak flow by about 15%. Planting the entire acreage of cropland on Camas Prairie to grass could lower the peak flow by about 25%, but the stream still has adequate power to move any size of rock found in the stream channel.

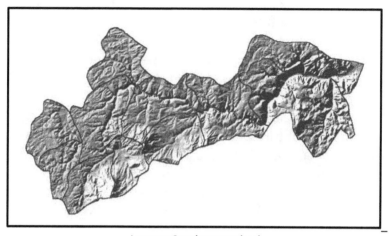

Lawyer Creek watershed.
Flow is generally left to right.
Kamiah is at the very right hand side of the picture.

To check the most extreme situation, the computerized hydrologic model was instructed that a dam had been installed in a tributary to Lawyer Creek. This imaginary dam held 100% of the storm runoff from the cropland above. Then this type of dam was modeled as installed on *three* of the seven tributaries to Lawyer Creek.

Again, although runoff was nonexistent from almost half the tributaries, the peak flow was only 20% lower, and the modeled flood and subsequent sediment deposition would still wreak havoc in Kamiah.

Breaking this news to the citizens of Kamiah was a little tricky. Models of any sort are not well understood by the public. Most are seen as giant black boxes that can produce any answer the modeler wants. Models have uncertainty, and a conscientious user has to explain the uncertainty along with the results. This uncertainty often sounds like the answers are guesses to the average listener.

A public meeting was held in the senior center in Kamiah. Rob went and showed the results of the model. His luck was good that day. Although Rob had not worked directly with the citizens of Kamiah in achieving the model results, he walked into a room with one of his former college professors at the University of Idaho. Dr. James Milligan had been the Civil Engineering Department Chair and an instructor in the hydraulics of open channels. Rob had taken that class his senior year. After presenting the model results and trying to use plain language to describe the complicated model and equally complicated hydrologic physics, Rob paused, turned to the last slide and asked the question he had worried about for the last week. "Are there any questions?"

Every head swiveled towards Dr. Milligan, who sat still in his chair except for a slight upturn of the mouth and a slight nod of the head. One of the citizen leaders paused for a moment, glanced again at Milligan then turned to Rob. "Dr. Milligan has been describing the same thing to us now for several meetings." There were no more questions or comments except those about future strategies and actions.

What should the Kamiah citizens do now? That is a harder question to answer. Citizens wanted to be able to bulldoze the rocks out of the existing channel and keep the current location as the main channel. After all, that is where the bridges are, and it doesn't do any good for the stream to not go under the bridges.

In the era of the Endangered Species Act (ESA) this action, at minimum, required a permit from the Corps of Engineers along with consultation with the National Marine Fisheries Service (NMFS). The effort with NMFS could involve the development of a Biologic Assessment (BA). The BA would describe in painstaking detail how the channel (re)construction would be done and the impact on Steelhead and Salmon habitat. Then the BA would be reviewed by NMFS and provided for comment to Idaho Fish and Game, US Fish and Wildlife Service, environmental groups and the public at large. All public comments must be addressed by the author of the BA, regardless of their weight, insight or validity.

This process is easy to derail. No one is in the wrong in this exercise; this is what the Act requires. It suffices to say that preparation of a Biological Assessment is out of the range of most County budgets and expertise. And bulldozing doesn't work in the long run. The channel is generally made too wide, as the popular thought is that more storage for gravel means longer times between maintenance actions. The wide channel however, means shallow flows and without deep water, the rocks drop out during all of the little storms. When a big storm comes, the oversized channel holds all the water but with no connection to a floodplain, the stress is too great and the bed and banks erode. This erosion means the channel will probably jump to a new location at some point.

As of 2013, Kamiah had not completed any flood mitigation provisions. There is very little they *can* do. Working in rural areas, Rob always found the hardest thing to tell a landowner is they were involved in the wrong land use for the location. Kamiah is virtually indefensible.

An old dairy along a creek that used to enjoy an annual cleanout of the pens during high water isn't viable if real pollution measures are required. Sitting at a kitchen table, talking to an elderly couple who are both crying is difficult. Sitting in a grange hall and explaining why flooding is inevitable, almost regardless of any act of engineering, is uncomfortable. But someone should, and the agency that manages no land of its own, and an employee with some credibility with the locals might be the best to deliver the word.

45

Big Canyon Creek

*"Telling a landowner that their house was in the wrong place
to coexist with a stream channel is difficult at best.
Landowners are often very attached to living by a stream."*

A story much like that of Lawyer Creek emerged from Idaho NRCS efforts on Big Canyon Creek. Yet, despite some similarities, the outcome at Big Canyon was different.

Big Canyon Creek drains an area north of Lawyer Creek and shares a watershed divide in some spots. Big Canyon Creek empties into the Clearwater River about 10 miles downstream from Orofino, Neil's posting in the 1960s. In 1996 and 1997, the Pacific Northwest experienced record flooding when rain, falling on an already warm snowpack, caused very large volumes of runoff.

Rain-on-snow flooding is a unique combination of hydrologic events. La Niña ocean currents push large amounts of moisture from the South Pacific up to the Northwest, often blanketing low and mid elevations with moisture-laden snow. As these storms gain energy, the snow changes to rain. The rain and the warmer temperatures from this 'Pineapple Express' result in floods much larger than that of a typical snowmelt runoff. Significant channel shifts and high amounts of streambank erosion in the lower-elevation streams often happen during these floods.

Big Canyon Creek is an ideal drainage for rain on snow flooding. Its watershed is large (227 square miles), and much of the catchment is at elevations lower than 4,000 feet. The slopes are steep, and the watershed is long and narrow with very short tributary channels. This combination of elevation and geometry funnels runoff very quickly to the main channel, where the community of Peck, Idaho straddles the lower reaches of the creek as it empties into the Clearwater River.

These large flows move very high amounts of cobble and gravel as stream bedload (in other words, sediment rolling along the bottom of the channel). The gravel and sand deposit in the channel as the flood recedes, and typically this would construct an alluvial fan similar to the one that Kamiah occupies.

However, since Big Canyon Creek is truly in a canyon, the typical fan shape is not formed. The location of the stream does shift as the water continually tries to find the steepest channel. This feature creates excellent spawning habitat for Steelhead trout, as there are usually fresh, well-sorted gravels, but also makes for very unpredictable river behavior.

A typical response by most counties after a flood is to try and remove the gravel deposits in the channel. The Nez Perce County road department mobilized a bulldozer just after the 1997 floods. The bulldozer started to push cobble and gravel from side-to-side in the channel resulting in a broad parabolic channel with cobble and gravel levees on both sides. Despite this being a typical practice, the cultural landscape had changed since the last time the channel was bulldozed. Steelhead trout were listed in 1997 as 'Threatened' under the Endangered Species Act. When the National Marine Fisheries Service (NMFS), the agency designated to protect threatened Steelhead, heard that the habitat was being disturbed they issued a cease and desist order to the County.

This left a frustrated County road department, and some very nervous homeowners, worried about what might happen during the next flood with the stream channel only partially cleaned.

Rivers and communities often have an uneasy existence with each other. In the case of Peck, the stream valley bottom is the only place flat enough for humans to live and build their infrastructure. Unfortunately, if flooding is controlled and forced to stay in the channel through the construction of levees, the forces are far too high for the existing bed and bank material to withstand. Conversely, if no levees are built, the stream regularly floods the people and structures built on the floodplain. Add to this the relatively steep (1 to 2 percent) channel and the large amounts of available bedload, and not only does the channel flood, but it often avulses[14] to a new channel location. This unpredictable behavior mobilizes the citizens to 'do something'.

'Something' generally takes the form of pushing the channel away from the homes and infrastructure, and an attempt to make the channel so big that the entire flood is contained. While channels can be made big enough to contain all the water, significant erosion and deposition will occur as the stream tries to move the sediments in the channel. As the channel fills with sediment, avulsion and flooding occur, arguably with worse results than if the channel had not been managed.

As a result of the 1997 flooding damage, the Nez Perce Soil and Water Conservation District (SWCD) obtained a grant from Federal Emergency Management Agency (FEMA) to repair the damage done on Big Canyon Creek. The SWCD requested the assistance of the Natural Resources Conservation Service (NRCS), and Rob was assigned the project.

NRCS started the project by collecting information about the stream, bridges, houses, levees and existing vegetation. Evidence from the data showed that these types of floods—and the resulting human actions to put the stream where it would not endanger houses and people—occurred fairly regularly. Similarly, it appeared that most of the human 'management' of the stream had probably made impacts from flooding and erosion worse.

The NRCS staff used an electronic transit (called a 'total station') to survey elevations and positions of the channel, the existing levees, the floodplain, homes and infrastructure. Using computer design software these elevations were mapped, and a very high resolution topographic map was developed. These data were then input into a hydraulic model that simulated the extent of flooding at different flows.

Two things became obvious. First was that there were several houses that were in locations indefensible to flooding or erosion. Second was that the channel, as a result of multiple bulldozing events, was

---

[14] Avulse means that the channel changes location abruptly and makes a new channel.

far too deep and wide and old remnant 'flood fight' levees exacerbated this problem. By the time the water got deep enough to flow out on the floodplain, and dissipate energy, there was far more force contained in the channel than the bed and banks could resist.

Using the information from the hydraulic model output, NRCS looked for an optimal combination of channel width and depth that would allow flood water to escape the channel onto a floodplain, move the expected sediment load in the channel, but not erode the bed and banks. The local NRCS field office set about trying to explain to the citizens of Peck what a stream might look like if it had access to a floodplain, yet still transported sediment in the channel. Unfortunately this included telling several landowners that their houses could not be defended regardless of anything NRCS did.

Telling a landowner that their house was in the wrong place to coexist with a stream channel is difficult at best. Landowners are often very attached to living by a stream. Similarly, most of the citizens of Peck had observed Big Canyon Creek for some time, and almost all had arrived at their own intuitive feel for how the creek could be managed. Unfortunately, stream behavior and hydraulics are often counter-intuitive, explaining why much of the stream 'management' that had occurred in the past had produced results that were opposite of those desired.

Ultimately, the County and SWCD purchased three properties that hydraulic models had shown to be the most susceptible to flooding and erosion. NRCS looked at the lower three miles of Big Canyon Creek that could be treated as a continuous stream reach, and began to formulate the project components.

Part of designing a stream modification project is to gather as much historic data as possible. The Lewiston and Orofino NRCS offices provided a wealth of this information as did the citizens of Peck. A picture looking up Big Canyon Creek from 1929 provided an excellent view of the channel and floodplain prior to the advent of large earthmoving machines.

The agency has always stressed the need for robust documentation of projects. There are the expected grumblings of 'just making paper' to put in the job file, but this folder fodder makes for a very good resource if you are trying to understand the history of a stream and a watershed. Documentation of past floods provides a great amount of support as the designer tries to understand the major forces at work and the practical way they can be counteracted.

The Big Canyon Creek project was implemented in 2000. The gravel levees were removed and hauled away, providing the stream access to its floodplain. Low rock weirs were installed to hydraulically narrow the low flow channel. Roughness elements such as the root ball of trees were anchored on the floodplain, and grasses and shrubs were planted. The remaining houses along the creek were generally protected from flooding but the landowners in some houses were informed of the risk of flooding.

In an attempt to complete the documentation at the end of the project, Rob looked for the same photo point to take a picture similar to one taken in 1965, another very bad year for rain on snow flooding. Finding a similar vantage point on the North side of the Clearwater River, Rob took the picture and for some reason decided to look on the back of the historic photo. In traditional agency fashion, a rubber stamp had been placed on the photo indicating the photographer, the date and other contextual information. Imagine his surprise to find that about 35 years prior, that photo had been taken by then District Conservationist Neil Sampson.

Big Canyon Creek, 1912 looking upstream

Big Canyon Creek, 1965 flood. Photo by Neil Sampson

Big Canyon Creek, 1996 Flood

Picture after project.
Truck is parked where a house once stood.
Gravel levees have been removed.

46

The Best Team

"The set of conservation practices that make up the alternatives
have to be explained to all of the participants,
local entities like road districts, and the politicians."

Rob's position at Idaho NRCS as State Design Engineer was challenging. Projects often had competing goals and uneven understanding of the natural resource concerns. Arriving at a project from out of town, and talking to the stakeholders and local technical folks while trying to build trust and fabricate a plausible set of alternatives is demanding.

If one alternative obviously will have the biggest positive impact on the natural resource concerns, the set of conservation practices that make up the alternative have to be explained to all of the participants, local entities like road districts, and the politicians. With the help of the NRCS Idaho technical team, and the great District Conservationists who ran the local offices, Rob got to travel the state and practice these skills. The jobs were similar to many of the conundrums faced as an Area Engineer, just larger in scale. Often, however, the stakes were higher in the form of damages if the selected conservation practices didn't work.

Since he had no supervisory responsibilities, Rob could concentrate on thinking about the science. With a talented group of other technical specialists, planning could truly be multi-disciplinary, generating more robust debates and more successful solutions. Working ing for Art Shoemaker was much better than Rob had imagined when he applied for the job. Art was steady and quiet, not saying much. When he did, his message generally was well thought out and had gravity. Art was always there to discuss a technical aspect to a project, or the method to analyze a set of alternatives, but he always let his staff have ownership in the solutions. He would, however, intervene if something looked like it might not work.

Art led by example, never asking his employees to do anything he would not do. In many cases he took some of the smaller, more distracting jobs so that his staff could concentrate on the bigger, more rewarding jobs. And Art had a great sense of humor, albeit dry as sand. You could get a full belly laugh out of him occasionally, but more likely was a very slight curl of the lip and look of total inner bemusement.

Terril Stevenson, the Idaho NRCS State Geologist was another reason Rob's job was so enjoyable. Terril was an NRCS legacy; her dad Jack Stevenson was a greatly respected Soil Mechanics Engineer as well as the Director of Engineering at the West Technical Center—and was the reason NRCS was a leader in the design and construction of earthfill dams. Although Terril had started her college education as an engineering student, she changed her major to Geology and spent the first part of her technical career with the Bureau of Reclamation (BOR) on their construction of Jordanelle and Upper Stillwater dams in Utah, among others.

Terril has immense skills in looking at landscapes as the sum of many parts. In that way of thinking, a good geologist is the perfect complement to a well-trained engineer. The engineer is trained in a process of narrowing down the factors that matter in the problem at hand. This allows a sharp focus on alternatives that will have the biggest impact on the identified problems. There are shortcomings to how engineers think about problems, however. If the objectives of the project are poorly defined, the solution an engineer comes up with could have unintended consequences or not fix the true underlying problems.

Geologist and geomorphologists put much of their professional energy into describing the physical processes that shape the form and function of the landscape they are observing. Observations, when first discovered, do not need to couple with one another. That linkage comes later, when the planner is trying to put all of the various physical processes in order.

The different methods of problem solving and analysis between geologists and engineers are quite complimentary to one another, if the two disciplines can communicate. This multi-disciplinary communication is strong in NRCS. Perhaps it is because at the field office level everyone has to understand all the positions, regardless of their job title. An engineer has to explain the parts of a published soil survey to a customer, and a range conservationist has to figure out pipe sizes when they are writing a conservation plan.

With Idaho NRCS's corporate culture of not being flashy and not getting too far from their core skills, and with the addition of a very high quality technical staff, Rob was quickly taken with his position and situation. This could be the last appointment of his career and he could well retire at Boise. Chris Hoag, Frank Fink, Jim Cornwell, Denis Feichtinger and John Kendrick all ended their career as State Office specialists, so working on the technical staff in Idaho must have had a great appeal or these top notch employees would have moved to work somewhere else.

Rob did want to travel as broadly as possible with NRCS, and he also wanted to train and teach. Art and then State Conservationist Rich Sims seemed willing to allow an excursion every now and then, and Rob kept his eyes peeled for opportunities.

At the request of the Hawai'i NRCS, Rob travelled to teach stream mechanics and work on the Big Island at a very special place on the north end called Waipi'o Valley. He was joined by his soon-to-be great friend and long time technical partner, Janine Castro, a fluvial geomorphologist. Janine had gotten her doctorate at Oregon State while working with the NRCS technical center in Portland. Rob had met her when he worked in Roseburg, where the two stream experts had loudly tested each other's skills and knowledge. Although this rigorous debate was as much about ego and educational hubris as anything, Rob and Janine ended up working together on many Oregon projects. When Rob left Oregon, she was one of the people he missed, so the opportunity to work with her in Hawai'i sounded great. Rob would learn later that it was Janine who had suggested his name to Hawai'i NRCS, and that without her good words, his trip to the islands wouldn't have happened.

The north end of the Big Island is very wet and steep. Waipi'o Valley is a small confined valley at sea level where native Hawaiians had grown taro root for many generations. Above the steep slopes was flatter cropland where several big sugar cane plantations had been located. Almost all sugarcane farming in Hawai'i had ceased, as the manual labor to harvest the cane became scarce. These cane farms had also diverted all of the headwaters of Wailoa stream for irrigation, and this had minimized the streamflow in Waipi'o.

This PL-566 funded watershed project was examining what would happen as the water distribution system from the now vacated sugar cane fields was dismantled. Putting the water back in the stream channel through Waipi'o would probably cause some major changes in Wailoa stream, and Janine and Rob were called on to develop a work-plan to analyze what these changes might be. Learning about the traditional cultivation of Taro and the diversion structures used to get water into the ditches feeding the lo'i basins was a great experience.

Working in the islands is exciting for any natural resource specialist. Lack of connection to a continent makes soils, plants, and even the humans evolve differently; and islands often have strong gradients in precipitation and storm patterns. Kona, on the windward side of the Big Island, gets about 10 inches of precipitation in a year, while Hilo, on the leeward side, receives more than 100. Volcanoes National Park on the top of the island between the two cities receives a whopping 200 inches of rain a year!

For a hydrologist and a person interested in stream behavior, each island is a fascinating puzzle to unravel. The relatively small size, the steep gradients, and the isolation are boundaries that sometimes makes answering scientific questions easier.

Later, Janine and Rob travelled to Alaska to teach a class and provide technical assistance on several projects. The State Conservation Engineer, Jay Cobb, had been Rob's counterpart across the Wyoming state line when Rob was in Rexburg. In those days they would meet in Jackson Hole for lunch under the auspices of making sure the Irrigation Guides were similar across the two state's borders. Jay had also been in the same NPEG three-week training that Rob had been in.

It was great to see Jay again, and Janine and Rob found their teaching styles complimentary. Their three day class in stream dynamics was well received; it would be a staple over the coming years and eventually evolve into bigger things. Similarly, the trip to Alaska was foreshadowing a future that no one recognized at the time.

Rob and Dianna had never been to Alaska so at the conclusion of the class, they rented a van, put the back seats in Rhoda Portis's garage and took a two week drive around Alaska, camping out in the back of the van. Their friend Rhoda was now the Resource Conservation and Development (RC&D) Coordinator for the Matanuska-Susitna RC&D Council. She had been the District Conservationist at Baker, Oregon when the Sampson's moved there in 1988. She was originally from Nebraska, as Dianna was, and Rhoda had always been a good friend to the Sampson's.

The shrinking degrees of separation between Rob and his professional contacts would continue. Teaching with Janine, at Jay's request, and having a chance to visit Rhoda seemed to be serendipitous. These parallel, yet crossing, professional and personal relationships would continue to be a theme in Rob's career.

47

Sheridan Creek

"...each stream is an original work combining
its disturbance history, valley soils and geology,
and water and sediment regimes."

Once back in Boise, the job of State Design Engineer continued to be stimulating and fun. Rob designed several wetland rehabilitation projects and was very proud of the work on Sheridan Creek in eastern Idaho. Earlier, the stream had been diverted to a ditch on the far side of the meadow, but the original channel still curved through the meadow, largely intact. There were some technical challenges at Sheridan Creek, but mostly there was a long and loud debate about whether and how the stream should be returned to its original channel. The Nature Conservancy had an easement on the large meadow, and the meadow abutted Harriman State Park. Each had retained expert consultants to review any design proposed by NRCS.

Ken Beckmann, earlier the Soil Conservation Technician in the NRCS St. Anthony Field Office when Rob worked in Rexburg, was now the District Conservationist of that same office and administering the Sheridan Creek project. In addition, Rob's first boss, Bob Lehman, was the engineer working on Sheridan Creek. This created an odd reversal of roles. Bob had been the technical 'father figure' teaching Rob many of his SCS skills. Now Rob played the role of the technical leader for NRCS wetland restoration effort, and the organizational chart suggested that Bob defer to Rob. But the actual hierarchy of the technical leadership on the Sheridan Creek project was murky at best.

In the late 1990's stream rehabilitation had taken a turn that would become a professional theme in Rob's career. Stream analysis and the practice of fluvial geomorphology had moved from being an observational science, to being a blend of observation, art and computation. The first generations of leaders in the academic advances of fluvial geomorphology were at the ends of their careers.

The academic literature now came out of several disciplines. Engineering and hydrology drew from the science of river mechanics and sediment transport. Geology departments taught geomorphology and sedimentation and stratigraphy (study of sediment and rock layers). Biology and Ecology departments taught classes about aquatic habitat, the life history of organisms, and theories of the food web that existed in streams.

Given the wide-ranging philosophies and paradigms at different universities and between departments, approaches to restoring streams and wetlands varied a great deal. At one end of the spectrum was the 'Humans can do no good' school of thought. The reasoning was that humans had such a low level of understanding of aquatic ecosystems that the best strategy was to keep all humans away from a certain section of stream, and it would adjust to some high level of function on its own.

The other end of the spectrum suggested we could examine a stream or wetland and determine the very best form and function for that natural system. That form could then be constructed and the stream or river would adjust to this constructed form with the desired functions.

There are some serious logical errors in both of these schools of thought. It suffices to say the different schools of thought don't end up with the same solution very often. The details of different restoration philosophies and the advantages of each technique, are complex and hard to summarize. Books written by Luna Leopold, Ellen Wohl and Stan Schumm[15] are great places to start for the science. The National Research Council has the best book in the philosophy arena.

---

[15] Leopold, L.B., 1994. A View of the River. Harvard University Press.

Wohl, E.E. 2004. Linking Rivers to Landscapes. Yale University Press.

Schumm, S.A. 2005. River Variability and Complexity. Cambridge University Press

NRC, 1992. Restoring Aquatic Ecosystems.

Sheridan Creek restoration was suffering from these opposing philosophies. After the dust cleared from the feuding scientists and practitioners, the project framework became one of gradual introduction of the live flow into the remnant of the old channel. Some types of vegetation were transplanted to different spots on the stream. Rough vegetation, like willow, was transplanted to areas just above where pools were expected to form. The willow roots and stems would cause eddies that would dig and maintain the pools. In spots where high energies were expected, strong vegetation like sedges and rushes were transplanted and established. Their dense root system would moderate the erosion caused by high stream energy and resist erosion. A very small amount of excavation was done to jump-start the pools in the stream, which had filled in over the years due to minimal water that had flowed down the original, but abandoned channel.

An aerial photo (next page) shows Sheridan Creek on 8/11/2011. Very little adjustment in channel form has occurred in the 10 years since the project was completed. Looking at this channel, it is hard to believe that one of the expert consultants had advocated removing over 700 dump truck loads of material while reshaping the channel. Would such a channel 'perform' better? Provide more habitat?

Since each stream is an original work combining its disturbance history, valley soils and geology, and water and sediment regimes, there is no way to do a controlled experiment because there is no way to find a second stream for a control. To compound the problem, measuring fish absence or presence or trying to measure bug populations that live in the stream is problematic.

Some statistical and measurement tricks can be designed into a restoration effort that help block some of the stream and biologic variability and can provide some signals through the noise. But the primary item that many restoration projects lack is a set of well defined, measureable objectives. The people looking at Sheridan Creek were similar to a group of blindfolded people touching different parts of an elephant and trying to describe what the animal looked like. Most people have a gut feeling about how streams should be. However, our history of stream and river manipulation over the years, when viewed in retrospective, does not give evidence that our intuition was particularly accurate or useful. We often got the opposite results from what we wanted.

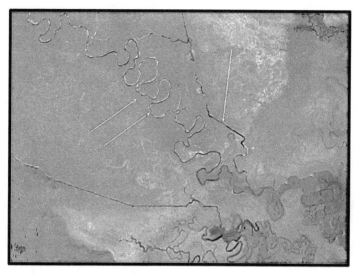

Sheridan Creek after restoration, 2011. Flow is top to bottom. The abandoned, straightened channel on the right (single arrow); the curvy (double arrow) original channel in the center.

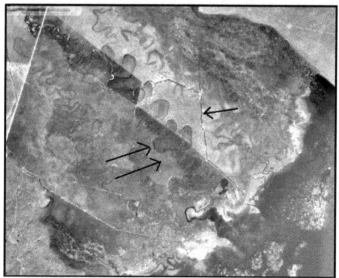

Channel in 1980. Active straight channel is marked by the single arrow. Abandoned curvy channel is marked by two arrows.

As a new century opened in 2000, there was little reason to expect any change in Rob's career. He had a great job as the State Design Engineer in Idaho. He got to solve difficult problems and work with an amazing group of technical specialists, especially Art Shoemaker, Terril Stevenson and Frank Fink. There were always new and more beautiful places to visit in Idaho, and NRCS supported Rob's travel to other states.

Everything seemed in order. NRCS as an organization had pulled through some quantum changes and survived. It was on the cusp of becoming the major conservation funding agency, bringing all of the responsibility, accountability and scrutiny that come with that distinction. That in itself was a victory won after years of political jockeying and controversy. The 1996 Farm Bill had provided NRCS with a new authority in the Environmental Quality Incentive Program (EQIP), and then the 2002 Farm Bill gave the control of cost-share dollars to NRCS rather than the Farm Services Agency (FSA, the old ASCS). This simple fact was a tectonic shift in how NRCS behaved and in their relationship and interaction with their sister agencies.

But major changes were in the wind; some foreseeable, many unexpected. Those changes would dramatically affect how the agency worked, what it valued and how its people would need to respond.

As NRCS was struggling to handle the changing stage of subsidies blended with some technical assistance, events were reshuffling some engineering positions at NRCS. The State Conservation Engineer who had hosted Rob's training and technical sessions in Alaska, Jay Cobb, moved to a similar position in South Dakota.

Rob and Dianna Sampson were sitting at dinner one night enjoying the company of Paul Pedone, a good friend and the State Geologist for NRCS in Oregon. Offhand, Paul stated that "Jay Cobb is leaving Alaska." There was silence at the table. Rob had thought Jay would stay in Alaska for the rest of his career. As Rob slowly tried to make sense of this new staffing vacancy at NRCS, it was Dianna that spoke next. "I guess we're going to Alaska".

That simple declaration loomed large in several dimensions. Popular thought in NRCS was that assignments outside the continental United States were great as long as your spouse and family were fully supportive of the change. The role Neil's family and particularly his spouse and Rob's mom, Jeanne, played in supporting his efforts at Harvard had been critical. Going to a place like Alaska had challenges simply due to the remoteness from friends and family. A typical joke about moving to the 'Great Land' was that if you thought the winter days were dark, short and depressing, try coming home to an angry spouse.

Dianna's declaration of support for a move that neither of the Sampsons saw coming was paramount. Of course Rob had to compete for the job, and there were still points of negotiation within the family as well as potential logistics to be decided. But a big hurdle, that of family consensus, had been cleared.

Within hours of the dinner declaration of a vacancy in Alaska, the Sampson's old friend from Baker City, Rhoda Portis sent an email. Rhoda was the Resource Conservation and Development (R&D) coordinator in Wasilla, Alaska. The subject line in the email, addressed to Rob was "Your Next Job."

August 15th, 2001 saw Rob and Dianna load a pickup, travel trailer and three cats and head north. Two weeks later they were parked in Rhoda's driveway in Wasilla, Alaska.

48

Alaska: Politics and History

*"Alaska's natural resources being exported to the 'lower 48'
with little return to the State has a history
dating well before the Statehood."*

The NRCS State Office was in Palmer, Alaska, recently relocated from Anchorage, some 45 miles south. The State Conservation Engineer position however, was still in Anchorage. Chuck Bell, the State Conservationist, had explained the location during the interview process as "Well, that is where the airport is." Needless to say, the ramifications of that simple explanation were lost on Rob, who was grappling with the logistics of the move and the promotion to a job he had never expected to have. In fact, the airport would become an important part of his life.

The Anchorage satellite of the State Office housed the State Resource Conservationist, John Copeland, a soil scientist, public affairs specialist, a secretary, and portions of Rob's staff: Rick McClure and Dan Kenny of Snow Survey, Lori Richter the State Design Engineer, and Jane Standifer-Trenton, an Engineering trainee. In addition, Rob supervised the Project Engineer housed in Fairbanks, Brett Nelson. The office itself was located in the Veco building (Veco was an oil field contractor with deep roots in Alaska politics and oil money). The company would prove to play a major role later in the decade in the downfall of Alaska Senator Ted Stevens.

The Anchorage NRCS field office was run by District Conservationist Michelle Schuman who arrived on the job the same day in early September as Rob had. Michelle had a great deal of SCS work background, but was returning from private practice to take the Anchorage DC position. The previous District Conservationist had been dismissed for running up several thousand dollars in personal purchases on the Government travel credit card. That seemed to Rob a very odd way to behave, but stories of Alaskans and excess behavior would prove to be normal in this assignment.

In late 2001, Alaska had offices in Fairbanks and Delta Junction to the north, Homer and Kenai to the south, and Wasilla and Anchorage in the south-central part of the state. All of these offices were, in local parlance, 'on the roads'. Driving from Anchorage to Fairbanks is a 6 hour, 360 mile drive in good conditions. Delta Junction is an hour beyond that. And the road system, consisting of three main highways, accesses a relatively small part of Alaska. The immense size of Alaska and the relative remoteness of most of its places dominated much of the NRCS's efforts in the state.

Even in early 2000s, communications with many of the bush Alaska Native Villages were difficult, and most of the access was by plane. A field office in Idaho was considered remote if it was 100 miles from the next closest NRCS Office, from Salmon to Arco for instance. Many counties in Idaho had clients that required a three hour drive to visit. Alaska field offices had many clients that to reach them required several airplane rides on increasingly smaller planes. And the schedule was often dictated by the weather and other mechanical, logistical and sometimes random events.

Alaska was listed as having 609 farms and ranches in 2002, of which over half had gross incomes less than $10,000. Over 400 of the enterprises were smaller than 180 acres. Very few of NRCS's standard technical assistance and cost share programs were tailored for a 'typical' Alaska agriculture scenario, if there was such a thing.

When Rob arrived, Alaska NRCS had 6 Field Offices, and about 60 full time employees. This would change significantly over the next several years and that change would have a big impact on Rob's experience in the state.

Senator Ted Stevens was an Alaska icon. He was the longest serving Republican in the Senate with 40 years of tenure. Stevens held many powerful positions, but the greatest impact during this time frame was his chairmanship of the Senate Appropriation Committee from 1996 to 2005. With a population of only 627,000, Alaska society in general has very few degrees of separation. People who travel around the State are a smaller subset of this already small population and it isn't long before many of the people boarding an Alaska Airlines 737 (the workhorse for jet travel in Alaska) look familiar.

It doesn't take long to understand why most of the political figures are referred to by their first name. In referring to Alaska's senior senator, most citizens even included a family modifier, and hence 'Uncle Ted' was how Stevens was discussed by the denizens of the Great Land.

The major line used by most Alaskans when debating with the other 49 states about who should have what, was "Other states have been in development for 100 or 200 years, while Alaska is just getting started." This argument was applied to everything from transportation projects to social services to defense spending.

Some facts about Alaska will help frame the story of Rob's experience there. It is difficult to understand the size of the state and the natural resource challenges and problems without some context. Alaska has a land area of 586,000 square miles. This is over twice the size of Texas alone, and led to the joke that if Texas continued to flaunt the size of their republic, Alaska would divide in half and Texas would be the third largest state. The population of Alaska is the fourth smallest, behind only Wyoming, Vermont and North Dakota. Alaska citizens provide about $3.6 billion dollars per year to the Federal Treasury, but they reap about twice that in Federal money with about $7.5B coming into the State.

The Alaska state budget was about $12.8 billion dollars in 2014, and the value of their savings account, the Alaska Permanent Fund was about $50 billion dollars. Much of the money in the Fund comes from taxes and royalties paid by the oil companies for oil that is moved through the Trans-Alaska Pipeline (TAP). The TAP came on line in 1977 and was pumping about 1.6 million barrels per day (BPD) of oil in 1980. Output of the TAP peaked in about 1994 with a daily average of 2 million barrels. In 2011, oil output was half a million BPD and dropping at 5% a year. That year oil and gas taxes paid to the State totaled over 19 billion dollars. Taxes paid by the oil industry compromise about 80-90% of Alaska's discretionary budget.

Natural gas fields in Cook Inlet near Anchorage had output that peaked in 1995. Of all the uses that natural gas could have had, much of the output was turned into nitrogen fertilizer at the State subsidized Agrium plant in Ninilchik. Much of that fertilizer was barged to the lower 48, similar to the oil coming out of the TAP. The Agrium plant shut down in 2009, despite calls for more state subsidy to keep the few high paying jobs at the plant.

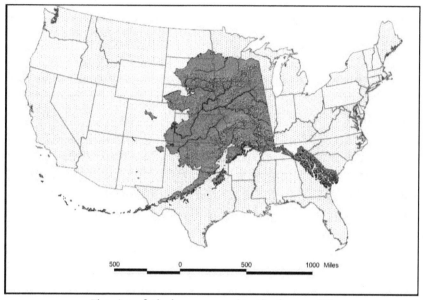

The size of Alaska compared to the 'Lower 48'

The oil output of the North Slope has declined to about 25% of the peak, and all forecasts point to a continued decline. Therein lies the double edged sword of using a feat of engineering for long term profit. Once the route of the pipeline is determined and constructed, the input and output points are fixed. Unless major oil reserves are discovered very close to the pipelines 500 mile route, there is no way to put more oil into the line except near the inlet.

The North Slope oil reserve has been declining, mostly due to the fact that the extractable volumes are finite. This presents problems for the TAP, as it was designed to transport up to 2.5 million barrels per day. Working at a much lower capacity, there are problems with build-up of sludge, the oil cooling too quickly and having to turn some pump station off or on to move the oil, although they were designed to operate continuously.

Why is so much information about oil and money in Alaska in-cluded in a book that has Soil Conservation as the primary theme? Because it describes the overall attitude of the people and corpora-tions that live and work in Alaska. There is a great deal of natural gas on the North Slope that is moved to the surface while mining oil. This is either re-injected down the oil wells or simply burned off by flares.

The oil companies and the State Government have been in al-most constant negotiation regarding a natural gas pipeline parallel-ing the TAP oil line to make use of this abundant resource. But the State and the Oil companies can't agree on the terms, despite offers of very low royalties to the State, because the oil companies want large Federal or State subsidies to pay for the construction. In es-sence, the oil companies want the pipeline for free, or less.

This is the attitude that permeates Alaska culture. If you say "no" long enough to any request for sacrifice or expenditure, eventually the Federal Government will step in and sweeten the deal. This is evident in all levels of society and government, and it is not a surprising result. Alaskans are big thinkers, and projects like the TAP, the Alaska Highway, the Red Dog mine in Kotzebue, or big timber op-erations in the Southeast part of the state, are all proof that thinking big, in a big state pays, at least for a little while.

Unfortunately for each of those very big successful projects, the landscape is littered with big ideas that were not sustainable in the long run, or even viable in the short term. Some examples of these projects provide a context to describe agriculture in Alaska.

The bridge to nowhere (BTN) is an engineering project to connect the town of Ketchikan to Gravina Island, where the airport lies. The idea behind the bridge that is publicly stated is that this bridge will allow easier access to the airport, and possibly increase cargo volume through the airport. The BTN last became a news item in the 'lower 48' when the recession of 2007-2009 forced federal budget cuts and a loud debate about 'earmarks'. Earmarks are amendments inserted into a spending bill that describe a specific project, usually in the home state of the Senator or Representative who proposes the amendment. The description is usually brief, and sometimes it is even hard to decide which agency or even which private group will ultimately administer the money. Congressman Don Young (Alaska's sole Representative, a Republican), sits on the powerful House Transportation Committee. Don has been in the House since 1973 and is known for his unapologetic nature when it comes to earmarks, as well as his folksy and often perplexing remarks.

Although earmarks make up a very low percentage of discretionary funding at the Federal level, they are something everyone loves to hate. Many State groups and citizens find it useful to be very selective in their criticism, however, often taking the form of hating all the earmarks except the ones that come to them. Although earmarks have finally fallen out of favor at the Federal level, Don Young seems not to have received the 'memo'.

With former Alaska Governor Sarah Palin as John McCain's selected Vice Presidential running mate in 2008, Alaska politics received a little more exposure and scrutiny than was normal. The BTN was roundly discussed and ridiculed by the press. None of this deterred Don Young from continuing to support the project. Palin learned early on in her brief and unsuccessful Vice Presidential bid to deflect questions about the bridge, because the proposed $400 million bridge was hard to defend.

Ketchikan Airport is a very, very small facility. After you get off the plane, you wander about 200 yards down to a ferry dock and sit on a ferry for about 15 minutes and one and a half miles to the mainland where a bus or taxi will take you the remaining 2 miles into town. The ferry costs $5.00 for a round trip. A version of these complex logistics is common at Alaska airports, as it is often hard to find enough flat ground to build a runway.

While Sarah and Don (Alaska politicians are referred to by their first name locally) were busy trying to spin truths about why this bridge should be built, there were parts of the story that never seemed to make the headlines. Although the specific earmark for the bridge was removed from the House Transportation portion of the 2005 Omnibus Spending Bill, funding for the bridge continued as late as 2011, contained in H.R. 662: Surface Transportation Extension Act of 2011. Even in the 2005 Omnibus, although the earmark language was removed, the amount of money going to Alaska remained the same.

"Bridge to Nowhere" stories abound, but only seldom does a news story state that although Gravina Island is small, there is some privately owned land on the island along with the airport. Former Governor Frank Murkowski, and current Alaska Senator Lisa Murkowski have 33 acres of family owned land and some lucrative mining claims on the island. Another BTN is on the books that would hook Anchorage up to Point McKenzie in the Matanuska Valley. And it is almost never mentioned that Don Young's family owns 60 acres of flat land with unobstructed views on the Point, very close to where the bridge would terminate.

This story plays itself out in many of Alaska's grandiose projects. Corporations who understand the high level of subsidy that occurs in Alaska, spend a great deal of effort looking for resource extraction projects with remarkably low operating or initial investment costs. Alaska's natural resources being exported to the 'lower 48' with little return to the State has a history dating well before the Statehood. Exports that made businessmen in Seattle rich included sea otter pelts, salmon and timber. Self-serving interests masquerading as public good develop partially feasible stories about the benefits these projects will bring. These convoluted notions about potential payback or profit only seem to make sense if you say them loudly enough or often enough.

This kind of background-story plays a consistent part in a description of Alaska's agricultural sector and even in describing the activities of NRCS in the State. The following chapters about NRCS in Alaska and Rob's role are not intended as criticism because foibles and strengths of a Federal agency operating in Alaska are not unique to NRCS. The atmosphere of Federal funding and politics and entitlement attitudes is just that, and it did not start with the agriculture sector or USDA.

49

Alaskan Agriculture

"In 2001 Alaska agriculture saw gross receipts of $48 million.
As a comparison, Rhode Island had $64 million
in gross agricultural receipts that same year."

The history of Agriculture in Alaska is vital to understanding the work of the NRCS in that State. Despite the State and Federal encouragement of development, few commercial farming operations in Alaska have succeeded. Handicaps to farming have included poor soil, a short growing season, permafrost, limited investment capital, high labor costs, expensive machinery and supplies, and haphazard marketing. In 1923, only 90 farms, each averaging around 15 acres in size, operated in the Anchorage, Matanuska, and Fairbanks areas. The farmers primarily produced grain and hay for horses, milk, eggs, and vegetables.[16]

The Matanuska Valley, lying about 20 miles across Cook Inlet, has some agriculturally desirable traits. It is mostly flat and the location people move to rather than dwell in urban Anchorage. In the late 1970's and early 1980's Alaska was awash in oil money courtesy of the Trans Alaska Pipeline (TAP) completed in 1977. The SCS did an initial Soil Survey of potential agricultural land in Alaska that showed a large acreage totaling some 20 million acres.[15]

The excess State revenue, combined with the soil survey and Alaska's desire to prove to prove itself capable of running a State that

---

[16] Alaska's Heritage. Chapter 4-17: Farming, Herding, and Lumbering. Alaska History & Cultural Studies Website, Alaska Humanities Forum.

[15] Snodgrass, R., C. Logsdon & B. Heim. 1982. Alaska agriculture, an overview. Also Davies, D. 2008. Alaska State-Funded Agriculture Projects and Policies: Have they been a success? Senior Thesis, University of Alaska Fairbanks.

was self-sufficient, resulted in several huge State-conceived and supported agricultural projects. The Delta Junction project, the Point Mackenzie dairy project, and the Anchorage fish processing plant are good examples where the SCS had a large role in supporting the development of these enterprises.

As Davies' Senior Thesis reported, authorities decided that Delta Junction was a good place to demonstrate Alaska's capability for large-scale agriculture. Project land was sold through a lottery system and winners were put on a development schedule and given large loans to get their farms operating. In the beginning of the 1980's, there were 84,000 acres of land sold by or leased from the State.

Other tracts of land were surveyed for agricultural production, and a few years later the Point MacKenzie dairy demonstration project was auctioned at lottery, as well as the Delta expansion. Support facilities, such as meat and milk processing plants and grain holding bins, were also planned and built.

Large-scale projects were a common effort in Alaska. Even before Statehood, President Roosevelt created the Matanuska Colony Project to breathe life into Alaska agriculture, assist farmers who had lost their farms, and get people working during the Great Depression. Impoverished families (202 of them) were moved from the lower 48 to Palmer, Alaska. The effort did prove that food and milk could be produced in the Great Land.[16]

One excerpt provides a quick view of the Colony project's trajectory:

"By 1949, there were 525 farms in Alaska and only 217 of them were commercial operations. Most of these farms were in the Matanuska and Tanana River valleys. That same year, the federal government created the Alaska Research Station at Palmer. The station sought to increase farm production.

"Within 10 years, farm production in Alaska had doubled. Milk accounted for 49 percent and potatoes accounted for 25 percent of

---

[16] Davies, Chapter 6: Federal Programs to Promote Resource Use, Extraction, and Development, USDOI: The Impact of Federal Programs on Wetlands, Volume II. 1994. Alaska History and Cultural Studies, 2002. Alaska's Heritage CHAPTER 4-17: FARMING, HERDING, AND LUMBERING

annual farm production. Beef cattle and sheep herds on Kodiak and the Aleutian islands increased. In the late 1960s, slaughter houses were built on Kodiak and Umnak islands. In 1969, the state established a meat inspection program.

"Still, farming in Alaska was not a great success. In 1964, the U.S. Department of Agriculture spent $7.5 million in Alaska, approximately $19,000 per farm. This expenditure was two million dollars more than the value of Alaska's agricultural production that year.

"In 1963, fresh milk transported by truck from Seattle retailed in Fairbanks for a dollar per half gallon. Of this cost, 40 cents covered transportation and handling costs from Seattle. The same year, the military began to enforce a contract requirement calling for a 48-hour limit between pasteurization and delivery. This requirement, in effect, stopped truck shipment of fresh milk from Seattle to Fairbanks. For a short period, dairies in the Matanuska and Tanana River valleys profited from the new regulation."

When Rob arrived in Alaska in 2001, there were 8 to 10 dairies remaining on Point MacKenzie. Matanuska Maid, the bottling and pasteurization plant, was in State ownership, and leased back to the producers, but the processing part of the facility only functioned intermittently. As of 2013, Matanuska Maid is defunct and offered for sale by the Alaska Board of Agriculture and Conservation, and there are no commercial dairies in the Matanuska Valley.

The Anchorage fish packaging plant was just down the road from Sampson's house. Although there was little commercial fishing out of Anchorage, the fresh pack plant was built with a business model that it would import fish from other parts of the state and turn it into value-added heat-and-eat products. Construction was subsidized by the State, which provided over $55M to build the plant in the late 1990s. With any transportation cost at all, fish from a remote location lost its appeal, its profitability, and arguably its freshness, Alaska Seafood International stopped operations in 2003. Instead of the 450 jobs that were envisioned in 1998, at its peak the plant employed less than 50 people.

In 2001 Alaska agriculture saw gross receipts of $48 million. As a comparison, Rhode Island had $64 million in gross agricultural re ceipts that year. The State agricultural statistics lists 3 farms that brought in over $500,000 gross. Of the 400 or so farmers, the statistics report about 160 with a positive net cash flow.

SCS and ASCS participated heavily in Alaska's agricultural development. Rob first learned of the SCS role in Alaska by listening to the stories of Alan Koester who was the District Conservationist at Condon Oregon, when Rob moved to Baker in 1988. Koester had a very sharp sense of humor and never missed an opportunity to talk about Alaska, a land he truly loved.

Koester described helping new landowners clear the black spruce and brush from the Alaskan fields-to-be. The best management at the time proscribed piling the trees and brush in long windrows running North and South to provide some protection from the winter winds and to collect snow for soil moisture. The USDA would subsidize the clearing if it was done in this way. Additionally, the farmer could get a low interest loan from the Alaska Revolving Loan Fund to assist with any cost the Federal Government did not pay. Unfortunately, this practice worked a little too well, and the farm ground near the windrows thawed out later in the season and remained too wet to farm.

The next effort by USDA was to pay farmers for burning the windrows. As the windrows remained very wet, this operation became multiple efforts of burning, re-piling the unburned material and burning again. Without the insulation of trees and brush, the ground often froze to a much greater depth over the winter and the soil remained cold and saturated longer into the growing season than it would have if the vegetation remained intact.

Alaska farmers then developed a distinct interest in the USDA's Conservation Reserve Program (CRP). CRP was intended to take highly erodible and other lands with special value out of agricultural production by paying an annual rental payment for keeping lands idle. As of 2013, Alaska had about 18,000 acres of crop land enrolled in the CRP program, out of the State's total of 31,000 acres.

In 2001, the Federal Department of Agriculture provided $140 million to Alaska for support of about 600 known agricultural enter= prises. NRCS had about 60 employees, with FSA and Rural Development adding about another 40.

NRCS had gotten word in 2000 that Senators Ted Stevens and Frank Murkowski, along with Representative Young, were interested in more assistance to rural Alaskans from USDA. An earmark added to the FY 2000 budget directed USDA in Alaska to open several new service centers to serve rural Alaska.

The 49th state has plenty of miles of paved road, but very little of the land is accessible from these roads. Still, most of the easily recognizable agriculture operations are, for obvious reasons, relatively close to the roads. NRCS had service centers in Homer, Kenai, Anchorage, Wasilla, Fairbanks and Delta Junction, roughly south to north, and all along the road system. Driving mileage from Homer to Delta Junction is about 550 miles and takes over 10 hours. Yet after the drive, you have traversed very little of Alaska.

NRCS set into motion efforts to open field offices in Juneau, Kodiak, Dillingham, Bethel, Nome, and Copper Center. This brought field office administration logistics to an entirely new level. Juneau is closer to Seattle than to Nome, and airplane flights, while regularly scheduled to all of these locations, were often at the mercy of the weather. The simple act of procuring an office space was a challenge, as suitable square footage that was heated and safe, let alone accessible to everyone, was a premium. The only available and marginally suitable office in Copper Center, even with the advantage of being on the road system, turned out to be a three bedroom house.

Each of these offices needed telephone lines, internet connections, furniture and a vehicle of some type, be it a truck, snowmobile or boat—or sometimes all three. None of these items are cheap in Alaska to begin with, but the added cost of shipping them by barge was high. By the end of FY 2002, offices were operating in Juneau, Dillingham, Bethel, Nome and Copper Center.

Finding employees to staff these offices who met the Federal standards for the position and who were willing to live in these towns was also a daunting task. To be qualified for the Soil Conservationist job series, you need to have 24 credits in soils and agriculture related classes, with at least 8 of the credits in soils. Many majors require one class in soils, but very few people took a second class. Once a person was found who met the qualifications and was interested in moving to Bethel or Nome, a rather low-key vetting process had to occur.

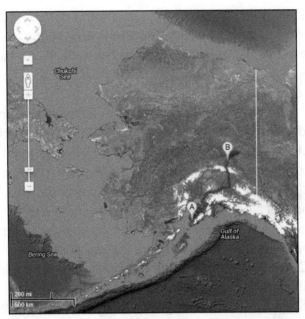

Image of the 550 mile distance from Homer (A) to Delta Junction (B)

Very few of the long-time residents of the towns were qualified for the jobs. Most career agriculture employees on the road system had minimal desire to move off the roads. Then there was a matter of pay. Alaska federal employees at the time had a 25% increase in their base pay added as a tax-free cost of living adjustment. In Anchorage, which has one of the busiest freight airports in the world, there was only a modest cost increase in most items compared to Seattle or Portland in the 'lower 48'. Living in Bethel, however, costs about 50% more than living in Anchorage. Despite that, employees in both locations received the same pay adjustment.

Even when a suitable applicant for one of the 'off-road' jobs was located, some subtle questioning had to be carried out to determine their motive and temperament. There are as many reasons to want to live off the road system as you can imagine, and many of them are noble and sincere. But there is very little sunlight in Nome during the winter, and the relatively large (by rural Alaska standards) population of almost 4,000 can start to seem very small. Add to this a harsh climate of cold and wind, and it takes a unique character to thrive in that environment.

The standard USDA agreement for transferring job locations was the Government would pay all charges for moving your household goods, and pay you for temporary quarters while you found a place to live. In return you would sign an agreement to remain with the Federal Government for three years. Shipment of household goods to Alaska often exceeded $100,000 and USDA wanted to get its money's worth.

Sometimes this match between employee and community was sustainable and stable. Yet, on more than one occasion, employees left before the end of the first year.

An even more pressing problem for NRCS was matching rural Alaska with typical USDA programs. The most popular programs for USDA were EQIP and CRP. The Environmental Quality Incentives Program (EQIP) provides financial incentives to install conservation practices. Everyone was eligible as long as they fit the definition of an 'Agricultural Producer'. Unfortunately the 'Producer' requirement specifically stated that a certain portion of income was derived from farm or agricultural sales.

It could be tenuously argued that the catching and smoking of salmon or killing caribou was an agricultural enterprise, but these commodities would need to be sold. Instead they were generally eaten so the 'producer' could stay alive. If they were 'sold' they were typically bartered. No cash changed hands and, even if it did, it was not reported to the IRS.

The USDA Conservation Reserve Program (CRP) planted highly erodible crop fields back to grass or trees. But in Nome, there were no crop fields other than some very small hay and grazing plots. At that time there was a program called the Wildlife Habitat Improvement Program (WHIP), and, at the time, the 'Agricultural Producer' limitation did not apply to that program. So to participate in WHIP, all that was needed was a project sponsor and degraded wildlife habitat that could be improved.

However, since WHIP was a cost sharing program, the sponsor needed to pay part of the cost. Finding individuals who had cash to put towards a habitat improvement project, and would sign a contract with the Federal government promising such was not the norm. And finding degraded habitat amongst thousands of square miles of relatively untouched tundra generally was an exercise in creativity. Some culverts could be replaced if they hindered fish migration, and a small amount of erosion around bridge footings could be moderated, but the argument that this improved critical habitat was generally difficult.

50

Alaska: Streambank Erosion & Flooding

"Floodproofing entire communities can be remarkably expensive, and is often unfeasible."

Where NRCS technical assistance could be of most value to rural Alaska was help in moderating flooding and streambank or shoreline erosion. But the scope and scale of many of these projects was several orders of magnitude larger or more severe than anything the NRCS would have tackled in the lower 48.

Alaskan rivers don't have many problems caused by humans. They are positively pristine compared to rivers in the Western continental United States. Irrigation withdrawals are unheard of, with the exception of some cabin lawns that get watered. Except for some hydropower facilities in the far southeast part of the state and a few mining ponds, there are very few dams. Bridges have caused some erosion and river pattern changes, but on the whole, these problems are localized; very few rivers have a large number of bridge crossings. Yet, the rivers and streams are changing for a host of reasons, many simply tied to the physical settings.

Alaska rivers are generally either very steep, mountain streams or very low gradient valley and estuary streams. An abrupt change in grade means the stream that was carrying bowling ball size rocks, now only has the capacity to transport silt size particles. Because the landscape is young and many streams are fed by glaciers, many rivers have a high sediment load of very fine silts and sand. Both the changes in gradient and the high sediment load suggest a stream that will change course as a normal tendency.

Due to a changing climate and receding glaciers, some Alaska rivers are changing their pattern even faster than before, and often changing to forms and patterns that are not consistent with their historical record. Due to the changing climate, many rivers are also experiencing changes in variability of flow and sediment load. This means high and low flows in patterns the river has not experienced, and this increased variability means more uncertain river behavior.

Similarly, rivers formed in permafrost landscapes where form was dictated by frozen streambanks are changing dramatically when that ice goes away. And even rivers that are not in permafrost were sometimes formed with streambanks being frozen solid when the ice breakup and peak flows occurred. If this ice goes out of the streambanks earlier or doesn't form at all due to warm winters, these rivers will change shape and form rapidly and dramatically.

Much of this is of little worry in uninhabited places. However as Alaska's Native Villages have changed from mobile hunting societies to living in a fixed spot with schools and clinics and water treatment plants, rapid river change can threaten these 'modern,' fixed facilities.

Picture a village in western Alaska. Although many miles upstream from the Chukchi Sea, the village is only about 20 feet above mean sea level. Flooding and erosion rates were generally taken into account during planning of school, clinic, and Village Council headquarters locations, but the severity of these events is increasing. Because construction materials and equipment must be barged or helicoptered to the site, construction is very expensive and in turn, village relocation is very expensive. As well, very few relocation sites exist that would not have the same problem as the current site.

If erosion of streambanks is the primary problem, there are many engineering techniques for stabilizing the streambank. Rock of various sizes (called riprap in engineering parlance) can be placed on the streambanks, and this is often successful in stopping erosion.

The practice is very expensive, costing hundreds of dollars per foot of streambank in the Western U.S. By comparison, in Alaska these projects can cost more than $1,000 per foot of streambank. And if the forces causing the river to change form are widespread due to melting glaciers or different ice patterns, the river could easily erode in a different location and change form dramatically enough to bypass the expensive streambank stabilization project altogether.

Rob, surveying McCarthy Creek in Alaska

Floods are a similar threat to rural Alaska Villages. Floodproofing entire communities can be remarkably expensive, and is often unfeasible. To put a dike all the way around the community involves a great deal of material that is not available on site and would need to be imported. There is generally no good way to keep the water pumped out from inside the dike, as most villages depend on diesel-powered generators for electricity, and this fuel is very expensive. Raising houses up is often an alternative, but this requires boardwalks to be raised, and utilities to be reconfigured. Of course, some facilities like airport runways simply can't be raised.

So coastal villages present a potential problem that is a combination of flooding and erosion mechanisms. As seas warm, the water expands, and sea levels are higher. Higher tides often cause severe erosion and the obvious threat of flooding. Couple this with the fact that as the sea ice forms later in the year than normal, early winter storms that used to occur over ice, may now occur over open water, creating flooding and erosion forces significantly greater than the ocean regime that formed the current shoreline.

Often it was NRCS engineers that were called to make the first visit to some of these communities. Although the village or town may not have any agricultural enterprises, the NRCS web site and public relations brochures touted our abilities to do flooding studies and to engineer solutions to erosion problems. Because the Federal Government has a 'Government to Government' status with the 200-plus Native Villages in Alaska, it was difficult to turn down a request from a Village Elder or Environmental Coordinator who needed some analysis and advice about flooding or erosion problems.

During Rob's four year tenure, he visited over 50 Alaska Native Villages. The newly staffed NRCS offices in rural Alaska provided a means of contact with people in more remote areas, and these offices were one reason for the high demand. But the rapid change in climate patterns and flood and erosion severity added to the demand.

A typical trip would involve getting on an Alaska Airlines jet and flying to Bethel or Fairbanks or Nome, where one of the regional airlines had scheduled service to one of the outlying Villages.   Someone on the Village Council or their staff would pick up the NRCS traveler from the Village airstrip, and provide transport by pickup, ATV or snowmobile to the Village proper. Since there were seldom motels at the Villages, arrangements would be made to stay in a rented room at a house, or to sleep on the floor of the school gymnasium or the Village Council office buildings. Sometimes a meeting with the Village Council Chair or Tribal Chief was arranged, but often it was the Council staff that provided background information and a tour of the area of interest.

It was not unusual for the investigation phase of the trip to be relatively short. Problems with flooding and erosion were often so severe that most feasible technical solutions could be discarded fairly rapidly, leaving Rob or the other NRCS engineers with a sinking feeling that they might be seen as just another Government worker who visited the Village, made some promises and went back to their comfortable house in the city. The return flight would not be scheduled for another day or two—and that was if the weather permitted.

2004 Storm damage on Main Street, Nome

The airstrip at Shishmaref

Rob usually resorted to trying to talk with as many people as he could, hoping that the collective knowledge would provide him insight and inspiration about a solution to the problem at hand. These discussions were enlightening on a number of levels. In many Alaska Native cultures, the background of the story was very important to conveying the overall picture of the problem. Such discussions then could often be long and detailed, but experience talking to farmers and ranchers in his previous jobs was useful in drawing people into conversation and being patient while they provided all the different bits of information they considered important. Sadly, in most cases, this assembled body of local knowledge did not make the problem less intractable or the solution more apparent

Shishmaref is an Inupiat Village between Nome and Kotzebue on the Chukchi Sea at about latitude 67. The Village is situated on the sea, on a sandy island, and is home to 300 people. Given the hummock-pocked, frozen silt lowlands that formed the bulk of the landscape, the sandy island provided a relatively flat, firm and clean place to reside. Erosion rates started to increase in the mid 1990's, and the shoreline retreat was threatening several houses and some fuel tanks.

NRCS, along with a host of other agencies began working on a multifaceted plan. The only long-term solution that made sense was to relocate the Village. But this is remarkably hard to do, and still harder to pay for. A relocation site needs infrastructure. Do you build the airport and sewage facilities and roads before the houses are relocated? Any one of the three items would probably take more than one construction season, and even if it was funded, no one wanted to see that level of investment isolated while three or four years go by. If the original village is scheduled for construction of a new sewage system, is that project put on hold while the relocation (possibly) moves forward?

Then there were the people and houses. Was the relocation voluntary, splitting the Village into parts, effectively requiring redundant services such as schools and clinics? Those services are modest and capacity limited to start with, and there is a lack of trained staff.

A failed erosion control project at Shishmaref

The alternative is a forced move for everyone, and no one was quite sure if any one entity had authority to require a move. The Army Corps of Engineers estimated a single relocation to be $80 to $200 million. At least 8 villages were in imminent danger of obliteration from erosion and flooding, and 184 out of 213 are impacted by flooding or erosion.[17]

Rob began working with the Shishmaref Erosion and Relocation Coalition in 2002. He led an NRCS team that assessed current erosion rates and five potential village relocation sites. The same NRCS group assessed a site across the lagoon at Tin Creek in more depth in 2003. Tin Creek is a traditional fishing and hunting area about 15 miles south of the current village. The Tin Creek site currently is only accessible by boat, so in order to maximize investigation time the NRCS team camped at the site, while they investigated the soils, vegetation and water resources.

[17] ALASKA NATIVE VILLAGES: Limited Progress Has Been Made on Relocating Villages Threatened by Flooding and Erosion. 2009. GAO-09-55.

While this NRCS effort was not a 'normal' conservation activity, Rob felt strongly that some entity of the Federal or State government should be concerned about the village and show good will and coordination to help the relocation planning. The Federal and State Agencies were not well-coordinated, and certainly no one agency assumed a lead role. NRCS and their small Alaska staff were in no position to lead any effort, but NRCS had set up an office in Nome and said they were there to help the citizens. It was important to show up, and provide something.

Rob later supplied some NRCS staff to do the construction inspection of a project to put rock on part of the eroding shoreline at Shishmaref. The project was not NRCS funded, but in an NRCS review of the initial design, it became obvious that the mix of sizes of the rock were very critical, and that construction logistics were going to be difficult. There was also no extra money to have construction inspectors assure that the design was adhered to. NRCS project engineer Brett Nelson spent three weeks in the late Fall and early Winter assuring that all the rock was installed correctly.

Although this project was not initiated or funded by NRCS, it was important to get it right. The shores around Shishmaref are littered with failed erosion control efforts. It seemed cynical to spend any more money for erosion control and fail to make sure it was installed correctly. The rock riprap did work and has remained intact and as designed for at least eight winters as of this writing.

Installing this heavily engineered solution to minimize shoreline erosion was not without controversy, and NRCS spent many hours discussing whether to be involved and endorse the project. What if the rock work provided a false sense of safety and derailed the relocation effort? What if the hardened shoreline increased erosion rates on the unprotected sections of the beach? Ultimately, there was no evidence that the relocation would create substantial forward progress on any known timetable, so NRCS made a decision to endorse the project and assist with a successful installation.

Village relocation and shoreline erosion were not typical NRCS projects, but NRCS has expertise that matters in the planning of these activities. Skills in soils and soil mechanics, pipelines, ponds and streambank stabilization projects are applicable as well as experience in talking with people about their needs, observations and goals. And NRCS was known for showing up, for travelling to the problem areas and talking to the people who are impacted.

51

Snow Survey in Alaska

*"SNOTEL data in Alaska has value beyond all monetary measures
in its documentation and use in analyses of climate change."*

The NRCS runs a small program that measures the amount of snow that falls in the mountains of the western states. These measurements provide the data for predictions of the volume of water that will come from the melting snow in the spring and the summer. The forecasts are used by farmers to decide what type of crop to plant, or how many acres could be farmed; but it wasn't only the farmers that appreciated knowing how much water was stored in the snowpack. Power companies with hydroelectric facilities on western rivers are keenly interested in the volume forecasts as are recreation interests like fishing and white water rafting. As noted earlier, Neil had been involved in the founding and operation of this program in Idaho.

Although some snow is still measured by hiking to the site and plunging a sampling tube into the snow to get a core, the workhorse of the Snow Survey program is now an automated measuring system collectively known as the SNOTEL (snow telemetry) system. A rubber pillow filled with antifreeze weighs the amount of snow that falls on the pillow. An electronic pressure sensor reports that pressure to a data logger and these data are relayed to a master station by bouncing radio information off a belt of meteors that constantly orbits the earth. This method of data transmission is reliable, inexpensive and unique.

It isn't hard to imagine the value of a snowmelt volume forecast in the headwaters of the Colorado or the Snake River. Irrigation water is scarce, and has to be divided up to meet State law and the needs of cities, manufacturing, power generation, and the biggest consumptive user, agriculture. Reservoir operators try to balance the goals of flood protection and irrigation storage.

In the Continental U.S., with its network of roads maintained on Federal Forest Service and Bureau of Land Management land, it isn't that difficult to access mountainous areas and install eight or ten SNOTEL sites at strategic locations to provide data and inform the volume forecast. But imagine the Tanana River in Central Alaska. The drainage area for this river is huge, similar to the Snake River in Idaho, covering almost 46,000 square miles. But almost no roads exist to access the drainage area of the Tanana. And there are no roads in the mountains.

Although it flows mostly through rural lands, the Snake River watershed is still home to almost a million people. By contrast, only 30,000 people at most live in the Tanana drainage. So why would measuring the snow matter in Alaska? The answer turns out sounding a lot like other answers from the Great Land: For very different reasons than down in the 'Lower 48'. One reason is similar: basic natural resource data is the foundation of many decisions and is the beginning of the framework for almost any kind of natural resources research.

It could be argued that snow measurement in Alaska would be useful in flood predictions. But flooding in Alaska is primarily driven by the formation of ice jams, and there is little correlation between the amount of snow and the severity of ice jam formation. Most Alaskan flooding outside of the Southeast part of the state that is not the result of an ice jam is a product of summer rainfall.

One of the best arguments for Snow Survey and SNOTEL sites is that in Alaska they function as remote weather stations. The grid of weather stations in Alaska is sparse, and mostly related to airstrips in the flat, lower elevations. In most cases SNOTEL data are collected and reported hourly, and these readings are used as remote 'eyes and ears' for everything from determining airplane and snowmobile trip routes to deciding if it is safe to take a boat out on the water, or whether a rural school should be open that day.

Skiers and boaters, as well as hikers, hunters and other outdoor recreationists, use the SNOTEL data to decide on a wide variety of activities. Slightly different from the rest of the U.S., is that the SNOTEL information might be the only available glimpse at the weather conditions, making the SNOTEL data all the more valuable.

One more hallmark of the NRCS snow measurement program stands out. SNOTEL data in Alaska has value beyond all monetary measures in its documentation and use in analyses of climate change. Northern latitudes are showing shifting climate patterns a good deal more dramatically than Southern climes. With some SNOTEL sites having records that extend 25 years or longer, changes in precipitation volume, variability and duration are beginning to be statistically meaningful in this important record.

Rob's four years of supervising the Snow Survey program for NRCS Alaska involved working with several very accomplished employees. Rick McClure, the lead hydrologist, and Dan Kinney, the hydrologic technician, made a remarkable impact on the availability of basic weather data in Alaska. During Rob's time there, at least 12 new SNOTEL sites were installed, and a number of sites were upgraded with new sensors or more reliable equipment. All of this was accomplished while maintaining the existing network of automated sites and measuring the manual sites. By 2013, there were 237 active manual and SNOTEL sites in Alaska.

Most of the SNOTEL sites in the continental US report to one of two 'Master Stations' in Idaho or Utah by bouncing radio signals off of an ever-present belt of meteors and meteor dust. Alaska maintained its own Master Station as the distance and geometry did not allow reporting to the Idaho station. However, because of the low angle of the meteor belt and the steep mountains, which rise abruptly from the valley floor, meteor burst communication is less reliable in the northland than the lower 48 states.

Alaska SNOTEL is now switching all of their communications over to satellite phone technology. At the end of 2013, at least 58 SNOTEL sites were communicating their data by satellite phone technology. Other than better data loggers and radios, this is the first big technology change since Neil was measuring snow on the Clearwater River in the early 1960's.

As dangerous as back country travel in Alaska can be, the snow survey program in Alaska adds even another element of risk. Since many of the non-NRCS weather stations are at airstrips, weather information is needed well away from the road or air transportation system. Installing new SNOTEL sites and maintaining the existing network requires back country travel in places that don't get visited by anyone very often. A focus on safety is paramount and Alaska NRCS's snow survey has a safety record that seems to defy all odds. Snow survey personnel, and to a lesser degree Alaska NRCS employees as a whole, spend a great deal of their time honing their safety skills. The low number of injuries over the last 25 years testifies to those skills.

At a minimum, NRCS Alaska employees attend school for safe operation of ATVs and snowmobiles, similar to field-going NRCS employees nationwide. But in Alaska there is additional training in gun safety and bear encounters. Aircraft safety, including Coast Guard-sponsored training in survival of emergency water landings and culminating in a simulated nighttime crash in cold water, is certainly beyond 'normal' NRCS training.

52

Restoration of an Urban Alaska Creek

"The developer wanted a stream that looked and sounded like a stream, with varying pitches and a rich palette of sound."

Chester Creek runs through Anchorage proper and provides a nice amenity for the relatively urban area. A pathway along the creek provided bicycle access, a walking path and place for fishers of all type to catch the different types of salmon that move up and down the creek.

Early in the 2000s, a development company contacted the local NRCS office because they had recently acquired property through which about three-quarters of a mile of Chester Creek ran. In the mid-1970s, the stream had been straightened to maximize space for single-wide mobile homes in a mobile home park. The new developer was interested in making the stream a hallmark of the mixed use development his company envisioned, and he was willing to grant a streamside easement of 50 feet on each side of the stream to make it more 'natural.'

Designing a stream channel in an urban setting is quite a bit simpler than designing one in wild land. Most urban streams have very little in the way of gravel and cobble moving through them. Although it may seem counterintuitive, there are more options that carry smaller risks in many urban streams.

As a potential designer of the stream project, Rob took a healthy skepticism to the table with the developer, but soon found quite a bit more common ground than he had expected. The developer and the designer wanted much the same thing for entirely different reasons. The developer wanted a stream that looked and sounded like a stream, with varying pitches and a rich palette of sound. To the designer this sounded like pools and riffles which are effective at distributing energy along the channel. This burns up stream energy and minimizes erosion—desirable stream traits that are also appealing to great number of people.

A straightened stream might be only two times as wide as it is deep. This is good for hiding habitat, but without some sunlight penetrating to the stream substrate, there may be very little primary productivity and a very narrow array of food for some fishes. Similarly, without the diversity of water becoming deeper in the pools and shallower in the riffles, there are no eddies for fish to find neutral velocities and wait for food to come without expending any energy.

The developer and United States Fish and Wildlife Service teamed up with NRCS and a local engineering firm, MWH. MWH completed the project, and NRCS assisted in funding and installing the design. The developer had his own construction company to complete the construction, and in 2004, the project was complete.

One of the highlights of the collaborative effort was contact with the developer's landscape architect, a Hungarian named Tàmas Deàk. Tàmas was a fascinating guy to be around and had excellent instinct in what would look contextually correct around the stream as it was envisioned to be.

Rob completed several stream projects during his time in Alaska, but it was this project that appealed to almost everyone that saw it. The re-construction provided a stream channel that, although limited by space and low tolerance for channel movement, provided some of the ecosystem traits that a wilder stream might if it was further from people and buildings.

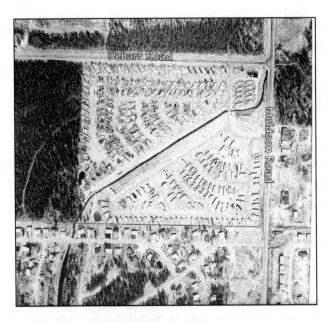

Chester Creek in the mid-1960s

Chester Creek under construction

53

Leaving the Alaskan Frontier:

It Takes Two Positions

"The Federal government, and by extension USDA, have statements in place to support co-placement for two career families."

Rob was impressed with the impact that the 40 to 50 NRCS employees in Alaska had compared to that of other agencies. Federal jobs in Alaska make up over 30% of all jobs in the state. Given the 150,000 salaried federal jobs in the 49th state, NRCS positions are barely worth counting (a third of 1%). Yet NRCS almost always had a place at the table in projects or decisions that involved natural resources, which was an element of nearly every Alaska planning effort and project.

NRCS in Alaska was involved in projects from invasive plant studies and management to demonstrating the use of bridges made from timbers rather than concrete and steel. Although typical USDA assistance programs barely fit any Alaska situations, these very few employees and the relatively few Federal dollars they administer have made an impact in every corner of Alaska.

Alaska politics are rough and tumble. Citizens know their Federal and State representatives by name, and because they often receive direct financial assistance from the State or the Feds, locals are not shy about calling a congressional representative. Nor are they afraid to tell a government official that the decision that was reached or the stance the official has taken is wrong.

Rob often fielded phone calls and personal visits from State and Federal congressional staff questioning decisions or policy stances taken by NRCS. While this activity is experienced by many upper-level

Federal officials, and being responsive to these inquiries is part of the job description, Alaska's citizens have learned that an answer of "No" is not the end of the debate. Weariness with this strong-willed manipulation of the allocation of Federal money and technical assistance ultimately played into Rob's decision to leave Alaska.

After the promised minimum of three years of service in Alaska, the rules of employment stated that Federal employees could sign a two-year extension of their service agreement or invoke their promised 'return rights'. The notion of 'return rights' from Federal Service outside the continental United States (OCONUS in Fed-speak) were developed to encourage employees to accept positions in remote locations. The basic agreement was that the Federal employing agency would pay to move a family to Alaska, Hawaii, Guam or the like, and in exchange for signing a three year service agreement, would be 'promised' a return to a similar position in the lower 48. Although this promise is codified in Department of Defense policy, USDA does not have such a specific policy, but rather alludes to the DOD rules.

Rob found that invoking 'return rights' simply involved hand shake agreement between managers. So the quality of positions offered to a returning employee was more dependent on the quality of employee's professional relationships than on a set of rules. It was up to the returning employee to assure their political currency was as strong as possible.

Rob's short span of service in Alaska had accomplished projects that advanced the agency's goals, but these achievements didn't necessarily align perfectly with the NRCS priorities in the continental states. Being skilled in planning Native Village relocation strategies, and having knowledge of wildfire remediation in permafrost areas are valuable skills, but NRCS managers in the lower 48 were more interested in irrigation planning and dam safety.

NRCS Nationwide has about 12,000 employees, but there are only 51 state conservation engineers, and these positions become available only sporadically. Engineering positions at the GS 13 pay scale are rare also, and the Sampson's were only interested in living in the Western United States. 'Return rights' boiled down to a search for only a handful of positions administered by management that may or may not have any knowledge, or any positive assessment of Rob's skills.

So began a delicate cat-and-mouse game. Rob notified the senior management that he was interested in exercising his 'return rights' and making phone calls to his contacts in the western States to determine what positions were available. Inherent in this process were questions to determine the power of Rob's negotiating stance, or put more simply, what perceived value managers and engineering leaders had regarding his skills and reputation.

This process is subjective even when changing positions between adjacent states, and that uncertainty was magnified by an almost four year hiatus from 'normal' NRCS program activity and a distance of several thousand miles that spanned 20 degrees of latitude.

Family dynamics are always at play in career changes, and the Sampson's case when deciding to leave Alaska was no different. But circumstances had changed since they moved to Alaska. Whether Rob could negotiate a job offer of a good position in a desirable location was a task with likely 50-50 odds to start with. Adding to the complexity, his wife Dianna was now employed with the Bureau of Land Management (BLM). In the short time of the Sampson's Alaska tenure, she had advanced several levels into increasingly complex and responsible positions.

Proving that Anchorage is a small town, after only six weeks of living in Alaska, Dianna had heard that the BLM state office would be hiring several Cartographic Technicians. She heard this from her hair dresser. A lively dinner-time discussion about the validity of the information gained at the beauty salon took place, but the information was true and Dianna applied and was hired as a permanent, full time Cartographic Technician. Needless to say, Rob's position regarding information gained while getting a haircut had to change.

BLM plays a significant role in conveying Federal land to the Alaska Native Villages and Corporations under the Alaska Native Claims Settlement Act (ANCSA) and the Alaska National Lands Conservation Act (ANLCA). These acts were part of the Alaska Native lands settlement that was reached when the trans-Alaska pipeline was constructed. BLM was charged with making sure the legal descriptions of these conveyed lands were accurate and recorded, and many people skilled in surveying and cartography were employed by BLM to generate and safeguard these records.

In the ensuing years, Dianna obtained a string of progressively more responsible positions, and when the Sampson's decided to attempt relocation to the lower 48, Rob's position was not the only consideration for the family.

If the Sampson's succeeded in moving back to the western U.S., it would be the family's ninth relocation on behalf of the USDA and the Federal government. The first several moves were without significant consequence to the two-career family. Dianna was versatile in her skills, and seemingly uncanny in her ability to navigate the Federal employment system. Her posts included working for the Targhee National Forest in east Idaho, the Wallowa Whitman National Forest in east Oregon, and the Routt National Forest in Colorado. Because of her versatility and the abundance of positions at the band of lower pay that most 20- to 30-year old Federal workers occupy, Dianna was able to move as Rob's career changed positions and remain employed with the Federal Government.

She took positions with the Forest Service as a cartographer, a fire fighter, a forester working to oversee the firewood cutting program, a silvicultural technician inventorying forest stands and wildlife habitat, and a fire dispatcher. Unfortunately, most of these positions were temporary, had little to no potential for advancement, and provided no tenure in the Federal retirement system.

An argument has been made that the Forest Service used their hiring authority for temporary positions excessively so the number of permanent full time workers would remain smaller. The Federal Government got the best of the deal: a very flexible workforce made up of dedicated professionals with many years of experience. Temporary employees then became more valuable as seasonal employees than as permanent full time workers.

Rotating through these temporary positions began to be a detriment to Dianna's professional résumé. Although her tenure with the Forest Service appeared continuous, she was not achieving the constant upward progression in pay or responsibility that is desirable for a strong employment record. Nor were her skills in natural resource management being fully utilized. Instead she became known as a strong team player who cheerfully accepted whatever job needed to be done next. Reputation as a versatile and hard-working utility employee is desirable, but often results in more of the same work in the Federal system. Hence, the role of utility worker tends to perpetuate itself in the Federal workforce.

As timber harvest slowed on Federal lands in the late 1980's and 1990's and Federal land management in the West shifted to resources other than timber, openings in full time jobs declined. After a less than satisfying experience working for the Forest Service in Colorado, Dianna confronted her need for a different career. While Rob was away doing research in the U.S. Virgin Islands for graduate school, Dianna tested careers in retail, library sciences, community theater and food service. While this list of jobs helped fill in the loss of a second full time income for the family, they had very little career growth potential.

Working through the Colorado State University career placement system, a rather unique, but obvious nexus for her skills presented itself in the field of graphic design. Dianna had always been interested in cartography and drafting. She had an aptitude for learning and running complicated computer software. The CSU career counseling center identified graphic design as a good fit for her
skills and arranged an internship with the University Creative Services.

At nominal pay, Dianna honed her graphic design skills as well as learning graphic design computer software. She also succeeded in acquiring a few clients as part of her own small business venture. This small business successfully transferred with the Sampson's after they left Ft. Collins and moved to Roseburg, and helped Dianna get a job with a small graphic design shop when the family moved to Boise for Rob's career.

Sadly, it soon became obvious that graphic design was a rapidly shifting profession. Better and better software titles were allowing people outside of the industry to meet their own needs in simple graphic design. Significant advances in printer technology relegated offset press production to only the highest volume printing needs.

Then, when Rob and Dianna moved to Alaska, it was obvious that graphic design, although encompassing Dianna's skills and interests, was not of itself a viable career path. Still, the career had allowed her to break ties with the Forest Service and gain some valuable new skills in art, software operation and business skills.

The Federal government, and by extension USDA, have statements in place to support co-placement for two career families. When one wage-earner gets a job in a new location, management is to support finding placement for a spouse or second Federal wage earner. Policies like this became necessary to recruiting and retaining talented workers as the number of households with two wage earners greatly increased between Neil's decades at USDA compared to Rob's tenure.

Positions for Rob that were discussed included the NRCS state conservation engineer jobs in Arizona and in Utah, the design team leader in Spokane, Washington and the environmental engineer position in Portland, Oregon at the newly re-formed West National Technology Support Center. All of these would be great positions for Rob but each was flawed in the context of opportunities for Dianna. As each of these positions were discussed, both with NRCS management and around the family dinner table, they each received a response of "those are great jobs, but not the best fit for our two-career family".

With each rejection, Rob knew that NRCS management was growing wearier of bending over backwards for him, and the pool of positions was dwindling quickly. Then Rich Sims, Idaho state conservationist called Rob on Christmas Eve morning of 2004. Art Shoemaker, Rob's mentor and friend had announced his retirement from the Idaho state conservation engineer position. Sims knew Rob's work as the State design engineer and must have thought of it as positive. Rich asked if Rob was interested in the Idaho state engineer job. Christmas presents for the Sampson family would never get any better than this, so while trying to keep a steady voice of tamped down enthusiasm, Rob accepted.

Offering the job to Rob was no small decision for Sims. Relocations from Alaska could run into the hundreds of thousand dollars range, and NRCS Idaho's budget for moving new employees was seldom more than $500,000 for an entire year of employee relocations. Sims also forfeited his ability to test the waters for stronger employees by advertising the position to all qualified applicants. So when Rob asked Sims about a 'co-placement' position for Dianna with the Federal Government, he knew he was pushing his luck. NRCS had made remarkable concessions for the family and asking for what amounted to another favor seemed cheeky to say the least.

After several days, Sims did deliver the news that of the several NRCS positions that fit Dianna's skill set, none were vacant, and none could be created. These NRCS jobs were the only ones in Sims' control, but he did offer to contact other Federal managers and see if they had a vacant position for Dianna. Once again NRCS was going above and beyond normal expectations and this effort was not lost on the family. Unfortunately, no other jobs in Boise were found within Sims circle of contacts, and the Sampsons were left with a dilemma faced by many two career families.

Weighing the good and bad aspects of all the alternatives, Dianna put her career on hold again. Together they decided to accept the state engineer position offered to Rob. Dianna would leave her position with BLM. To say that this decision was difficult is an understatement. Luckily, Dianna received some advice that was a powerful positive turning point when viewed in the long run. Rather than resigning from BLM, she asked to be placed on leave without pay (LWOP) status, thus preserving her status as a current Federal employee.

In the world of Federal personnel management this status is very important, as it allowed her to apply for positions advertised only for 'current Federal employees'. Allowing the LWOP status was not a trivial decision for BLM management, as they most likely could not fill Dianna's Alaska position until she officially resigned.

In the first part of March, Rob and Dianna Sampson loaded up the truck with a dog and three cats and started the nearly 3,000 mile drive to Boise. The days were getting longer at a very rapid rate, something no Alaskan wants to miss. Dianna was leaving a very successful career and they both would miss the 'Great Land,' tingeing the trip with bittersweet. But they were headed to a city they knew and loved, and the backdrop of advancing springtime as they travelled South was an obvious metaphor for their move. As they arrived in Boise and checked into temporary housing in an apartment complex, their spirits were high. St. Patrick's Day celebration with old friends in Boise was very sweet for Rob and Dianna.

The saga of Dianna's career and her concessions on behalf of Rob's NRCS career advancements would be remarkably incomplete if the story was stopped at St. Patrick's Day in 2005. She had career momentum that provided her an advantage if she were to continue Federal service, but that momentum had a short shelf life. She had been granted permission to use her accrued annual leave and about six weeks of LWOP, so she would need to find a position in less than eight weeks after leaving Alaska.

Finding an open Federal position with the right qualifications and description in this time frame, and making successful application for the position, is the equivalent of threading a needle in the dark.

Then, through friends and contacts she learned of a position at the BLM Idaho state office in the Fire and Aviation branch. Given her experience in dispatching and fighting fire as well as her knowledge of the Federal Incident Command System, she seemed an excellent fit with this branch with the exception of the job description: the position was as an administrative assistant. A secretary. Now, not only was Dianna putting her name in the ring for a non-technical job, but she was tumbling significantly back down the Federal pay scale.

Given the dwindling time frame of her Federal employee status, she once again dusted off her well-worn resume and SF-171 and began the competition with over 50 other applicants.

During interviews for the position, some obvious questions arose, that while not discriminatory, display the difficulty of being flexible in the name of a Federal spouse's career: 'Did she feel overqualified for the job?'; 'Did she think the position would be challenging enough for her?' Dianna beat the odds and started with the BLM only six weeks after leaving Alaska.

The new-found job did come at a price. Despite trying to keep a positive and 'team-player' attitude, inevitably someone would treat her as a 'lesser-secretary' to be ordered about, rather than a skilled member of the staff. Having been on a career track of ever-increasing responsibility in Alaska, and having one of your co-workers shove a pile of envelopes onto your desk with a curt request to stamp and mail them, was not a career high point for Dianna. Inevitably this led to more dinner table discussions about the level of sacrifice required of a spouse. Luckily for Rob, Dianna's fortitude held out long enough for lightning to strike again.

The Boise District of the BLM encompasses the southwest corner of the state and oversees three field offices: Owyhee, Four Rivers and Bruneau. A Geographic Information Systems (GIS) analyst position at the District level, but stationed in Marsing at the Owyhee field office, was advertised in April 2006. Once again, Dianna dove back into the job search fray and emerged from a huge pool of applicants as the successful job applicant.

She found herself back in a technical position at a GS-9 pay scale that had potential for promotion, and the obvious advantage of no one shoving a stack of unstamped envelopes onto your desk. Taking this position was not without sacrifice, as it included a 30 mile commute one direction on a crowded and dangerous state highway.

Dianna thrived at the position and received many awards as well as a pay raise. She only sustained one minor accident during the 60 miles of daily driving. Her skills and progress were eventually awarded when she was named the GIS coordinator and her position was moved back to Boise in September of 2009.

Four and a half years after resetting her career to an entry-level position, Dianna had regained her pay grade and technical status. Without her tenacity and success in applying for and receiving positions and upgrades, this story may have written itself quite differently. A two career family proved difficult, but not impossible for the Sampsons. Rob's path seems relatively easy compared to Dianna's experience, but two Federal careers were managed successfully, and, in this case, Dianna is the hero of the story.

Although this book is about a father and son's shared experience in a Federal agency and the world of conservation, one of the object lessons is that employees are hired not in a vacuum, but in the context of their family's goals and needs. When Neil decided to compete for the Graduate Studies program and relocate the family to the east coast, that decision changed the lives of all the family members just as surely as it changed Neil's fortune. Similarly, Rob and Dianna made choices about mobility and location that undoubtedly improved Rob's employment status, but reset Dianna's goals. Luckily, no one ever knows where the path not taken leads to. In the case of moving back from Alaska, that decision worked well in Rob's favor. He had a job in familiar geography, in a system he had helped create. He knew the players at the Federal and State level and had experience all over the State of Idaho. Dianna triumphed professionally due to her skills and persistence.

54

Boise Part II

*"The Idaho NRCS engineering staff that greeted Rob upon his return
from Alaska was a talented group of engineers
and engineering technicians."*

In 2005, NRCS Idaho had about 200 full time positions, of which 13 were engineers, 8 were Civil Engineering Technicians and some 30 were Soil Conservation Technicians. Although everyone in Idaho contributed to the planning and design of conservation practices considered to be 'engineering', it was these 50 or so employees that shouldered the bulk of the design, layout, construction inspection, and final acceptance of the engineering practices.

When Rob returned to Idaho from Alaska, Idaho NRCS was managing a budget of about 12-15 million dollars annually, of which roughly 70% was expended on engineering practices.

NRCS has a detailed process for distributing authority for the design and approval of engineering practices, based on the complexity and scope of the situation. Authority is obtained through demonstrated and continued competence, and the State Conservation Engineer (SCE) ultimately determines who can design and approve the installation of a certain level of engineering practice.

Because engineering is regulated by the state, one of the duties of the SCE is to meet with the State Board of Professional Engineers, and explain the NRCS method of review and approval of engineering practices. Ideally, the SCE can obtain Board concurrence that the delegated authority method, as well as NRCS design standards and a robust program of quality assurance, allows the SCE and NRCS to undertake engineering practices in the State.

In order to make these negotiations possible, NRCS requires each SCE to be a licensed professional engineer (PE) in the state where they work. If the Board is in agreement with NRCS's engineering protocol, the SCE becomes responsible to the Board for all engineering done on NRCS's behalf in the state. Essentially then, each of the employees across the state who are designing and accepting engineering practices are practicing under the SCE's Professional Engineering license.

Rob was registered in Idaho as an Agricultural Engineer, as well as holding licenses in Alaska and Oregon in the disciplines of Civil and Environmental engineering. In order to meet licensure requirements as well as participate in the spirit and rule set forth in Idaho law and the professional code of conduct, active participation in the profession is required. Thus some effort to participate in Professional Societies, to stay current with select scientific journals and to give back to the engineering community specifically, and the technical community in general, is an essential part of the job.

Of these responsibilities, increasing the quality of undergraduate and graduate level technical education, as well as providing mentoring and support for early professionals in engineering and technical positions has been a constant effort and source of rewards for Rob. If SCS had not taken a chance on a barely proven freshman and offered a Student Trainee position to Rob in 1981, this story would either not be written at all, or would be very different.

Support of the larger technical community and improving the skills of NRCS employees in Idaho were goals for Rob that were driven by a sense of professional responsibility, but also much broader motivations. Much of the State Conservation Engineer's time is expended on risk management. Conservation practices must work, and work well, under a wide variety of conditions. The terms of "professional engineering," the agreement with the State Board of Professional Engineers, and a simple sense of expending public funding in an optimal manner, demand a high level of quality.

Formal and informal training, as well as continuous mentoring, were already well-woven into Rob's Professional psyche. But that value had been gained in a different time. In 2005, fewer NRCS offices had the stereotypical Soil Conservation Technician (SCT). In the early 1980's a SCT had been was an older employee, one who more than likely served in the military in Korea or Viet Nam. SCT's almost always had some family ties to the community they served, and all had been trained rigorously in agency policy, engineering practice design, and practice documentation.

Thirty years later the demographic profile of SCT's had changed significantly. A typical SCT was younger, often with a professional degree in natural resource management. They seldom had ties to the community they served, and often had no background or experience in farming and ranching. Many of these young professionals had applied for a SCT position in order to get permanent full time status and experience with the agency allowing them to be competitive for a soil or range conservationist position.

All of these factors combined to favor a technician who did not stay in the same position for long. From 2005 to 2010, technicians in Idaho NRCS had changed at 24 of the 30 field offices. This short tenure was very different from the situation at beginning of Rob's career when, during the 5-year period of 1980 to 1985, only 2 of the technician positions changed at the 30 field offices that had a technician on staff.

This churn created a constant training need that simply could not be met by one-on-one training and mentored professional development. In order to address these needs the Idaho NRCS leadership team instituted two new policies. One required new professionals to acquire engineering job approval authority prior to their first promotion. These employees were also required to attend a special course in engineering methods.

Engineering job approval authority is one of the primary methods NRCS and its state conservation engineers use to assure that an employee has engineering skills to design high-quality conservation practices. This authority is described in policy manuals and is based on a sliding scale of complexity. For instance, a sprinkler system with a single irrigation pump and a pipeline might be described as a 'class II' level of complexity, while a sprinkler that covered 400 acres and had a complex piping scheme might be categorized as a 'class V'.

Different levels of authority for a wide variety of engineering practices are delegated from the state engineer to the area or field engineers. They in turn delegate authority to each employee with the need to plan and design conservation practices. The rules of this delegation are very simple: the need and skills must be demonstrated, and any upper-level engineer cannot pass on authority to another employee that is more complex than their own assigned authority.

With much of the NRCS staff across the state trained to do some engineering design, this system provides several benefits to the public and to the state engineer. Planning of conservation practices tends to be more accurate and realistic when the planner can do some rudimentary conceptual design as they talk with an interested farmer or rancher. Handling the workload of planning, design and installation at the field office level also liberates field engineers to devote time to more complicated engineering practice design.

Idaho NRCS state conservationist Rich Sims supported the policy that all newly hired planners and technicians would obtain some amount of job approval authority as a prerequisite to obtaining their next promotion. Without this prodding policy, engineering skills by the staff at the field office level were uneven. Newer employees that had math and design aptitude tended to receive engineering training and approval authority, while newer employees who were not familiar with engineering design could avoid (and possibly ignore) conservation practices that required engineering skill to size and locate.

The Idaho NRCS engineering staff that greeted Rob upon his return from Alaska was a talented group of engineers and engineering technicians. The engineers had an average of 18 years of professional experience. Perhaps more importantly, almost all the engineers were quite skilled in training and technical communication in general. After convening a meeting with all of the Idaho NRCS engineers and engineering technicians, all agreed that a focused effort to provide the basics of engineering and practice design was needed. A syllabus describing different training topics was developed by the Idaho engineering staff, and Rob delivered the concept and training outline to the Idaho NRCS leadership team.

A carefully constructed argument describing the growing engineering workload coupled with increasingly complex conservation practices was laid out for the managers, along with a proposed solution: a mandatory two week 'boot camp' to study and demonstrate the planning and design of conservation engineering practices. The managers were being asked to devote as much as three staff years state-wide to improving the engineering skills of their employees. The Idaho leadership team vote was unanimously in favor, and Rob and his staff put the first training session into motion.

NRCS corporate culture encouraged a higher level of professional development of its employees. Management support of this expensive, but valuable engineering training in NRCS Idaho never wavered. This was quite a commitment through several years of uncertain budget situations.

A hallmark of the two week engineering training was that each student had to complete the design of a conservation engineering practice from their field office. This design had to be reviewed and approved by an engineer with the appropriate engineering job approval authority. In this way, many NRCS employees who were not engineers by training gained a great deal of skill and experience in a highly focused and efficient manner. A mix of classroom and field exercises along with nightly homework assignments provided as many as 30 NRCS employees an immersion in engineering topics and techniques at each session of this training.

Although the success of the engineering training effort was difficult to measure, there is excellent anecdotal evidence that the quality, timeliness and engineering skill had improved in Idaho NRCS. This is attributed as a direct result of policy requiring engineering job approval for each employee, as well as successful attendance at an engineering boot camp.

In 2006, Idaho NRCS had approximately 800 engineering practices that were late or backlogged in the eastern part ('Area 2') of the State. These numbers were reduced to less than 100 by 2010. Spot checks of completed work state-wide indicated an error rate of about 10-20% on engineering practices in 2006. By 2010, this rate was lowered to less than 10%.

Because most of the easy conservation practices had already been installed, complexity of engineering was increasing as more variable site topography, more problematic soils, and more intensive use of the water supply were encountered. To be increasing the quality of the engineering practice planning, design and construction in the face of decreasing employee experience and increasing site complexity was rewarding for the NRCS engineering team in Idaho.

55

The USDA Model – and How it Changed

"SCS had acquired some pseudo-regulatory duties in the 1985 farm bill and this had changed their relationships with farmers."

For much of the 1960's, 1970s and 1980s, the model at the USDA service centers had stayed about the same from the farmer's point of view. Generally housed together, the Farmers Home Administration (FmHA), the Agricultural Stabilization and Conservation Service (ASCS) and the Soil Conservation Service (SCS) were in the same building, often entered by a common door.

To the farmer, the face of the Department of Agriculture was that single door opening into a bland office building housing these three agencies that oddly overlapped in name and function. The (FmHA) made loans for rural development, including some small town sewer and water projects. This was where a farmer went to get the year's operating loan if it was needed.

ASCS provided the subsidies. Grain support payments, direct purchase of commodities for the Commodity Credit Corporation, and paying farmers for work to improve soil and water conditions. The Soil Conservation Service, working in cooperation with the local Soil Conservation District, provided planning and technical assistance to farmers and ranchers to help them solve soil and water problems on their land.

The flagship conservation program for the ASCS was the Agriculture Conservation Program (ACP). Farmers signed up to do a conservation practice such as a grass waterway. A referral form was filled out by the farmer and ASCS, along with a black and white photocopy of an aerial photo with the location of the practice sketched on it.

The form and map went to the SCS District Conservationist, who assigned a technician to perform a 'needs and feasibility' study that consisted of going to the farm, taking some measurements for the proposed conservation practice, and starting to sketch a design. If the practice proposed by the farmer was 'needed and feasible' the referral form was returned from SCS to ASCS for funding approval.

ASCS employees were an odd bureaucratic hybrid. They were employees of the County Committee (a USDA committee of local landowners, elected by local landowners) and they were paid with Federal funds. The ASCS County Executive Director (CED) brought the funding requests to the County Committee, who would approve or disapprove the requests for conservation funding.

In small rural counties this decision amounted to a fair bit of power. Often the local Soil Conservation District Board of Directors was involved, but there was no doubt the power was held by the County Committee. The subsidies for the ACP conservation practices were small, generally a few hundred to a few thousand dollars. A running joke in upper USDA management was that the maximum federal subsidy for the ACP program coincided with the minimum amount of money that would buy a landowner's loyalty to the USDA.

If the conservation practice was approved, the practice referral (form AD-862) went back over to SCS, who contacted the farmer, designed the practice, oversaw the installation, and certified that the installation met 'SCS Standards and Specifications'. Documentation of the practice extent, location and dimensions, along with some measurement of the conservation benefit, such as tons of soil saved, was recorded. This documentation then went back to ASCS who made payment to the farmer.

From inside the government, however, the model was that ASCS had the money and SCS provided the technical knowledge to design and apply conservation practices. Both of the small agencies needed each other, but there was always a distinct undercurrent of jealousy and conflict.

To some in ASCS, the SCS and its 'Standards and Specifications', its measurement of soil loss, and its insistence that a practice be installed correctly before it could be technically certified often was just an impediment. Why not "just let the farmers install what they need to?" ASCS reasoned. The ASCS could check to see that something had happened on the farm, just as they checked to see if grain was in the bin that the government had just purchased. The farmer knew what needed to be done, and after all, ASCS knew how to get farmers in the door and signed up for the ACP program. The ASCS performance was measured in how effectively they distributed money, so trying to make sure that terraces in a field all had the correct dimensions didn't seem as important to ASCS as it did to SCS.

To many in SCS, what mattered was that the conservation practice was the right thing in the right place to improve conservation performance. The SCS technician knew that what was difficult was to locate the furthest upslope terrace correctly, make sure the terraces were constructed with enough soil moisture, compacted correctly and had the correct dimensions and elevations. ASCS's function of writing the checks seemed like a simple afterthought to an SCS soil conservation technician. ASCS didn't have any specific technical knowledge, the currency of trade in SCS. How hard could it be to write a check and report same to headquarters? For the SCS, all of the archaic forms that ASCS filled out and filed to document the government payment to the farmer didn't have anything to do with whether the conservation practice worked or not.

SCS also valued the planning that occurred *with* the farmer. Often the farmer had signed up for a practice, like terraces, when the erosion the farmer observed was actually a symptom of other problems. SCS planners were at their finest when they could identify the fact that the farmer's erosion was caused by a compaction layer left from a plow, and the wrong crop rotation that did not leave enough residue over the winter to slow spring erosion. The gold standard of planning was to help the farmer understand the underlying cause of the erosion, and, if needed, change to a different plowing and cropping scheme. These practices were then documented in a farm plan, analyzed for secondary impacts, and the plan was agreed to by the local Soil Conservation District.

The result of these differences between the agencies meant that to each the ASCS and the SCS, the other was superfluous and could go away. Some of these jealousies were on display when Neil and Rob attended a House Agriculture subcommittee hearing in 1994. Budgets had gotten tight, and with SCS and ASCS jockeying for position as the threat of a major reorganization became imminent, the tactics got a little rougher. A member of the subcommittee held up a fax printout and read a few sentences about how useless SCS had become and how ASCS could carry on conservation programs just fine without them.

But what really seemed to blow the doors off the hearing chamber was that the fax was sent using a government fax machine. This type of direct lobbying of Congress by a Federal employee was frowned upon and probably illegal. It is impossible to tell now if that event changed the arc of the future. From Rob's standpoint then, ASCS was winning the tug of war. The ACP program was going away, but ASCS funded the wildly popular Conservation Reserve Program (CRP) to plant erodible land back to grass or trees.

SCS had acquired some pseudo-regulatory duties in the 1985 farm bill and this had changed their relationships with farmers. Consider, for example, who got the warmer reception from a farmer: The ASCS employee coming out to measure the grain bin for payment, or the SCS employee documenting that wetlands were being farmed and that penalties might be assessed? To the farmer, the two-agency model used by USDA was a little confusing and more complicated than it had to be.

Rural coffee shop talk often focused on the insanities of the Federal Government:

> "Two government agencies with the word 'conservation' in their name! And why would a producer have to go to two different agencies just get their grant[18] of $3,500 a year?
>
> Heck, those farmers are always doing some sort of conservation work. Why does that guy from the one agency measure how full the grain bin is, then another different person surveys for the ditches?

---

[18] This was a common misperception. The ACP program provided cost-sharing, typically about 50% of the project cost. The landowner had to show receipts, then payment was made for half of the total. The very maximum amount on a single contract was $3,500. No matter how often this was explained, many landowners argued they were 'owed' $3,500 if they put in a conservation practice.

And why go to all the problem of drawing a set of plans for those terraces? The bulldozer operator knows how to put in terraces. All those flags stuck in the ground out in the field will just get ran over..."

Today, there is a better relationship between the agencies at the field level, but after the ACP program went away, there was less need for close coordination. There are some instances where NRCS and FSA are consolidating offices between counties, and in at least two instances breaking up the two offices, placing FSA in one county and NRCS in another.

In spite of the differences in philosophy and approach, there was seldom much controversy at the local office level. The local people in SCS and ASCS didn't make the policies and design the program rules. They just did their best to carry them out. And because they worked closely together in very small towns, they were often personal friends. They might complain about the inconsistencies, but they didn't usually let those prevent a good working relationship. At the state and federal level, as Neil was to find, competition between SCS and ASCS grew more intense, the personal relationships between agency people less close, and the political struggles between the agencies and their primary supporters often flared up into major confrontations. That agency conflict probably peaked in the jockeying around the 2002 Farm Bill, when the final transfer of fund management responsibility for EQIP was transferred from FSA to NRCS. Looking back with the luxury of time, it seems that both agencies got some of what they asked for, with some unforeseen consequences. With the Farm Bills, reorganization and a shift in the philosophy about agricultural subsidies at the Federal level, by 2013, NRCS and FSA had both changed significantly, when seen from a conservation programs standpoint.

By 2013, FSA had very little to do with the flagship conservation financing program, EQIP. NRCS now does all the advertising, application, ranking and contracting with landowners to install conservation practices, a job completely handled by ASCS under the old ACP program. NRCS still plans, designs and certifies installation of the conservation practices, but now they also write the financial contract with the farmer and document and authorize payment.

FSA still funds the Conservation Reserve program, but it is the last conservation program they administer. FSA also administers a small loan program, arguably on the budget chopping block, and makes payments for the remaining subsidy programs. However, these direct crop subsidies are disappearing, as they have no favor on the international stage and their existence penalizes the US in trade negotiations.

With new responsibilities comes oversight. NRCS's new-found financial authorities raised it to a level of scrutiny that was very unfamiliar. The Office of Management and Budget (OMB) determined that with the level of spending at NRCS, a financial audit of their control and accounting systems was in order. The results of the 2007 Audit were a disaster. Deficiencies were identified in 9 of 20 categories, NRCS was found as having "deficient, poor or nonexistent controls and auditing procedures." Suddenly, the agency that valued a technically sound, well written conservation plan had to worry about accruals, signatory authority to enter into contracts, and farmer's legal 'control of the land'.[19]

The administration of the Farm Bill Programs had been increasingly dominating field office activities since 1996. As technical leaders, Rob and his colleagues were constantly pushing field staff to get the conservation plan right. But time in the field, helping a farmer and learning about their operation did not do anything to rank an EQIP application, write a contract or make a payment.

At some point around 2005, it had begun to seem farcical to lecture a field office administering 60 EQIP contracts that they needed to follow the conservation planning process and spend more time with the landowner. The financial audit hammered one of the last nails into the coffin of conservation planning. Audit performance became part of the State Conservationist's performance plan. More EQIP contracts brought more money to pay salaries; the contracts and the payments *would* be done right. These priorities were very clear to the field offices.

---

19 http:www.usda.gov/oig/rptsauditsmres.

.   Pearlie Reed, when he was Chief of NRCS, once told Neil Sampson that "this isn't the same agency you worked for," and the description above certainly validates that statement. The NRCS of today is not the SCS of half a century ago. Not in agricultural or conservation technology, not in policies or programs, and not in people's attitudes toward government.

To most observers, including the authors of this book, that represents a lot of progress. But progress sometimes comes at a price, so it may be useful to explore what costs may have been incurred in the transformation of soil conservation services. In many ways, it wasn't much fun to be trying to promote soil conservation when there were active federal policies and USDA programs that were providing solid economic incentives for landowners to do otherwise. Those pressures seem to have abated somewhat, with a more consistent policy and program approach to conservation.

Attempting to line up Federal conservation programs under a single agency had caused conflict between the agencies for decades. One flare-up in 1958 was centered in South Dakota, and though it was finally won by the conservation districts and SCS, the political jockeying was bitter, particularly between the National Association of Soil Conservation Districts (now NACD) and the Agricultural Lime Institute.

The Lime Institute, led by Robert Koch, a former ASCS County employee, sent out "reams of mimeographed material to South Dakota farmers, ASCS Committeemen, and Members of Congress" saying that all of the USDA conservation functions should be carried out by ASCS since "with SCS in the picture it creates unnecessary overlapping of Federal agencies which certainly creates taxes, expenses and headaches."[20] An editorial in *The Morbridge Tribune* in Corson County, SD accused the Lime Institute of having "no interest in South Dakota other than its fight with the Soil Conservation Districts who advocated the dropping of the cost-share for liming from the Agricultural Conservation Program (ACP)."

---

[20] Sampson. R. Neil. 1985. *For Love of the Land: A History of the National Association of Conservation Districts,* Washington, DC: NACD. pp. 110-111.

SCS and districts won that fight, but the rancor continued to poison relationships across the decades of Neil's career. A continuing thorn in ASCS's side was the success of the Great Plains Conservation Program, where SCS handled all of the contracting and cost-sharing in a limited number of states. Efforts to de-fund that program continued for years, and Neil was involved in a successful effort by the Conservation Coalition to block one of those efforts during the Reagan Administration in 1986. The fallout from that interagency fight had implications for the Clean Water Act Programs in the 1970's, and for other USDA conservation efforts.[21]

Winning the fight for NRCS was not totally painless, either. When the 2002 Farm Bill fight ended up giving NRCS almost sole control over the conservation programs, the staff of the House Agricultural Committee, who had opposed the move, were furious. They launched a federal audit of NRCS focused on its use of grant funds with non-governmental partners, primarily the National Association of Conservation Districts.

The resulting political pressure on NRCS caused it to pull grant support for NACD's local programs designed to help conservation districts improve their capacity to assist in carrying out their new responsibilities. At the Washington level, NACD was told by influential people on the Hill that unless they fired Ernie Shea, who had been NACD's Executive Vice President for 18 years and served as their "point person" with Congress, that political retribution against NRCS and NACD would be unremitting. So Shea was fired, becoming one of the "victims of the victory".

What Neil (and probably many other NRCS and NACD participants) didn't foresee was what would happen to NRCS when they won the fight. Like the dog that caught the car, they suddenly had problems that they were ill-equipped to address. From Neil's viewpoint, the most important question was not if NRCS could successfully administer the programs, including the financial management. He thought they could, once they learned what all was involved, and

---

[21] Many of these stories are told in R. Neil Sampson, 2009, *With One Voice: Wheatmark,* December, 2008.

got the proper training and systems in place. The evidence now suggests that is happening.

But the critical question became "what will be lost in the process?" Will the "conservation conscience" of the USDA give way to the "support the farmers" political driver? Will NRCS field people still find the time to learn the technical skills needed to evaluate complex landscape problems and guide landowners toward a plan that addresses the entire system, or will their energies be so captured by the need to administer programs and successfully support farm income that they become what ASCS was criticized for being in the 20th Century?

Currently, in 2013, there is talk among stakeholders that the administrative people seem to be replacing technical competence at many field offices.

56

Bob Lehman

"The economics and stability related to Federal jobs in very small,
natural resource-based communities was very apparent
the day of (Bob Lehman's) funeral."

As Rob settled into the State Engineers position in 2005, one of his first phone calls was to Bob Lehman, who was then serving as the Area Engineer for the eastern half of the state. The call involved many memories. The turnabout of Rob being the technical supervisor of his mentor and friend had an odd feeling, but as always, Lehman had several sound ideas about changes that could be made in engineering policy and procedure which the new State engineer quickly implemented.

Lehman, the long-time civil engineer in Rexburg was Rob's first supervisor when he got out of college. Bob had graduated from Colorado State University in 1961, and began his career in Colorado Springs, Colorado in 1962. He worked at several places in Colorado, but his favorite post was in Durango, CO, where he served as the field engineer for the several SCS field offices in the southwest part of the state.

Bob's passions lay in all things outdoors, and Durango offered unlimited possibilities. He was on the ski patrol at Purgatory ski area, rode motorcycles and snowmobiles in the San Juan Mountains, and also hiked, fished and hunted. Bob's other passion was for all things mechanical. His garage was stacked floor to ceiling with parts from a broad spectrum of snowmobiles, motorcycles and autos. In Durango, many weekends were spent going to the local Polaris dealership and fixing snowmobile engines along with the occasional lawn mower. In this way Bob got to know the owners, and that friendship eventually led to formation of the local trail riders club, and provided fuel for endless stories about motorcycle and snowmobile riding.

Next, Bob was posted to Longmont, CO, and Steamboat Springs, CO. He applied for several other jobs higher in SCS in Colorado, but was never offered these positions, so he applied for the position in Rexburg, Idaho, leaving behind his beloved Colorado in 1977. It was only months after the Teton Dam had failed that he began his career in Idaho overseeing flood cleanup.

Bob was an excellent designer, and kept a comprehensive library of his favorite design references and examples in a seemingly random bunch of paper piles that covered every flat surface in his office. A design question asked of Bob inevitably brought a series of several muttered answers accompanied by reaching into at least two of the piles and removing exactly the correct piece of paper to answer the question.

Training was another love for Bob, in that he truly liked people and wanted new SCS employees to know the background and lore of the agency. His communication style often consisted with starting in the middle of the process he was trying to describe. Bob's brain just moved faster than most folks could follow and he had generally solved the problem at hand, and had long ago moved on to the next steps. So although Bob had a high level of passion for training, the trainee had to listen carefully and ask questions in order to get the whole story, and then learn the correct steps in the correct sequence.

Rob's previous stint in Idaho as state design engineer had created an odd juxtaposition of technical hierarchy. Reviewing the designs that Lehman now submitted for approval brought flashes of memory for Rob, so that it was a little disconcerting to be reviewing Bob's designs with snippets of Lehman's training echoing in his head. Often Rob would realize he was providing advice to Lehman that the elder engineer had preached to Rob 15 years earlier.

Several projects of Lehman's were high profile, and had encountered some problems. These problems were very seldom technical in nature, but more often revolved around local controversy regarding how water should be managed or how stream and habitat restoration should be accomplished. These 'controversies' were the natural province of the State Conservation Engineer, and Rob found himself travelling to east Idaho every month or so to meet with various groups and discuss these projects.

Almost always there was more common ground than not and almost always Lehman had very good ideas, backed by sound analysis, but sometimes the controversies were rooted in communication. The strategies and design proposals that caused friction between NRCS and its partner agencies or local advocacy groups benefitted from being described from a different angle or by using different words.

In this way, Rob and Bob found a comfortable common ground and some complementary roles. Since the newly arrived state engineer could provide very little in the way of technical advice to the senior engineer that had not originated in part with the senior engineer himself, Rob became the spokesman and sounding board for projects that needed a slight push to move ahead.

Then, in 2008, Bob's years of spending time in the great outdoors, mostly at high elevation, resulted in skin cancer that ultimately took his life on May 12th of 2008, a month after his 69th birthday. The funeral service was held in St. Anthony, about two blocks from where the Sampson's had lived from 1985 to 1988. The small community of St. Anthony, and particularly the Presbyterian Church, lost one of their leaders that day.

The economics and stability related to Federal jobs in very small, natural resource-based communities was very apparent the day of the funeral. The Targhee National Forest Supervisors office had moved to Idaho Falls in 2002. The lumber mill closed in 1990, having been dependent on Federal harvest contracts of insect-killed lodgepole pine.

Bob's family had lived in St. Anthony for 30 years, providing a profound continuity in the community. Outside of production agriculture, Bob's salary was easily in the upper quarter of salaries in the small town and probably in the upper 10%. Bob knew everyone and knew of most events that shaped the town.

In this way the Federal Government, with its long lasting presence in a community and the salaries paid to professional, life-long

312

civil servants generates stability. Federal professional salaries pale to those of professional private sector positions, but are quite attractive compared to that of a grocery clerk or nurses aid at the clinic. Federal employees living in small towns also bring professional skills that wouldn't be present in some areas. Soil scientists, civil engineers, and professional planners, buoyed by the stability of a permanent, full-time position, serve on school boards, rural fire departments and city councils.

Someone had to clean out Bob's desk after he died. Someone had to sort out current projects from historical information, and separate out personal things that belonged in the hands of Lehman's family. Sorting through Bob's belongings was a specialized task, since a technical knowledge of project names and time-lines was needed in order to know if a design or some calculations needed to be filed at the Project Office, retained in a reader file, or simply thrown away. The task, of course, fell to Rob.

Bob had been such a dominating figure in Rob's professional development that despite the sorting being a technical task, it had a strong emotional component. This would have been the case for any other NRCS employee who knew Bob, had they been assigned the duty. Post mortem continuity and keeper of the institutional knowledge were responsibilities that were not written in the job description of a State Conservation Engineer. Yet, during this three day effort, Rob became the institutional memory of engineering in east Idaho. Metaphorically, he became one of the older employees who were the engine that kept NRCS effective, and could speak authoritatively of the Agencies history and values.

At a career mark of 26 years, his role as mentor and keeper of the NRCS culture became clear to Rob. After always feeling like the 'young employee' surrounded by, and listening intently to professionals who had served the public for 30 or 40 years, his role was reversed.

Mixed in with literally thousands of designs was the evidence of Bob Lehman's 48-year Federal career and 31 years of living in St. Anthony and working in NRCS Field Offices all over the eastern half of Idaho. The design work proved to be difficult to sort. Multiple copies of drawings and specifications in various stages of completion had to be cataloged, organized, and distributed to the correct office where the information would be useful. But many of the pieces had special meaning, and some of the technical products saved by Bob and sorted in his filing 'system' had a direct meaning to Rob.

Tucked in a corner of the office in yet another pile, Rob found his own first design that Bob had signed as approved, certifying it was ready for delivery to the landowner and for construction. These drawings and calculations to design a grassed waterway were fairly simple, but Bob had still found items that needed corrections prior to approval. In a hand-written letter on plain white tablet paper, Bob had written a recommendation to management that Rob be promoted to a GS-9.

Another pile contained a design for a steel irrigation diversion structure designed by Rob on which Bob had made a series of corrections. Rob remembered the design and that he had felt some of Bob's corrections were stylistic rather than rooted in engineering design. The changes were made in the name of getting Bob to approve the design. Particularly stark were the comments written in blue ink. These changes were written by Bob after Rob had delivered the design to the farmer. Bob had visited the farmer the day after Rob delivered the design, retrieved the drawings and specifications and made further 'corrections.'

Mixed in with design material, photos, slides, old calculators and other odds and ends were the things that taken together described Lehman's Federal career. His letter to four western states detailing his interest in engineering positions was dated the day after he was notified of not being selected for a promotion in Colorado SCS. Several job applications to Colorado SCS dated after 1977 showed Bob's interest in getting back to Colorado, including one during Rob's tenure that had been unknown to the junior engineer.

A 1993 letter from the SCS Administrative Officer during a time of low budgets and preparation for a possible reduction in work force (RIF), directly requested that Bob strongly consider taking an early retirement. There was a letter of reprimand for Bob's hauling his personal snowmobiles on the Government's trailer. Bob had always

314

trusted his own machines that he knew inside and out, and the fact that there was only one letter of reprimand was remarkable.

Much of the material retrieved and cataloged from Bob's office was bittersweet. Letters of job application rejections, attempts to run computer software that ultimately were abandoned for hand calculations that Bob trusted. The increasing shaky hand lettering as cancer treatments took more and more of his energy. Letters and plaques detailing people's gratitude for Bob's high quality work, almost entirely from entities outside of SCS hierarchy such as Conservation Districts, Watershed Councils and environmental groups.

At the funeral, Bob's children eulogized their Dad, each with a personal touch of a story or a parable or an outdoor activity with their Dad. But to a person they also said that they had never known their Dad designed and built things that improved fish habitat, made irrigation water easier to apply, and slowed erosion on farmer's fields. Their Dad was more of an environmental activist than they had ever known. While initially surprised, Rob found this easy to rationalize after some thought. Bob would never have bragged about work, or even described it to many people.

He did what he did, because the clients and the impacts resonated with him, and this generated quiet passion that often had him working on nights and weekends. This cross of passion, humility and deep desire to 'get it right' was what Rob found embodied in Bob's professional papers and library. As he went through the body of work, Rob soon realized that Bob had never planned to retire from the NRCS. There was no evidence of provisions made for a life after NRCS. Observing this intense loyalty to the mission of NRCS, rather than to the people who made up the leadership of the agency, was stark, but enlightening, for Rob. It helped explain many of Bob's baffling behaviors.

Rob's intimate glimpse into Bob's life, gleaned from the cleanout of his office, was humbling. Bob hadn't gotten as many 'good breaks' in his career as Rob had. His propensity for just 'doing the good work' but not telling anyone had left his reputation with upper level managers slightly tarnished but had gained him a sterling standing with the people he thought mattered, his customers. In several ways Bob was a metaphor for the agency as a whole. Always put the farmers first. Always put the natural resources first. A deep sense of humility coupled with rural sensibilities such as to 'do the little things well and that will take care of the big things'. Never bragging. Never refusing to do work even when budgets were slashed. And never taking the easy way out when dealing with land owners.

In 2010, Rob was asked by Colorado NRCS to tour the state and provide a retrospective on their recent stream and wetland restoration efforts. That trip took him to western Colorado and specifically to a constructed wetland plant nursery, as well as a streambank stabilization effort on the Animas River just outside of Durango. After drifting away from most of the group, Rob and the landowner were debating some ideas about wetlands, and the quality of service he had received from the NRCS.

In the midst of this conversation, the landowner mentioned he had once owned the Polaris dealership in town, and had also sold Yamaha motorcycles. As the hair rose on Rob's neck, he asked the landowner if he remembered a person named Bob Lehman. Given the shock on the landowners face, it was evident that Bob's protégé was now talking with Bob's best friend and mechanic partner from the time Bob had lived in Durango. Both the Government bureaucrat and the mechanic landowner shed a quick tear. And somebody smiled from above.

Rob and Bob Lehman at Sheridan Creek, about 2006

Part III

By Neil and Robert Sampson

57

Patterns of Change?

"Conservation is the result of a scientifically-based communication effort that blends the professional's skills with the land manager's knowledge of their own situation."

The Soil Conservation Service and later, the Natural Resources Conservation Service, grew out of the Soil Erosion Service, created on September 19th, 1933 by Congress and Franklin D. Roosevelt. Hugh Hammond Bennett was named Chief. As of this writing, SCS and NRCS have had 15 Chiefs. Collectively, Neil and Rob have worked for all but the first two.

To a person, these leaders have been dedicated to conservation and to the good of the agency. Obviously, there were differences in policy emphasis, as called for by the situations each faced. Neil was opposed to the shift from a professional chief chosen from within the agency's ranks to a political chief from outside that occurred in the 1980's, arguing that this would damage the professional thrust. Did it? That's hard to say, even with over 30 years of hindsight. It seems most likely that the changes wrought in the agency and its programs were more driven by changing times, challenges and opportunities than by the personal sway of a leader. That could be argued, for sure, but there doesn't seem to be much hard evidence either way.

What is certain is that a great deal *has* changed in the 79 years of the agency. Calculations once completed by slide rule are now figured in a spreadsheet or possibly an application on a smart phone Memos typed by a secretary in the typing pool from hand-written notes on a legal pad are now typed by the executive who signs the document. All the surveying is done by electronic machines, and very few of the newer technicians could set up a manual transit, let alone 'throw a chain.'

The temptation to write about 'change' as a theme is there, but at least as instructive is a look at the unchanged. NRCS and Soil and Water Conservation Districts still represent a unique Federal partnership with a local government group. Districts still provide an essential conduit of communication to private landowners. Although the meeting may be held in a chilly Grange hall late in the evening, if the District votes to support a certain Federal effort, it carries weight. And that small piece of legitimacy is transferred to the local NRCS field office and provides the beginning of a discussion.

Technical assistance still consists of the day-to-day effort of showing up at a farm or ranch and looking at the situation. Discussions and agreements with the local manager, the person that works the land, are still the only way to change land management. NRCS thinks of itself as a technical agency, so technical knowledge and skill are prized in the agency, although the focus on program administration has grown in recent years. If technical skills, the ability to read and understand the land, and the planning acumen to lay out a conservation system that works *are* the backbone of NRCS credibility, the agency will need to decide how this coexists with program administration and the intense and consistent pressure on effectively spending the program money that Congress has appropriated.

It still takes a unique blend of communication skills and technical knowledge to spread a map out on the hood of the pickup, point out several things that the landowner may have missed and talk about grazing patterns. When you can hear the landowner's voice trail off just a little bit, as the facts and combinations just discussed start to work in their head, and their finger points to a new place on the map, you just did it. You just laid out some evidence in an understandable form, and related it to things that fit this operation. You didn't talk too much and you didn't talk down; you showed interest in things important to that landowner. And they bought it; so your idea has become theirs. Not everyone can do that, and it's probably a learned skill, not an inborn one.

The skills involved come not just from formal education, but also from experience. A technician that works with dozens of land managers a year gains an increasing knowledge reservoir of problems analyzed and solved. Each solution builds competence that is more than technical – it also represents an approach that worked and might work elsewhere at some future time. As NRCS field people spend more time in the office working with program documents and rules, and as staff levels stay the same or go down, there is less opportunity to be in the field solving conservation problems. Whether this will have a negative effect on the overall technical competency in the agency is a concern.

Surveying is still the only way to get the information you need to design a complicated conservation system. Remotely sensed elevation, digital images, and geographic information systems are not precise enough, but more importantly, those technologies don't know the right questions to ask. They don't know the right survey shots to take. A trained planner or engineer is designing the conservation practice while they are collecting the data—and possibly still carrying on a conversation with the farmer. They are seeking facts and asking questions that will be essential in planning and proposing the right solutions for the situation they find. There are very few shortcuts available, and that means that there is little or no way to "wholesale" conservation practices. One size does not fit all situations, and one riparian buffer design does not fit every streamside.

Conservation is the result of a scientifically-based communication effort that blends the professional's skills with the land manager's knowledge of their own situation. The limiting factor to planning and designing conservation management and practices is trained planners and technicians. That hasn't changed.

Some of the change that is worth mentioning is not necessarily so positive. NRCS is pushing 10 times the money out the door as they did 25 years ago. The impact of the 1985 Farm Bill and its effects are readily shown by the graphs below, initially published by NRCS. Coupled with the steady reduction of field staff resources discussed in earlier chapters, it is no surprise that the shift from a technical focus to an administrative one has been evident.

Although some may bemoan the fact that the programs are driving the agency's agenda, every signal the field staff gets from the National and State Offices is driven by allocating the money and passing the audit. There is no pretense anymore—program regulations and dollars rule the day. Ask a local technician how wide a riparian buffer should be and they are more likely to quote a program rule about width or a condition of providing Federal money than they are about sediment trapping or nutrient uptake.

As of this writing, NRCS has successfully avoided being a regulatory agent. Even the 30 year old Swampbuster rule that dirtied NRCS's white hat has become status quo with the landowners. But NRCS's voluntary model of conservation is coveted by agencies who desire to gain access to landowner's property and their knowledge. Recently EPA released an interim rule for the Clean Water Act (CWA) that had a list of more than 50 NRCS conservation practices that would be exempt from CWA permitting. NRCS was not very interested in certifying practices that they did not plan or design at a specific location to accomplish a conservation goal for the purpose of helping the landowner avoid a permit. This particular rule is predicted to be rescinded, but other advances from the regulatory agencies will happen.

NRCS enjoys the privilege of being invited onto private land and being trusted. That needs to be preserved or some other way to deliver Soil and Water Conservation programs will need to be devised.

There is still political controversy over the topic of climate change, but the scientific consensus is strong – the next century will not be a repeat of the past century in terms of the environment facing farmers, ranchers, and foresters. The climate is changing, and will continue to change at rates much faster than what is seen in the historical record. This has major implications and technical importance for agriculture and forestry. As precipitation patterns and temperatures change, the challenge will be adaptation to new and, in some cases, unprecedented conditions.

Some of the impacts are particularly challenging for soil and water conservation. Species changes in the face of changing climates will mean new crops or management strategies for farmers, while ranchers and foresters are likely to see the fade-out of the species they are most familiar with while new species move in to fill the landscape. Whether these new invaders are useful, in terms of grazing or timber value will have a significant impact on these operations.

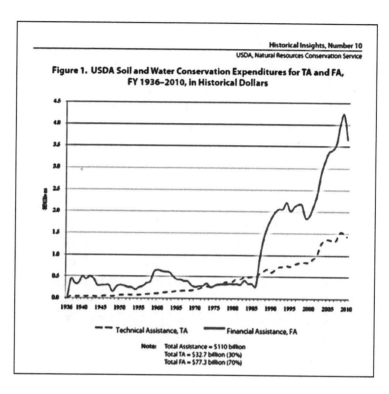

Figure 1. USDA Soil and Water Conservation Expenditures for TA and FA, FY 1936–2010, in Historical Dollars

Technical Assistance, TA   Financial Assistance, FA

Note: Total Assistance = $110 billion
Total TA = $32.7 billion (30%)
Total FA = $77.3 billion (70%)

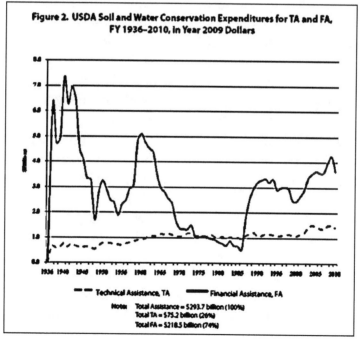

Figure 2. USDA Soil and Water Conservation Expenditures for TA and FA, FY 1936–2010, in Year 2009 Dollars

Technical Assistance, TA   Financial Assistance, FA

Note: Total Assistance = $293.7 billion (100%)
Total TA = $75.2 billion (26%)
Total FA = $218.5 billion (74%)

Storm events are going to become more severe, perhaps more persistent, and the patterns will be harder to predict. Conservation practice design procedures will need to be modified, and the best conservation practices for a certain combination of conditions will change. There may be more regional variation to accommodate. The result will be a continuing need to update research and the technical skills of the field force of NRCS. Where landowners are challenged to maintain their economic viability, there may be less attention and money to invest in conservation and development of their land and its resources.

NRCS is finding pressure and reward in focusing on conservation practices that are out outside the standard concerns of soil erosion, water quantity and water quality. Wildlife plantings for pollinators, sage grouse habitat and locally grown food are real issues and real concerns, but if you are trying to keep 2000 acres of corn and soybeans profitable, these may not be on the top of the list of priorities.

NRCS is also being pushed by Congress to address big issues. The hypoxic 'dead zone' in the Gulf of Mexico, oyster die-offs in the Chesapeake Bay, and drought in California are very real issues, but success on this scale will not come solely from a small Federal Agency. Unless agricultural technology and practice is changed across entire regions, the chance of success is limited. The odds of accomplishing this with a small conservation program or by regulation or edict are low, so long as market economics press for maximum output.

Hopefully NRCS will continue to work on many conservation problems one farm at a time. The result is not just a problem solved, but a land manager that "owns" the solution and is likely to be more capable of solving new or repeat problems as they arise. Congress and Administrators want efficiency, but a land manager wants answers that work. That takes confidence in the plan, and the planner, and that takes time and skill. Hence agency leaders need to understand that while creating a catchy and colorful web page may bring kudos from Congressional staff and environmental groups, it may just elicit a collective sigh from the local field office staff and their conservation district partners. Those local people, and the American land that is in their daily care, deserve far more from national policy than a public relations program. We can only hope they continue to get it.

R. Neil Sampson is a career conservationist with service in the Soil Conservation Service (now Natural Resources Conservation Service), the National Association of Conservation Districts, and the American Forestry Association (now American Forests). As President of Vision Forestry LLC, a forest and land management consulting firm in Salisbury, Maryland, he also serves as Executive Secretary of the External Review Panel to the Sustainable Forestry Initiative

In 2001, he was the F.K. Weyerhaeuser Visiting Fellow at the Yale School of Forestry and Environmental Science, involved in research and teaching on public policy as it relates to private forest management and sustainable forestry. He has been a Technical Advisor to the Utility Forest Carbon Management Program of Edison Electric Institute, the International Carbon Mitigation Program of The Nature Conservancy, and the National Carbon Offset Coalition. He has written many popular and professional articles on a broad range of natural resource topics, focusing on soil and water conservation, forest management and health, climate change, and public policy.

Rob Sampson was born in Burley, Idaho, went to high school in Washington DC, has degrees from the University of Idaho and Colorado State University, and is registered in Agricultural, Civil and Environmental Engineering in Idaho, Oregon and Alaska. His professional interests are in water resources, stream and wetland restoration, and river hydraulics and sediment transport.

Rob has worked for the NRCS in Idaho, Oregon, Colorado, the Virgin Islands, Alaska and Washington DC. He moved from being the State Conservation Engineer in Idaho, to his current position as the National Water Management Engineer at NRCS headquarters in Washington DC. There Rob is the technical lead for issues involving irrigation, drainage, water quantity and water quality. His current activities include Drainage Water Management in the upper Mississippi River Basin, improving irrigation efficiency around the Ogallala Aquifer, and assisting the drought response for the Central Valley in California.

Rob was named a Berg Fellow by the Soil and Water Conservation Society in 1993 and was nominated from the Western Region as SCS Engineer of the Year in 1994. In 1995, he received an Honor Award from USDA for "Innovative Technical Leadership".

CPSIA information can be obtained
at www.ICGtesting.com
Printed in the USA
FSHW020924130119
54997FS

9 781508 604884